PSYCHOLOGY OF POVERTY AND DISADVANTAGE

"Advances in Psychological Research in India Series"

1. *Perspectives on Psychology and Social Development*
   U.N. Dash and **Uday Jain** (Eds.)
2. *Psychology of Poverty and Disadvantage*
   Ajit K. Mohanty and **Girishwar Misra** (Eds.)
3. *Perspectives on Indigenous Psychology*
   Girishwar Misra and **Ajit K. Mohanty** (Eds.)
4. *Psychology of Reading*
   Shantilata Sahu

About the Institution

The Centre of Advanced Study in Psychology, Utkal University, is the first such centre for psychology in India. The centre specializes in broad areas of Educational and Developmental Psychology, Social and Organizational Psychology as well as Comparative and Physiological Psychology. Members of its faculty, one of the largest among the university departments of psychology in India, are highly qualified and internationally reputed for their contributions in various fields of research and applications in social psychology, cognitive development, information processing, early childhood education, psycholinguistics, testing and measurement, and exploratory behaviour. The centre which has a large number of acclaimed publications to its credit, has currently launched a publication series "Advances in Psychological Research in India". Its teaching programme includes Diploma in Early Childhood Education, besides Masters, M.Phil. and Doctoral work in psychology.

About the Editors

Ajit K. Mohanty is Professor and Co-ordinator at the Centre for Advanced Study in Psychology Utkal University, Bhubaneshwar. A Ph.D. from the University of Alberta, Canada, he has been studying the various aspects of bilingualism, language development and reading process. His teaching and research experience spans over nearly three decades. He was a Fulbright Fellow at the University of Wisconsin, U.S.A., a Visiting Scholar in the University of Geneva and a Senior Fellow at Central Institute of Indian Languages. He has published papers in national and international journals and authored *Bilingualism in Multilingual Society* and edited *Perspectives on Indigenous Psychology*. He has contributed a chapter to Vol. 2 of the second edition of the *Handbook of Cross-Cultural Psychology* on language acquisition and bilingualism. He has been President and Convenor of National Academy of Psychology (NAOP), India and has delivered a keynote address in the International Congress of Applied Psychology at Madrid, Spain.

Girishwar Misra is Professor and Chairman of the Department of Psychology and Dean, Faculty of Arts, at Delhi University. Earlier he has taught at the Universities of Gorakhpur, Allahabad and Bhopal. He is on the editorial board of *Psychological Studies* and *Culture and Psychology*. Apart from numerous articles in journals, he has written or edited *Psychological Consequences of Prolonged Deprivation, Deprivation : Its Social Roots* and *Psychological Consequences, Foundations of Social Psychology, General Psychology, Applied Social Psychology in India, Psychological Perspectives on Stress and Health* and *Perspectives on Indigenous Psychology*. He was a Fulbright Fellow at Swarthmore College and the University of Michigan. His areas of interest include cultural psychology, applied social psychology and human development. He is on the Executive Committee of International Association of Cross-Cultural Psychology (IACCP). He has also been elected President of National Academy of Psychology, India.

Advances in Psychological Research in India Series — 2

PSYCHOLOGY of POVERTY AND DISADVANTAGE

Edited by

Ajit K. Mohanty and **Girishwar Misra**

Utkal University, Bhubaneshwar — Delhi University, Delhi

CONCEPT PUBLISHING COMPANY, NEW DELHI - 110059

ISBN 81-7022-805-0

First Published 2000

Published and Printed by
Ashok Kumar Mittal
Concept Publishing Company
A/15-16, Commercial Block, Mohan Garden,
NEW DELHI - 110059 (India)

Phones : 5648039, 5649024
Fax : 091-11-5648053

Dedicated
to
The Memory of

PROFESSOR DURGANAND SINHA

who pioneered psychological research
on poverty in India

Those who have put out the people's eyes
reproach them of their blindness

— John Milton

Foreword

During the current phase (1997-2002) of the University Grants Commission's special assistance, the Centre for Advanced Study in Psychology, Utkal University has launched a new series of publications under the title *Advances in Psychological Research in India.* Through the publications under this series, we seek to project the recent developments in psychological research in India. The first volume under the series *Perspectives on Psychology and Social Development*, edited by Professors U.N. Dash and Uday Jain, attempted to bring together the current trends in various areas of psychological research in India with relevance for social development. The present volume focuses on the theme of poverty and disadvantage. Research on poverty has traditionally been considered an exclusive domain of economics. Contributions from other social science disciplines have been acknowledged, but, they have generally been viewed as peripheral. Psychologists in the western world have been interested in the phenomena of poverty and disadvantage for at least fifty years. In India, however, systematic psychological study of poverty is about three decades old. Despite this, it is unfortunate that planners and policy makers do not seem to have taken the psychological analysis of poverty very seriously. Psychologists are at least partially responsible for this neglect; their attempts have been sporadic, analyses casual and integrations conspicuously absent. With the single exception of the volume '*Deprivation : Its Social Roots and Psychologial Consequences*' edited by D. Sinha, R.C. Tripathi and G. Misra published in 1982, there has been no other comprehensive work in this area. Poverty and disadvantage are not just economic phenomena, they are psychological and social. And hence, study of poverty is incomplete unless it is viewed from a multidisciplinary perspective. The present volume seeks to broaden the existing framework within which the phenomena have been analysed so far and, at the same time, to project more clearly the psychological dimensions of poverty and disadvantage.

The Centre of Advanced Study (CAS) in Psychology has been well known for its pioneering work in the area of social disadvantage. It perhaps remains the only post-graduate Department of Psychology in India to offer a course on Psychology of the Disadvantaged. Its publication in 1979 of the monograph *Cognitive Abilities and School Achievements of Socially Disadvantaged Children in Primary Schools* by R. Rath, A.S. Dash and U.N. Dash was the first major Indian work in the area and is widely cited by researchers in the field. The CAS in Psychology at Utkal, keeping to its tradition in this area of study, organised an interdisciplinary seminar on "Psychology of Poverty and Disadvantage : A Fresh Look" from 18-20 December, 1997, overlapping the Eighth Congress of the National Academy of Psychology (India). This book is an outcome of this seminar. Through this work the CAS in Psychology seeks to provide an integrated approach to the study of poverty and disadvantage in India and, we hope, it will be considered useful by our colleagues in psychology and other social science disciplines. I thank Professor Girishwar Misra for joining me as a guest editor in putting the volume together. He has been involved in this area of study for long years and his association has definitely contributed immensely to the quality of this work.

Late Professor Durganand Sinha, to whose memory this book is dedicated, delivered the keynote address in the seminar on December 18, 1997. This was his last visit to Utkal and his paper in this book is based on his keynote address. It was received by me the day before he breathed his last at Delhi. Professor Sinha's absence leaves a void in this area of research, as in many others in which his contributions were phenomenal. But, I think, the trends set by Professor Sinha would continue to dominate psychological studies of poverty and disadvantage in India.

Professor Ramashray Roy not only presided over the keynote session of the seminar but also guided the deliberations significantly contributing to the overall interdisciplinary framework which this volume has sought to preserve. I am thankful to Professor Roy and to all other colleagues in various sister disciplines and to the social activists from many NGOs, all of whom contributed to enriching the quality of the papers, some of which were substantially modified after the seminar.

The seminar was supported by the UGC special assistance to the CAS in Psychology and by the UNICEF, whose contributions are gratefully acknowledged. All my colleagues at the centre have made it possible for me to organise the seminar and to undertake the production of this work. I am grateful to them. I thank Shri Ashok Mittal of the Concept Publishing Company for his effort in launching the publication programme of the CAS in Psychology at Utkal. As the Coordinator of the Centre, organiser of the seminar and as one of the editors of this book, I would consider my contributions meaningful if this work meets the expected standard to merit attention of researchers and scholars in psychology and other related disciplines.

Ajit K. Mohanty
Coordinator,
Centre of Advanced Study in Psychology
Utkal University

Utkal University,
Bhubaneshwar

Acknowledgements

While preparing this volume, a number of colleagues and friends have extended various kinds of help for which we are grateful to them.

We thank Dr. Prabir Patnaik, M.S. Law College, Cuttack for the conceptual design of the cover-page for this book.

We thank our senior colleagues Professor R.C. Tripathi, Pro-Vice-Chancellor, University of Allahabad and Professor Janak Pandey, Director, G.B. Pant Institute of Social Studies, Allahabad for their enouragement on this project.

The publication programme of the CAS in Psychology at Utkal University supported by the UGC has made it possible to publish this work based mainly on the National Seminar that the Centre organised on the theme. The support is gratefully acknowledged. The publication has been undertaken by the Concept Publishing Company, New Delhi with active interest and supervision by Shri Ashok Kumar Mittal to whom we are thankful.

We are grateful to the UNICEF field office in Orissa for partial support to the Seminar on "Psychology of Poverty and Disadvantage" which made this publication possible.

Help in reviewing the papers and editorial support from a number of people have facilitated our task of putting this volume together. We are thankful to Professors U.N. Dash and Anand Prakash, Professors of Psychology, University of Delhi and to all our colleagues in the CAS in Psychology at Utkal.

The Department of Psychology, University of Delhi provided hospitality to the first editor whose visit to Delhi made it easier for us to work together on this project. The infra-structural facilities for the work at different stages was also available from the Psychology Department in the University of Delhi. We are grateful for the support received, particularly from Ms. Monica Gupta, Ms. Moni Mishra, Dr. Suneet Varma and Mr. Deepak Sharma. We thank Mr. Manoj Sethi, Computer Assistant at Utkal for handling the organisation of references and other details of the manuscript of this book.

While the work was in progress both at Bhubaneswar and Delhi, our families had to bear with our lack of attention. We can only offer our sincere feelings of gratitude for the emotional support received from all the members of our families.

Ajit K. Mohanty
Girishwar Misra

CONTENTS

Contributors

Anjali is Reader in Psychology at Allahabad Degree College. She completed doctoral work on language development in the disadvantaged children. She is interested in socio-psychological interventions and implementation of social policy for the uplift of the poor. (Add : Psychology Department, Allahabad Degree College, S.C. Basu Road, Allahabad-211 003).

Ajit K. Dalal is Professor of Psychology at Allahabad University. He has worked extensively in the areas of information integration, attribution, multivariate methods and health psychology. He was a Fulbright Fellow at University of California, Los Angeles. Recently he has completed an international project on community rehabilitation. His publications include numerous journal articles and *Attribution Theory and Research* and *Human Resource Development : Psychological Perspectives* (Add : Department of Psychology, University of Allahabad, Allahabad-211 002).

U.N. Dash is Professor of Psychology at Delhi University. Earlier he has taught at Utkal University, Bhubaneshwar. He has been KILLAM scholar and a visiting professor in Canada. He has published extensively in national and international journals in the area of cognitive and educational psychology as well as research methodology. Schooling and cognition, and statistics are the areas of his special interest. He is author of *Schooling and Cognition* and edited *Perspectives on Psychology and Social Development*. (Add: Department of Psychology, University of Delhi, Delhi-110 007).

Uday Jain is Professor and Head, Department of Psychology, Barkatullah University. Earlier he taught at the Universities of Rajasthan, Allahabad, North

Eastern Hills and Sagar. He was a Fulbright fellow at the University of Chicago and Swartmore College. He has published in reputed journals in the area of social and environmental psychology. He is the author of *Psychological Consequences of Crowding* and has edited : *Perspectives on Environment and Behaviour* and *Perspectives on Psychology and Social Development.* He has been the Principal co-investigator of CIDA — Shastri Indo-Canadian project on *Community and Regions Overcoming Ecological Crises.* (Add : Psychology Department, Barkatullah University, Bhopal-462 026).

R. C. Mishra is Professor of Psychology at Banaras Hindu University. He was at the Queen's University as a National Fellow, and later as Shastri Fellow. He has published extensively in the areas of perception, schooling and acculturation. He is author of *Ecology, Acculturation and Psychological Adaptation* (Add : Psychology Department, Banaras Hindu University, Varanasi- 221 005).

Janak Pandey is Director, G.B. Pant Social Science Institute. He has been Fulbright Scholar-in-Residence and visiting professor at Wake Forest University, and visiting Commonwealth Fellow at University of Manitoba. Prof. Pandey has taught at the Indian Institute of Technology, Kanpur and at the universities of the Ranchi, Patna and Allahabad. He is interested in research on social influence processes and contemporary social issues which are relevant to socio-economic change in developing societies. He has been president of International Association of Cross-Cultural Psychology (IACCP). He has contributed articles to several reputed journals and has edited *Perspective on Experimental Social Psychology in India, Social Reality : Perspective and Understanding, Psychology in India : State of The Art, Asian Contributions to Cross-Cultural Psychology* and *Handbook of Cross-cultured Psychology*, Vol. 1 (Second Edition) (Add : G. B. Pant Social Science Institute, Jhusi, Allahabad-211 019).

Sudhakar Rath is Reader in Psychology at Utkal University. His main interest is in cognitive style and interventions for overcoming cognitive deficits in deprived children. (Add : Department of Psychology, Utkal University, Bhubaneswar-751 004).

Damodar, Suar teaches psychology in the Department of Humanities and Social Sciences at I.I.T., Kharagpur. His areas of interest include community psychology, operations research and intervention strategies. He has also taught at Xavier Institute, Ranchi. He has authored '*Psychologial Aspects of Polarisation Phenomenon*'. (Add : Department of Humanities & Social Siences, Indian Institute of Technology, Kharagpur-721 302).

Durganand Sinha was the founding Head and Professor of Psychology, Department of Psychology at the University of Allahabad. He has been the President of the International Association for Cross-Cultural Psychology, as also its Fellow. He has published extensively on psychological dimensions of poverty and deprivation, cross-cultural psychology, and indigenisation in psychology. His publications include *Indian Villages in Transition : A Motivational Analysis, Motivation and Rural Development, The Mughal Syndrome, Psychology in a Third World Country : The Indian Experience, Social Values Development, Effective Organisations and Social Values,* and *Asian Perspectives on Psychology.* (Add : 8, Malviya Road, George Town, Allahabad-211 002).

Tara Singh is Senior Lecturer of Psychology at Barkatullah University. He has published papers on cognitive development and was also associated with project on coping with ecological crisis under the Partnership Programme of Shastri-Indo-Canadian Institute and did field work in British Columbia, Canada. (Add : Department of Psychology, Barkatullah University, Bhopal-462 026).

Anoop Kumar Singh is Professor at Management Development Institute, Gurgaon. He has been a visiting scholar at Institute of Social Research, University of Michigan, Ann Arbor. His area of interest includes attribution, poverty, and organisational development. In addition to articles in Journals he has authored *Social*

Psychology of Poverty and edited *Human Resource & Development : Psychological Perspectives.* (Add : Management Development Institute P.B. 60, Meharauli Road, Sukhrali, Gurgaon-122 001)

Aparna Vajpayee is post doctoral fellow at Psychology Department, Banaras Hindu University. She is interested in deprivation and cognitive development. (Add : Department of Psychology, Banaras Hindu University, Varanasi-221 005).

SECTION-I

CONCEPTUAL ISSUES IN POVERTY AND DISADVANTAGE

1

Introduction

AJIT K. MOHANTY AND GIRISHWAR MISRA

Psychological research on poverty and disadvantage in India is over three decades old. Indian psychologists have variously focussed on the problems of poverty, deprivation and disadvantage along with several related and applied issues such as rural development, malnutrition, illiteracy, population growth, health and sanitation etc. Psychological analyses of the problems of poverty and disadvantage— their concomitants and correlates, processes involved in growing up under these conditions and in coping with them, and the question of intervention at the individual and/or societal level— have enormous application potential and policy implication. But, in reality, Indian psychological research in this area has had very little impact on the policies and programmes for the poor and the disadvantaged. Over the years the volume of research relating to poverty and disadvantage has grown, but, barring a few attempts (e.g. Misra & Tripathi, 1980; Sinha, 1969; Sinha, Tripathi & Misra, 1982), not much has been done towards a comprehensive understanding of social and psychological processes underlying poverty and disadvantage. In respect of some aspects of the phenomena, for example, in characterising the conditions and psychological consequences of social disadvantage and poverty, there exists a substantial bulk of studies but, overall, in the absence of any clear conceptual framework and theoretical perspective, the gap between research and application remains formidable.

Other social sciences like economics and sociology have found their forte in this domain of human interest but psychology with a narrow disciplinary perspective has lagged behind in making any appreciable impact. This is unfortunate because poverty and disadvantage are being increasingly viewed as not just economic phenomena but as social and psychological in nature. Even the affluent societies have built-in inequalities which give rise to perception of certain individuals or groups as poor, deprived or underprivileged. Various socio-cultural conditions interact in complex ways to create inequality of opportunities which put some in an advantaged or privileged position and, others, to disadvantage, deprivation and, possibly, to a state of economic poverty at least in a relative sense. True, that the differences between the privileged and the deprived or the poor and the others within a society as well as between societies may not always be very sharp in objective terms, but, they are psychologically real.

The perceived states of deprivation, poverty and disadvantage, however, are not just subjective experiences; they are grounded in physical realities of income, caste, class, housing, nutrition, health and all other socio-economic conditions which are linked to well-being and quality of life. The nexus between the objective socio-economic conditions and subjective experience of being poor or disadvantaged becomes evident when one finds that in any given society the chances of upward mobility and success in terms of the accepted criteria are also differentially distributed. In the modern scientific and technological societies, for example, success or chances of upward mobility are associated, to a large extent, with scholastic success. However, scholastic success itself is an unevenly distributed phenomenon. While some succeed, quite a few meet with failures. Of the ones who fail, most share some common characteristics— they belong to the lower social strata, low income groups, minorities and socially discriminated groups etc. In other words, in any society individuals belonging to certain groups, with some marked characteristics, have a higher chance of failure in terms of the criteria valued in the society as indicators of success and upward mobility. Such groups are at a disadvantage because their members have a limited chance of success and upward mobility.

Whether or not an individual feels to be so disadvantaged or the extent to which the criteria of success or failure are just would matter but so would the group belongingness biasing the chances of success. Disadvantage, thus, is both real and relative. It is real in the sense that within a given social framework the chances of success and, hence, resources are unevenly available. It is also relative because, as social values and priorities change, individuals may find themselves at different ends of a success-failure or advantaged-disadvantaged continuum. A very successful university professor may become more disadvantaged in a tribe of hunters because of his lack of prowess with bows and arrows. The notion of deprivation and disadvantage, therefore, is linked to the risk of lacking resources which are valued in a given society.

Poverty is commonly understood as a lack of economic resources, although this in itself would be inadequate for identifying the poor; one would have to view poverty as a set of social, economic and psychological conditions. Thus, the concepts of poverty and disadvantage are embedded in the socio-cultural, political, economic and psychological contexts. The dichotomies of disadvantaged-advantaged, poor-nonpoor and deprived-nondeprived are the conventional labels essentially of a relative nature. In a complex pluralistic society like India they cannot be viewed as discrete categories. Contrasts, such as Harijan vs. Brahman, urban vs. rural, tribal vs. nontribal and even, female vs. male, based on caste, class and other demographic parameters are not to be viewed in the manner in which the Black-White dichotomy has often been treated in American psychology. Given the complex multidimensional nature of poverty and disadvantage, it is not surprising that this area of research often shows ambiguity in conceptualization.

As has been stated, the phenomena of poverty and

disadvantage are related to the question of inequality of resources, wealth, income, skills etc.— and the question of social inequality. Hence, the parameters of poverty and disadvantage are both objective and subjective. Poverty is indicated by the aspects of standard of living or the economic quality of life as well as by a perceived status in the society. It is generally observed, however, that the perceived poverty is related to objective economic indicators. People often have a somewhat realistic view of the quality of lives of their own and of others resulting in a general agreement regarding 'visible' poverty. But what really compels a psychological or multidisciplinary approach to the problems of poverty and disadvantage is the in-built and self-defeating nature of poverty and disadvantage. They seem to be associated with a set of characteristics which entail psychological barriers towards change and development (Sinha, 1990). In other words, besides being linked with economic indices of quality of life, poverty and disadvantage are also associated with some social, psychological and cultural features which help explain and predict differences between the relatively less and more poor and disadvantaged in a given society. Somewhat consistent relationship between the conditions of poverty and disadvantage and such socio-cultural and psychological characteristics have given rise to concepts like *poverty syndrome* or *culture of poverty*.

Unfortunately, terms like "poverty syndrome" or "culture of poverty" tend to be value loaded. In an era of search for alternatives and pluralism in thought and world views, labelling of individuals/ groups/cultures as "deprived", "disadvantaged" or "poor" because they do not conform to certain preconceived criteria, sets in motion a series of processes which perpetuate inequality. Use of phrases like "culturally deprived" or "socially disadvantaged" is fraught with biases of imposed values of the dominant segments of the society. Unfortunately, social scientists and researchers, often knowingly or unknowingly represent such biases. However, psychological studies of poverty and social disadvantage are now turning away from a *deficit* approach (blaming the victims of poverty for its consequences) in favour of difference approaches which show that 'culture of poverty' does not entail a 'poverty of culture' and suggests that the poor and the disadvantaged are *different* from the dominant society. Issues of cultural relativism cannot be divested from the study of poverty and disadvantage. The cultural implications of intervention programmes for the poor and the disadvantaged need to be examined from a *difference* perspective because such programmes often bring about cultural assimilation and subjugation under the guise of development and modernization.

Yet another issue fundamental to psychological research and applications in the area of poverty and disadvantage is the level of analysis. Psychologists have appreciated the social and relative nature of these phenomena but have felt more comfortable in dealing with the same at individual level. The context of development of individuals as well as groups incorporates several subsystems of environment— social, physical and psychological— which interact leading to the processes of poverty and disadvantage in a society. Preference for individual focussed micro level approaches have led to a peculiar intrapsychic framework being too narrow. The problems of micro-level approaches are quite evident in the limited and short-term success of some of the psychological interventions directed at changing the individuals living and growing in poverty and disadvantage through training, motivational and attitudinal reorientation and other means without any effort at attacking the problem at a higher level of social analysis. In fact, sometimes micro-level interventions generate greater amount of frustration with raised expectations getting thwarted by a relatively static or change-resistant social structure. Thus, while the value of individual focus on micro-level analyses in understanding and ameliorating poverty and disadvantage cannot be denied, there is an urgent need to adopt a macro-level and multidisciplinary perspective.

Extreme poverty usually involves a number of conditions of enduring deprivation such as malnutrition, illiteracy, ill health and a host of other socio-cultural and economic factors. The phenomenon has, therefore, to be understood from a variety of perspectives. Poverty and disadvantage cannot be treated as a unitary social, cultural, economic or psychological condition. They reflect combination of several mutually interacting conditions which are yet to be fully understood. Further, as has been pointed out earlier, these conditions are usually associated with certain groups in the society such as the Scheduled Castes (SC) and the Scheduled Tribes (ST) which are enduringly deprived of economic resources and social privileges. This relationship between group belongingness and deprivation is invariably linked with the vicious nature of the poverty cycle and the cumulative effects of early deprivation. However, poverty and disadvantage are not, simply, characteristics of sub-populations, they are also the consequences of social conditions; they can be viewed both as causes and consequences of specific patterns of social development.

Contextualization of poverty and disadvantage is, thus, imperative. At the same time, individual or, at least, process level micro-approaches are warranted. Poverty and disadvantage as social processes must also be understood in terms of processes of human development under difficult circumstances (UNICEF, 1986) such as severe malnutrition, child abuse, forced prostitution, child labour, broken family and family violence, street childhood etc. The relationship of these circumstances with development under conditions of poverty and disadvantage remains to be fully explored. Further, in a contextual and process view of poverty and disadvantage, systematic variations in these conditions must be properly understood. For example, poverty under rural and urban settings perhaps needs to be viewed as somewhat separate phenomena. While rural poverty is characterised by absolute economic disparity, lack of motivation and resistance to changes, urban poverty is perhaps a more relative phenomenon without some common syndrome of rural poverty. In fact, change proneness and motivation may be higher among the urban poor. The urban society seems to be characterised by a sharper cleavage between the rich and the poor whereas in a rural society the gradient of poverty appears to be more continuous. This has implications for the perception of poverty whose psychological ramifications cannot be ignored.

Thus, it seems there is a need for psychologists to broaden the conceptual framework for the study of poverty and disadvantage to address the problem with a macro-level and interdisciplinary perspective and a focus on the underlying processes at a micro-level. One objective of this volume is to assess the existing theoretical and conceptual bases of psychological research in India on poverty and disadvantage and to bring together the work of some leading researchers to facilitate the emergence of a broader multidisciplinary framework for further work in this area.

The Indian researchers interested in the psychology of poverty and disadvantage have so far been largely confined to demonstration of differences between groups sampled on the basis of caste, income, region, socio-economic status (SES) and other sub-cultural or group differences and labelled as disadvantaged/deprived/under privileged. A variety of cognitive and intellective measures, and measures of motivation, personality, mental health, attitudes and academic achievement are some very common grounds of comparison, preferred by the researchers, between the disadvantaged and non-disadvantaged. Such comparisons are fraught with several methodological problems and problems arising out of test biases as well as sampling artifacts. Treatment of poverty and disadvantage as gross variables without any reflection on the processes underlying the operation of these variables have also added to the confusion and equivocal nature of our findings. Despite these and other limitations, some earlier analyses (e.g. Misra, 1983, 1984; Rath, Dash & Dash, 1979; Sinha, Tripathi & Misra, 1982) have shown some trends. In general the groups in poverty and disadvantage are found to perform poorly compared to their privileged counterparts on most of the cognitive tasks.

The differences in performance, however, are not so pronounced in respect of basic ability to learn. Further, while the poor and the disadvantaged tend to show similar performance as their counterparts in early years of development, the gap between them tends to increase over the years. Such cumulative deficit in performance is also found in respect of academic achievement. This is particularly significant because it is estimated that in the developing countries 20 million of the 100 million children in the primary school age do not attend school and an additional 30 million drop out by grade four (UNICEF, 1990). In India, drop out rate among some disadvantaged groups is estimated to be 80 percent by grade five. As discussed earlier, educational failure forms an important aspect of social disadvantage and, therefore, it needs to be viewed more comprehensively.

The poor, and the disadvantaged, contrasted with the mainstream or the dominant and privileged groups, seem to lack the qualities, dispositions, skills, motivation and values needed for upward mobility in a harsh and competitive world which adversely affects their motivation rendering them passive and feeling helpless. However, it must be pointed out that these findings depict a relationship between poverty/disadvantage and performance which is more correlational than causal and usually inferred following comparisons of extreme groups. Poverty and disadvantage are grossly viewed both as causes as well as consequences of poor psychological performance in various dimensions. Further, as noted earlier, the processes by which the relationship between specific aspects of poverty/disadvantage and psychological performance is mediated need to be addressed rather than treating them (i.e. poverty and disadvantage) as global or unitary phenomena. In the Indian studies on consequences of poverty and disadvantage there seems to be a conspicuous lack of diversity perspective blurring the distinctions between the difference vs. deficit approaches (Cole & Bruner, 1971). In this volume, an attempt has been made to review the Indian studies on this aspect of poverty and disadvantage and to show some trends towards a better and authentic understanding of the processes underlying the problems, their causes and consequences.

Earlier, we have noted that the processes involved in bringing about quick economic growth with social justice and overall improvement in the quality of life to bridge the gap between the rich and the poor through interventions at the individual or group level may be somewhat unsettling with possible psychological repurcussions. By and large, psychological interventions have been viewed as micro-level approaches shunning away from the complex realities. It is essential to widen the horizon, focus on systemic and structural macro-level variables and to become multidisciplinary. Schemes and programmes for alleviation of poverty and disadvantage, primarily based on limited perspective(s), have also contributed to failure in realizing the desired results. As pointed out, poverty, deprivation and disadvantage are primarily environmental phenomena related to distribution and availability of resources as well as complex socio-cultural dynamics. It, therefore, requires a multipronged strategy at the levels of the individual, the community and the society at large.

It is evident that the poor and the disadvantaged come from conditions which are discontinuous with those prevailing in the mainstream of society and which are made complex by the prevalent strategies, biases and discriminations making them more vulnerable and leading to feelings of helplessness and hopelessness. Under such circumstances, the mechanisms for promoting individual competence and social empowerment, which would break the expectancy frame of non-contingent relationship to foster the feelings of self-efficacy need to be introduced. Changes in school practices, compensatory education and enrichment programmes, social policies, and economic input through gainful employment opportunities are necessary along with individual interventions.

In this context, intervention efforts by the psychologists have been generally very narrow and individual-focussed and very little has been done in terms of analysing the successes and failures of large scale interventions and social welfare programmes from a psychological perspective. In respect of welfare and subsidy oriented programmes, it has been suggested that, "support may lead to dependency which may further perpetuate the problem rather than solve it. Support should be of such quality that people feel competent enough to take initiative and feel responsible for their actions and have the experience of personal causation and self-efficacy" (Misra, 1990). Thus, while individual level psychological interventions have to be embedded in a wider social context, broader community level social interventions need to consider the psychological processes at the level of individuals and groups. To conclude, the assumptions of current interventions for poverty and disadvantage call for a fresh look which this volume seeks to provide through analysis of interventions at different levels, their successes and failures, scope and limitations.

On the whole, in bringing together various views, findings, theoretical integrations, and practical insights in respect of the major themes and concerns in psychology of poverty and disadvantage, particularly in the Indian context, this volume seeks to advance our understanding of the problems and their remedies. The contributors are involved and experienced researchers in the field and offer divergent perspectives and approaches amid a unity of concerns to make psychology in India more meaningful and relevant for the poor and the disadvantaged.

Organisation of the volume

The chapters in this volume are thematically organised into three substantive sections reflecting the major concerns in psychological studies on poverty and disadvantage and a concluding section in which we have sought to draw some broad trends and future prospects. The major sections dealing with conceptual issues, concomitants of poverty and disadvantage and intervention do not consider the themes as mutually exclusive as would be obvious from the views and analyses presented under each section. Rather, the organisation reflects certain dominant concerns of the researchers in the area as well as the manner in which scholars in the field of psychology generally classify the studies on poverty and disadvantage. Each section begins with a chapter in which one or both the editors have sought to provide a general overview delineating the various perspectives in the context of which the papers by the contributors may be viewed. There is a broad set of ideas and positions on which there is general agreement among the contributors but they put forth their own points of view and their own definition of the problems and issues are presented. The opening chapter in each section, therefore, is intended to put these points of view into perspective.

The first section deals with issues in conceptualizing poverty and disadvantage. To speak of poverty and disadvantage inescapably implies certain assumptions and value judgements about the individual and the social order. Various disciplines in social sciences have their own dominant perspectives and priorities which imply certain values. Part of the problem in psychological research on poverty and disadvantage resides in a failure to reconcile these divergent perspectives. As we have argued earlier, psychology of poverty cannot be diverted from the economics or the sociology of poverty. Girishwar Misra has sought to review comprehensively the perspectives from different disciplines in defining and conceptualising poverty and disadvantage. He has discussed various approaches and the problems arising out of an exclusive adherence to any one of these approaches. Concepts of poverty, deprivation and disadvantage have been analysed with a focus on the issues in definition, identification and measurement. The remaining papers in the section are in a general agreement with Misra that the phenomena of poverty and disadvantage are to be holistically viewed. However, there seems to be some divergence of views in respect of the degree to which the focus in psychological approach ought to be on the individual or group in poverty and disadvantage or on the social context of the phenomena. While Sinha views the individual's family and social conditions as constituting different interacting layers in his ecological model, Pandey's focus is more on the individual's perception of his/her state of poverty within this totality. Uday Jain and Tara Singh seek to move the focus to the social context pleading that poverty and disadvantage are socially constructed realities. On the basis of his analysis of language issues, Mohanty argues that psychological disadvantage is perpetuated by social inequalities and differential privileges associated with languages and cultures resulting in the lack of opportunities for socio-economic mobility for some. These conceptualisations of poverty and disadvantage are consequential for research and applications in the area.

Sinha traces a brief history of Indian psychological research on poverty since the seventies. In his view, psychology of poverty is more concerned with identification of "attendant conditions" of poverty than with its definition or causes. Poverty has certain adverse impacts on individual's functioning rendering him/her less competent to deal effectively with the demands of the environment. Study of such effects of poverty is essential in Sinha's view, for devising intervention programmes. He also points to some positive aspects of people growing up in poverty, such as cohesiveness, tolerance, interdependence, which should find a prominent place in psychological literature. Sinha's paper discusses an ecological framework for identifying the conditions and the psychological processes related to poverty and deprivation and a model relating poverty to its psychological consequences and behavioural outcomes. The major trends in Indian research on psychological correlates of poverty are briefly discussed. However, Sinha observes that these studies have not had much impact on policy formulation and intervention strategies and pleads for greater attention to 'systemic' and structural variables associated with poverty and a more macrocosmic approach.

On the basis of his review of various measures of poverty, Pandey shows the need for incorporating various social psychological dimensions in conceptualisation of poverty. He discusses measures of perceived poverty, relative poverty, perceived social status and rated quality of living conditions and goes on to discuss some research findings relating these measures to caste and socio-economic mobility. He also shows interesting aspects of perception of causes and functional nature of poverty. Studies by Pandey and his colleagues show that people with leftist ideology and rickshaw pullers who do not own their rickshaw tend to blame the government and others for poverty which also is perceived to be somewhat functional by the middle class, more so by middle class women. Pandey discusses the implications of these interesting findings and of the significance of studying the perceived and socio-psychological dimensions of poverty in developing societies.

Jain and Singh view psychological research on poverty as having been primarily undertaken within the 'deficit' or 'deprivation' paradigm which has often led to a 'blame-the-victim' view of poverty. This dominant paradigm has, in their view, came as a relief or a convenient apology to planners and implementers of policy for the failure of intervention. Further, there is an exclusive focus on the individual in psychological analyses as well as interventions which, according to Jain and Singh, will remain ineffective or at best temporarily successful in the absence of structural changes at the societal level. They question the epistemological bases of psychological research on poverty— the conceptualisation of the problem as well as the basic methodological approaches, and discuss a contextual view of poverty which focuses on poverty as a social process in the context of the environment and the socio-cultural milieu. Such a social perspective according to them is useful in understanding the psychology of poverty and extending help to plan for interventions. Finally, they advocate a social constructionist approach to bridge the gap between research and practice in psychology of poverty.

The plea for a social-contextual approach to poverty is also taken up in the next chapter by Mohanty in which it is argued that inequality perpetuated by the society through its policies and institutions forces certain groups and cultures to a status of disadvantaged and poor. The point is sought to be substantiated through an analysis of the issue of the language of the disadvantaged. It is argued that the mismatch between the home language of the minority mother tongue speakers and language of their schooling is one of many ways in which groups are put at a disadvantage. The nature of Indian multilingualism and positive consequences of bilingualism are discussed to argue that denial of rights of the speakers of minority mother tongues and 'nonstandard' varieties to use their language often leads to educational failure and lack of social mobility. Cultures and languages are rendered powerless by social neglect and discrimination which are sought to be justified on the grounds of weaknesses of those languages and cultures leading to a viscious cycle of disadvantage. Mohanty advocates a mother tongue based multilingual education for all children in order to confront this viscious cycle. The debate on individual centred versus social centred approaches is carried a step further by showing how disadvantage does not constitute an inherent property of individuals, groups or subcultures, but a condition of the society which perpetuates inequality by various means. In view of the pluralistic nature of Indian society, this approach seems to carry a forceful appeal.

The Section II in this volume is devoted to an analysis of the psychological correlates of poverty and disadvantage. In the first chapter in this section we have sought to provide a comprehensive picture reviewing the Indian literature on the psychological consequences and correlates of poverty and disadvantage. The review touches upon all the major areas of psychological dimensions of disadvantage which Indian researchers have addressed. Discussion of Indian studies on health, nutrition and development under conditions of poverty and disadvantage includes problems of malnutrition, mental health, and emotional adjustment problems associated with these conditions. The processes of poverty and their role are discussed under the group of studies dealing with socialisation of children in poverty and personality and motivational aspects of poverty and disadvantage. Cognitive and scholastic consequences are reviewed next in light of the major Indian studies in this area. The review also touches upon the explanations of the consequences of poverty and disadvantage as reflected in the Indian literature. Some methodological limitations of these studies are discussed.

While our review seeks to provide as nearly a complete picture as possible offering a bird's eye view of the Indian literature, the remaining chapters provide more specific and detailed illustrations without any claim regarding their representativeness. The study by Anjali and Sinha reported in the next chapter shows social class differences in children's expressive skills and their syntactic and semantic development. The study also shows that lower class families are characterised by a poor linguistic environment for the child which was assessed in terms of quality of the linguistic interaction, speech variety, language learning opportunities and stimulation available to the child in the family and outside. Social class and linguistic environment were found to be highly inter-related.

Social class difference in intelligence has been a major concern in psychological research throughout the world although the concept of intelligence is perhaps in the process of being thrown out of fashion. In India, SES and intelligence-related aspects of intellectual functioning happen to be very popular variables in psychological research. Anup Singh's paper addresses itself very specifically to this issue of the relationship between poverty and IQ, also touching upon the question of heritability of intelligence and the biases in IQ testing. This review article is included in the volume more as a recognition of the centrality of the theme for the issues which concern this section of the book. Singh reviews Indian studies as well as others in different parts of the world relating poverty to intelligence. He finds the evidence inconclusive particularly in view of the controversy regarding the nature of intelligence and problems inherent in testing the IQ of disadvantaged populations. He also examines the nature-nurture issue in relating poverty to intelligence and questions the findings in respect of heritability estimates of intelligence. In conclusion, Singh points out that differences in intelligence are not as important as the question of maximizing the potentials of the poor and the disadvantaged.

Apart from the questions of cognitive consequences of poverty and disadvantage, Indian psychologists have shown a major preference for the analysis of motivational concomitants of poverty and disadvantage. As such, a lot has been said about the lack of motivation of the poor and disadvantaged. In the last chapter under this section, Misra and Jain examine the cognitive bases of motivation of the disadvantaged in terms of their causal attribution. They integrate the findings of a series of studies on attribution for achievement among the disadvantaged compared to the more advantaged groups. Disadvantaged groups were found to attribute success to external factors and failure to internal factors. The opposite was noted with the nondisadvantaged groups. It seems that the poor blame themselves more for their poverty. However, studies reviewed by Misra and Jain also show that such processes of attribution are affected by class stereotypes as well as by the feelings of helplessness rendering the motivation of the disadvantaged groups dysfunctional. The authors examine the various explanations of the observed attributional characteristics of the disadvantaged groups and their implications for motivational interventions.

Section III in the book is about interventions with poor and disadvantaged individuals and communities— issues, strategies and problems in such endeavours. Unfortunately, interventions are most often talked of but rarely attempted. Reports of most psychological studies in almost all the areas, particularly the ones dealing with disadvantaged populations, usually end with suggestions for intervention or remedial actions but, very few, really get translated into actual practice. Of the few that are attempted we seldom hear of or read about the ones that failed. Further, psychological input into many large scale intervention programmes with the disadvantaged groups usually supported by the state, is very little indeed. Usually, psychologists remain contented with small scale interventions or training studies. In the first chapter (Ch. 11) of this section Girishwar Misra and Uday N. Dash provide an analysis of the various levels of intervention efforts for alleviation of poverty and disadvantage. They discuss studies to evaluate the success or failure of some major and large scale intervention efforts supported by the Government. Their review also focuses on psychological intervention and training studies which are directed at changing some aspect of individual's psychological functioning to enhance his/her chances of overcoming the drawbacks associated with poverty and disadvantage.

Rath (ch.12) discusses the scope of intervention with the disadvantaged groups within the cognitive behaviour modification paradigm. He demonstrates specific application of verbal self-instructional (VSI) training in improvement of cognitive-academic performance of disadvantaged tribal children. Another psychological intervention study is reported by R.C. Mishra and Aparna Vajpayee in the next chapter (Ch. 13) in this section. Mishra and Vajpayee begin by reviewing various intervention efforts which they group as structural change and behaviour change attempts— a distinction which closely parallels Girishwar Misra and Dash's view of large scale state sponsored intervention and psychological intervention. Mishra and Vajpayee view both the social level and the individual level interventions as necessary. They report the findings of their own intervention study with low and high-caste children in which training was successful in levelling off the difference between the two caste groups on cognitive measures. The effect of training was also shown to persist after six months. In the light of their findings and review of studies, Mishra and Vajpayee discuss the role of caste variable in India and the nature of effect that training produces under different conditions. They also discuss some general issues in respect of intervention programmes and their policy implications.

As pointed out earlier, the literature on intervention carries an inherent bias. Not only do the negative findings often go unreported, the reports of positive findings also seem to grossly exaggerate the extent of success. Intervention programmes are conducted under complex conditions the dynamics of which are often beyond the control of those responsible for implementing the programmes. As such, more often than not success is mixed with failures and frustrations which get glossed over amid the euphoria of a successfully implemented programme. In this context, Dalal's (Ch. 14) account of a community based rehabilitation (CBR) programme for the disabled is refreshingly down-to-earth. As a good psychologist, Dalal is able to stand back and dispassionately reflect upon the success and failures, problems and prospects of a community based rehabilitation project sharing his experiences which may provide a lot of insight to any one planning intervention with the disadvantaged.

In the next chapter (Ch. 15) Damodar Suar goes beyond his own experience of development programmes with the disadvantaged rural people to show the enormous complexity of such programmes and to suggest some practical approaches to handle the same. He begins by listing some commonly observed characteristics of the disadvantaged in rural settings which have implications for intervention efforts. Based on his analysis, Suar proceeds to recommend systematic steps as a guideline for the development professionals involved in interventions with the disadvantaged rural people. His suggestions are practical but tentative and can be taken as a broad set of guidelines for those involved in the process of social and psychological change and community intervention for the poor and the disadvantaged.

In an area like this with its multidimensionality, pervasiveness and complexity, many questions are bound to arise. The chapters in this volume address some of the vital issues in the psychological study of poverty and disadvantage although there may still be some loose ends. As an area of study grows, new questions crop up and new insights develop. Hopefully, the present volume can contribute to a reappraisal of the field of psychology of poverty and disadvantage in the Indian context by facilitating some insights and, at the same time, raising new issues. Our discussion in the last Section IV (Chapter 16) is an attempt to bring to focus the vast scope of this area of study and the challenges and possibilities. In this chapter we have sought to take a fresh look at the issues, put forth our view on the necessary changes in the approaches and the perspectives and to show some trends and directions for future developments in this important and interesting field of human enquiry.

2

Conceptualization of Poverty, Deprivation and Disadvantage

GIRISHWAR MISRA

Notwithstanding the fact that while poverty and deprivation conditions subsume approximately two-third of world's population, its study as a significant theme has remained marginalized in the field of psychology for a long time. Confined largely to the modern and developed part of the world, the discipline of psychology shares most of its concerns with understanding the social reality of the industrialized countries. Psychology texts, even those specializing in social behaviour, never bothered to talk about the nature, causes and remedies of poverty. Such an avoidant attitude reflects psychologists' emphasis on variables and constructs. Its commitment to the ideology of individualism, and its reductionistic bias have made the mainstream psychologists indifferent towards the study of issues involving complex political, economic and structural considerations. The decontextualized mode of psychological scholarship under the positivist tradition has further contributed to this attitude. Psychologists in India too were preoccupied with the same set of issues and problems (Sinha, 1986). As a result, attention to the issues like poverty had to wait for a change in the focus of national planning as well as recognition of the academic legitimacy of such research. As Moulik (1981) in the second ICSSR Survey commented, the research in this area indeed reflected "poverty of psychology". The third ICSSR Survey included several contributions (e.g. Muthayya, 1988; Panda, 1988; Saraswathi & Dutta, 1988; R.C. Tripathi

1988) which examined poverty and deprivation in contexts of rural development, education, human development and applied social psychology. In general, the researchers documented adverse effects of poverty and deprivation on major psychological functions.

During the last one decade, a number of reviews and volumes on poverty and deprivation have been published (Misra, 1983, 1990a; Misra & L.B. Tripathi, 1980; A.K. Sen & Anima Sen, 1984; Anoop K. Singh, 1991; D. Sinha, 1982a,b, 1990; D. Sinha, R.C. Tripathi & G. Misra, 1982). Researchers have opted for one of the two foci i.e., (i) Macro-level social and economic processes, and (ii) individual's experience of poverty and its socio-psychological consequences. Among allied disciplines like economics the nature and assessment of poverty have remained central (Gupta, 1987; Jalan, 1992; Minhas, 1974; Myrdal, 1968; Rede, 1990; Roy, 1972; Singh, 1969). It has also become a concern for the students of environment (Chambers, Saxena & Shah, 1989), development (Chand, 1987), social work (Singh, 1980), political processes (Jain, Krishnamurthy & Tripathi, 1986; Kohli, 1987; Kothari, 1989; Lewis, 1991; Ommen, 1988; L. Rudolph & S. Rudolph, 1987), and law (Baxi, 1988).

The different disciplines have analysed poverty from different vantage points looking at diverse aspects of the problem. In fact, studies show what Chambers *et al.* (1989) have termed *a professional poverty trap* which leaves many aspects of poverty unrecognized. For instance, the urban concept of 'employment' and villagers' notion of 'livelihood' point to two different modes of thinking. It has been observed that the study of poverty differs from the lived experience of poverty. The researchers who are not poor, often represent well to do socioeconomic background. Their scholarship lies in refined analyses of poverty and suggesting policy which can gradually enhance the quality of life of the poor. Economists often choose some aspect of poverty (e.g.; static and standardized wants and needs) amenable to measurement, particularly the flow of income or consumption (Chambers, 1991). It has been found that income and consumption are not inclusive (Jodha, 1986).

Also people's wants, needs, priorities change over time and are determined by a host of social and demographic factors (e.g., age, ethnicity, occupation etc.).

The interest of psychologists in the study of *poverty* has been focused on considering it *as* an antecedent or a consequent *variable*. However, the bidirectionality of the relationship between the causes and consequences of poverty often makes poverty an unmanageable construct. It is difficult to capture its essence through any simple unilinear and microscopic strategy. A social group or community termed 'poor' or 'deprived' is constituted by diverse types of people who vary along several characteristics (e.g., age, employment status, residence, caste, gender, health status). Viewed in this context "children", "women", "tribals", "migrant slum-dwellers", "beggars", "untouchables" and "labourers" all can be categorized as poor. However, they share little commonality in terms of the particular psychological characteristics. Psychologists, unfortunately are not well prepared to undertake the analyses of macro variables. They examine the issue of poverty and deprivation within the broad context of environment— human development linkage. This leads to conceptualizing poverty mainly as a negative condition along the environmental— experiential continuum supposed to restrict and interfere with the process of growth and development.

As hinted earlier the study of poverty and related phenomena have been pursued from many angles and different construals of poverty have emerged. The complex and often fragmented understanding that has emerged in this process does not offer any simple conceptualization of the phenomena. The psychological analyses may be grouped under three broad categories i.e., *poverty, deprivation* and *social disadvantage*. Poverty is basically a comparative economic concept rooted in the notion of inequality. It has usually been looked at as economic hardship. If a large section of society's population is incapable of satisfying the basic needs then this situation is termed as poverty. Thus if a group lacks resources to meet the needs for accommodation, nutrition, clothing, education and health which are essential to maintain one's capability then that group is termed as poor. The term deprivation stands for a sense of loss/lack or suffering. Such an experience is associated with poverty but psychologists tend to localize it in the individual. Disadvantage is related to the structurally determined socioeconomic conditions. It involves socially imposed discrimination/handicap as found in the case of scheduled castes (SCs) and the scheduled tribes (STs). Theoretically deprivation can be experienced by any group or individual but the deprivations experienced by the socially disadvantaged groups emanate from individual's group membership. Let us examine these concepts in some detail.

Poverty

Poverty has been understood by social scientists in a variety of ways. Being multifaceted and relative in nature any unidimensional characterization of poverty fails to encompass the range of factors bearing on it. However, expanding the definitional range of the concept often-times leads to confusion between the causes of poverty and its consequences (Roy, 1982). The socio-economic definitions of poverty necessarily presuppose some notion of welfare and involve value judgement. The notion of *poverty line* separates population into two categories i.e., those who have an adequate level of welfare and those who do not. This is often achieved by adopting various criteria which select and label different groups as poor. These include *calorie intake, protein intake, food ratio, life expectancy, gross national product (GNP), per capita income, per capita consumption, the cost of a minimally adequate range of food, and clothing and shelter compared to income.* It may be noted that these criteria are not independent. Their adoption, however, leads to differing criteria to identify the poor. Of all these criteria, income or consumption level has been the most frequently used. Roy (1982) considers poverty as a 'relative lack of or inaccessibility to resources and/or inability to utilize resources to achieve what is needed or desired' (p. 14). To him, an adequate analysis of poverty should concentrate on both the social-institutional as well as individual-relevant characteristics.

Literally poverty refers to a state lacking material possessions and refers to the condition of having little or no wealth, indignation and want. It can be approached from an absolute or relative perspective. Thus reference to 'bare subsistence level' illustrates the use of an absolute objective approach while linking it with a specific income level demonstrates a relative view. Expressed in calorie terms the poverty ratio is at best an indicator of "food poverty". It does not function as a good indicator of the state of the overall social infrastructure such as hygiene and sanitation, drinking water, access to health, education and other facilities. An absolute definition of poverty does not help much because "people's needs, even for food, are conditioned by the society in which they live and to which they belong, and just as needs differ in different societies so they differ in different periods of the evolution of single society" (Townsend, 1979, p. 39). Two persons with the same expenditure at a particular level may experience different levels of well-being. A family below the poverty line in a relatively economically more developed region may have better Quality of Life (QOL) in terms of health and education than a family above the poverty line in a relatively "poor" or backward region. Thus the concept of poverty ratio as defined in terms of calorie intake does not help in identifying the families that may or should be covered by poverty eliminating programme in a given area.

More recently attention has been paid to evolve and use both macro indicators and micro norms of poverty in a given region. The Human Development Index (HDI) is such an attempt. The Human Development Report (HDR) 1997 focuses on poverty. It argues that it is in the deprivation of the lives people lead that poverty manifests itself. Poverty can mean more than a lack of what is necessary for material well-being. It can also mean the denial of opportunities and choices most basic to human development, to lead a long, healthy, creative life and to enjoy a decent standard of living, freedom, dignity, self-esteem and the respect of others. HDR 1997 brings together in a composite index the different features of deprivation in the quality of life to arrive at an aggregate judgement on the extent of poverty in a community. The human poverty index (HPI) as given in this report focuses on longevity, knowledge and a decent living standard. The first dimension relates to survival— the vulnerability to death at a relatively early age— and is represented in the HPI by the percentage of people expected to die before age 40. The second dimension relates to knowledge— being excluded from the world of reading and communication— and is measured by the percentage of adults who are illiterate. The third aspect relates to a decent standard of living in particular, overall economic provisioning. This is represented by a composite of three variables— the percentage of people with access to health services and to safe water, and the percentage of malnourished children under five.

This approach draws on the income perspective and basic needs perspective and concentrates on capability perspective. However, since everything cannot be included in a composite index several aspects of poverty are not included. Thus lack of political freedom, inability to participate in decision-making, lack of personal security, inability to participate in the life of a community and threats to sustainability and intergenerational equity. Also, it is argued that poverty depends on context. In the developing countries the HPI value for India is 36.7 per cent and the rank is 47 amongst 48 countries.

The definition of poverty tends to vary with change in the general level of affluence in a given society. It is the relative poverty which is sometimes manifested in the form of inter group conflicts. Relative poverty results from iniquitous institutional framework, uneven distribution of national income, increasing concentration of income and absence or ineffectiveness of the policy makers to check such inequalities. It is linked to differentiations in socioeconomic status (SES). Hierarchy and its psycho-social consequences are triggered of by attempts to emulate or achieve the position occupied by reference groups which a particular low SES group sets as its model.

In social scientific analysis poverty has been approached from one of three perspectives i.e. *functionalist, conflict based* and *interactionist*. The functionalists hold that poverty turns into a social problem when it no longer performs the function of motivating people to make productive contribution to society and poses threats to society. The conflict perspective assumes that poverty becomes a problem when a group feels that the distribution of resources in society is unfair and that should be redressed through some action. The interactionist perspective asserts that poverty is a function of shared expectations. Poor people in society internalise the negative images of themselves propagated by the significant others and behave according to these images. The functional perspective maintains that poverty fulfils several important functions for special interest groups. These include performing dirty work, guaranteeing the status of the non-poor, assisting upward mobility of the non-poor and absorbing the economic and political costs of technological and economic change (Gans, 1972).

In sociological thought, cultural and situational perspectives have been important (Rainwater, 1970; Valentine, 1968). Both of them have their ideological implications. The culturalist position proposes that the poor manifest patterns of behaviour and values which are characteristically different from those of the dominant society. The *culture of poverty*, as Oscar Lewis (1961, 1966) proposed, is a culture of multiple disabilities and gets transmitted across generations through socialization process. Because of instability and discontinuity in family life, low motivation, sticking to present-time orientation and being fatalistic the poor are at a disadvantage. In contrast, the situational perspective fails to treat the behaviour patterns of the poor as pathologies, nor are they seen as being derived as the products of a unique value system. They are normal outcomes of situations where the dominant social structure is unfavourably disposed and restricts the choices.

The assumed homogeneity of the characteristics of poor and the assumption of somewhat a closed relationship between the individual and society implied in the culture of poverty explanation are problematic (Anandlakshmy, 1982). The category of poor is heterogeneous. In an interesting analysis Shivaramayya (1988) has identified the following categories of the poor:

1. Those who do not have any means of livelihood except the 'charity' of the society, like the nonprofessional beggars, destitutes etc.

2. Those who are in a position to earn livelihood but whose occupational income is of a precarious or seasonal character or is highly susceptible to the vagaries of nature (e.g. agricultural labour).

3. Those who have a fairly steady occupational income—even if it is meagre and inadequate.

The cultural view does not take into cognizance the perspective of the poor. It is blind to the factors such as lack of opportunity, the discriminations and the prejudices that cause much poverty. It fails to explain minority groups and women/children who are poor. Also it obscures the vitality and resilience exhibited by at least some of the poor. The study on which cultural view is based was largely uncontrolled and the criteria of poverty were adopted in the context of middle social class. Rodman (1971) has advanced the concept of "lower class stretch" to meet some of these problems. He thought that the poor actually share the mainstream values but must "stretch" them to fit their circumstances. If freed from poverty, they will fit into the culture of the dominant people. This view goes in favour of the 'structure of society' explanation. Its problem is that it frees the poor from responsibility. Another alternative has been proposed by those who talk of a relational perspective on poverty. It situates poor within the social structure and underlines the significance of attitudes and actions of the non-poor toward the poor and the effects of these, in turn, upon the poor themselves.

Dreze and Sen (1995) have proposed that poverty may be analyzed in the context of the notion of capability. Capability denotes alternative combinations of functions from which a person can choose. It stands for freedom or the range of options a person has in deciding what kind of life to lead. Thus, poverty 'lies not merely in the impoverished state in which the person actually lives but also in the lack of the real opportunity. It is ultimately a matter of capability deprivation' (Dreze & Sen, 1995, p. 11).

Poverty Scenario in India

In India poverty has existed in varying degrees since long. According to a rough estimate approximately 82 per cent of the people in India lived in extreme poverty around the beginning of the later half of 19th century. In 1947, the percentage of poor was estimated at 59 per cent (Zaheer, 1976). In this way; Independent India inherited a large section of its population living under the societal condition of abject poverty.

The absolute level of poverty has been estimated in terms of indices such as calorie intake, national minimum expenditure for a household, per capita money expenditure and per capita income. Most of the studies are based on common expenditure surveys of National Sample Survey (NSS). In perhaps, the first systematic study of Indian poverty Dandekar and Rath (1971) used the norm of calorie intake. The estimate of poverty has been attempted by several of other scholars (Ahluwalia, 1986; Bardhan, 1970; Dandekar, 1981; Sen, 1985; Sukhatame, 1981) as well as by the Planning Commission of the Government of India. As has been said earlier measuring poverty using a single norm has its own limitations. For instance absolute poverty might increase even with increase in expenditure if there is a shrinkage of common property in the villages and if the public expenditure on social services contracts. If institutional framework becomes more negative, it is possible for a person to be above the poverty line getting trapped in the vicious circle of low level of health and productivity because of low level of social expenditure. Unfortunately the line of poverty approach to poverty measurement ignores and denies the experience of the poor in its analysis (Beck, 1994).

There are important regional differences in the incidence of poverty in India. In general its incidence has increased upto 1983 and declined thereafter for rural areas but increased in urban areas. The incidence of poverty in 1987-1988 was estimated at 48.7 per cent in rural area, 37.8 per cent in urban area and 45.8 per cent for the whole of India. Despite the decline in the head count ratio (H) the absolute number of the rural poor has increased. The Expert Group Report of the Planning Commission identified poverty base line of Rs. 49 (rural) and Rs. 57 (urban) at 1973-1974 prices anchored on the recommended per capita daily intake of 2400 calories and 2100 calories respectively, with reference to the consumption pattern of 1973-1974.

Rural Poverty

Being an agricultural country, vast majority of the Indian population lives in villages, a large section of which is poor. As Rede (1990) has pointed out, the H shows increase in poverty between 1960-61 to 1968-69. Between 1968-69 to 1973-74 rural poverty ratio shows a decline, rising again between 1973-74 to 1977-78. Between 1977-78 to 1988, rural poverty incidence again shows a decline. There is decline in the upper bound of poverty fluctuations, with lower bound being slowly approached in the rural sector. It seems that relative deprivation of the poor has been partly reduced (Dayal, 1989).

Rural poor come from the group of landless labourers, artisans and marginal/small farmers, most of them depend on wages and small farm products. The wages are usually seasonal. Due to inadequate earnings, the female members of poor families are compelled to go out for work. They, however, are vulnerable as the incidence of ill-health, under and mal-nutrition and poverty is very high amongst them. The rural poor are low in sociopolitical and economic status and are powerless. They fail to control important events in life.

Urban Poverty

The urban population in India is increasing due to natural

growth rate as well as the continuous influx of the people from villages. According to one estimate, 26 per cent of India's population is presently urbanized. Urbanization has led to rapid growth of slums and informal settlements in which people live without necessary physical amenities (e.g. water, sanitation, roads, drainage, education, health).

The available data indicate that India has the largest number of poor people than any other country in the world and though the proportion is declining, the absolute number of very poor people is still increasing. It has 27 per cent of the world's absolute poor. It is estimated that by early twenty-first century India will have the largest single concentration of poor urban people in the world.

Deprivation

Psychologists use 'deprivation' as a hypothetical construct as well as an empirical variable to characterize procedures and conditions in laboratory studies as well as studies done in natural settings. In the context of socio-economic and cultural variations in societies, it has been frequently employed interchangeably with other expressions such as 'cultural deprivation', 'environmental deprivation', 'parental deprivation', 'psychological deprivation', 'social deprivation', 'economic deprivation', and 'social disadvantage'. Most of these terms point to the deficient environmental conditions and impoverished experiences characteristic of the socially disadvantaged people (e.g., SC, ST, OBC). Literally 'deprivation' stands for the dispossession or loss of opportunities, privileges etc. However, researchers have virtually used as synonymous with 'privation', that is, lack or insufficiency of the basic necessities for survival of the individual. Thus the empirical studies of deprivation include both lack as well as loss of factors considered necessary for the growth and adaptation of the individual. In doing so, as G. Misra and L.B. Tripathi (1977) have noted, the researchers have often confused consequents with antecedents and have taken a very narrow range of variables in isolation somewhat arbitrarily. Also, the notion of deprivation is used to refer to a variety of states or conditions. R.C. Tripathi (1982) has identified three criteria to classify the states of deprivation i.e. — organismic vs. environmental; objective vs. subjective and absolute vs. relative.

The Indian researchers have usually regarded deprivation as a global characterization of environmental impoverishment, without dilineating the constituent environmental dimensions and the magnitude of differences amongst them. Deprivation is often viewed at through nominal categories such as caste, residential area or membership of a cultural/ethnic group. The resulting dichotomous groups are treated as deprived and non-deprived in "either/or" fashion which certainly is not the case. This has led to considerable confusion in understanding the specific features of deprivation. Use of SES scale which provides a composite score based on combination of factors such as income, education, occupational prestige, material assets and caste etc., has been a frequent practice. This, however, does not help in understanding deprivation. Also, there is no common area of agreement in SES scales (Reddy-Sujatha, 1986). As G. Misra (1983) observes "differences in these variables have been assumed to represent differences in environment's wealth or deprivation without delineating or specifying the exact nature of differences in environmental characteristics" (p. 14)

Some efforts have been made to go beyond the mere categorical or nominal level treatment of deprivation, by considering it in terms of proximal experiential variables. L.B. Tripathi and G. Misra's (1975) proposal of *prolonged deprivation* is such an attempt. It refers to a broader spectrum of variables constituting the basic sources of experiences of the individual. It is considered as a prolonged process relative to a defined socio-cultural setting. Socio-cultural life in any community can be conceived of as a continuum, at one end of which lie those who have all their physical, social and economic needs gratified, leading to varied experiences of life, while at the other end lie those who are physically, socially and psychologically most handicapped in fulfilling their needs, and are thus unable to have varied experiences. The members of various social groups undergo specific types of experiences and at times lack in experiential width and depth. This shift in conceptualization has led to significant changes in measurement of deprivation in the real life conditions. These authors (G. Misra & L.B. Tripathi, 1978) constructed a Prolonged Deprivation Scale (PDS) to assess the life conditions and experiences across 15 areas i.e., housing condition, home environment, economic sufficiency, food, clothing, formal educational experiences, childhood experiences, rearing experiences, parental characteristics, interaction with parents, motivational experiences, emotional experiences, religious experiences, travel and recreation and miscellaneous socio-cultural experiences. A factor analysis revealed two factors i.e., *physico economic deprivation* and *experiential deprivation.* Its variations have been developed by Misra and A. Shukla (1986) and Pushpa (1990). Recently, Mukherjee, Chatterjee and Gupta (1991) found three factors i.e., of prolonged deprivation, viz. *Physico-economic, cultural* and *emotional.*

Chambers (1991) has identified five dimensions of deprivation: *poverty proper* (lack of income and assets); *physical weakness* (under-nutrition, sickness, disability, lack of strength); *isolation* (ignorance, illiteracy, lack of peripheral location); *vulnerability* (to contingencies, to becoming poorer); and *powerlessness.* Based on the study of the priorities of the poor people, he has articulated a hierarchy of priorities consisting of survival, security and self-respect.

The perceived and subjective aspects of deprivation have also been attended to. For instance, Reddy (1992) has focused on the feeling of being deprived and developed a measure of *awareness of deprivation.* Pandey and Anoop K. Singh (1985) have developed a measure of *perceived poverty.* It involves subjective assessment of (a) income in relation to household expenditure, (b) dissatisfaction with economic condition, property, standard of housing, food, clothing and, (c) anxiety concerning resources for essential expenses (e.g., festivals, marriage rituals) and unexpected events (e.g. illness, accidents and death. This measure was modified by Nanda Biswas and Pandey (1996). It was observed that perceived poverty correlates positively with per-capita income and quality of living conditions. Also, the measure of perceived poverty in comparison to objective indicators has proved to be a stronger predictor of an individual's reactions to poverty, in terms of coping and adaptation (Pandey, 1999).

The human environment is often viewed as comprised of a system of nested hierarchies (Bronfenbrenner, 1977; G. Misra & K.N. Tripathi, 1993). Extending this approach to the Indian context, D. Sinha (1982b) has proposed an ecological model of deprivation consisting of two concentric layers of factors (See ch. 4 this volume). The studies of Saraswathi and Dutta (1990, 1992), and G. Misra and B.K. Tiwari (1986, 1992) have demonstrated the efficacy of ecological framework in relating poverty and deprivation to social and cognitive development.

Venkatamma and Rajamanickam (1984) found that in Tamilnadu, there was greater degree of deprivation, in motivational experiences and low in travel and recreation areas of prolonged deprivation. The number of children in the family was positively related to deprivation level. K. Pandey (1988) has developed a deprivation scale related to the deficiencies in social, emotional, economic, parental and educational areas. Similarly Upadhyaya (1986) developed an inventory to assess the deficiency in home and school environments. Tharakan (1992) has developed an SES measure including education, occupation, social participation, monthly income and material possession. G. Misra and B.K. Tiwari's (1986) measure of home environment consists of seven factors i.e., *intellective stimulation at home, perceived home environment, verbal interaction, parental concern, perception of school environment* and *parental pressure*. Amar K. Singh (1983) has used an additive index of social advantage/disadvantage consisting of four components i.e., (i) *income*: high/low, (ii) *social status*: high/low caste or tribe, (iii) *sex*: male/female, and (iv) *place of residence*: urban/rural.

Thus, it is clear that measurement of deprivation has been undertaken in diverse ways and with varying degrees of emphasis on dispositional and/or experiential features in one's life. Also most of these attempts use an additive model in which different components are equally weighted. While multidimensionality of the concept is often accepted the differential contributions of various factors and the degree of interrelatedness of parameters in the deprivation environment have often been ignored (Tripathi, 1982).

As a psychological construct, the study of deprivation suffers from several problems. They emerge from conceptual diversity in studies, level of measurement (microscopic vs. macroscopic) and investigator's specific concerns. L.B. Tripathi (1982) proposes microscopic treatment and analysis of deprivation. In another analysis Chatterjee (1982) has noted that there is a need to distinguish the variables with which deprivation correlates monotonically and nonmonotonically. In assessing poverty and deprivation, attention should be given to the needs and priorities of poor people as experienced by them. In this context, special care has to be taken not to miss or misperceive the poor.

Social Disadvantage

The Indian society presents a context in which vast differences still continue to exist in the life conditions of the people. It presents a hierarchically arranged social structure in which the lowest strata of society, constituted by the people of some backward and SC as well as ST groups is deprived of economic, cultural and social opportunities for considerable period of time. Areas with a high proportion of tribals notably in central and eastern India are amongst the poorest. In rural areas many low castes are still relegated to menial roles and are put to severe discrimination. The extent of admission to various socio-cultural and religious ceremonies and activities depends on the caste of a person. A majority of these castes make their living as agricultural or urban labourers as employees of the landlord. Their cultural, social and religious life somewhat differs from that of the higher castes. The prevailing power structures, partially reflecting the distribution of land ownership and wealth often create social discrimination.

The official measures adopted after independence (e.g., social legislation, industrialization, spread of educational facilities, Zamindari abolition) have made financial, educational, social and cultural activities partly independent of caste structure and upward social mobility has been on increase. However, the equality of opportunity is not yet realized. The efforts to accelerate the process of socio-economic uplift of the disadvantaged groups through positive discrimination have not been able to achieve much. On the other hand, the erosion of traditional way of life and making caste independent of occupation have created economic hardships for the high caste people. This has resulted in a category of economically disadvantaged people in the high caste strata too and caste alone cannot serve as an adequate criterion of poverty. Caste and class do go together to some extent but their relationship depends on many other contextual factors.

In brief, the nature of disadvantage and its dimensions in Indian context are characterized by an extreme degree of poverty, overpopulation, vertical social structure and varying degrees of agro-economic development. The structure of disadvantage is related to the broader socio-cultural configuration of society which transmits and maintains deprivation. As Amartya Sen (1982) has rightly noted, in India lower castes were traditionally in a disadvantageous position in the overall socioeconomic structure and they have lived for long in perpetual poverty. They include untouchables, tribals, weaker castes, women and certain minority groups (including refugees and internally displaced people). In this way disadvantage becomes a systematic application of handicap. Thus various social groups suffer from intergenerational continuities of deprivations due to structural disadvantage. Caste, gender, ethnicity become linked with deprivation because of the features of social structure. As noted by Edwards (1979) "membership in a social group is the source of problem and makes disadvantage a phenomenon of socio-cultural origin" (p. 27). Disadvantage involves systematic unfairness in the distribution of rewards and the opportunities of life (Brown, 1983).

Several protective, developmental and preferential measures have been adopted by the Central and the state Governments for the upliftment of Dalits since independence. However, despite of constitutional safeguards, the socioeconomic condition of weaker sections is deteriorating.

Children constitute another important category of the disadvantaged. They bear the heaviest burden of poverty. Child poverty is increasing at a much faster rate than adult poverty across rich as well as poor countries. Its effect on children is direct as well as indirect. The direct consequences include ill health, poor nutrition, poor housing and lack of poor education. The indirect influences are diverse. They include less than optimal parental interaction, inadequate child care and child labour. While child labour does contribute to family income some of its forms are exploitative. Children become commodities and market forces tend to exploit them in many ways.

Women and girls constitute another important disadvantaged group. India has increasingly adverse sex ratio, the reason for which are poorly understood. However, it does point to the low status of women as well as discrimination against girls. The sex ratio in 1991 was of 929 women per 1000 men. The sex ratio has deteriorated over this century and it is particularly adverse in the northern and western states and urban regions. Women have restricted access to the social security programmes of the state, to health care and to education which restrict the development of children. Girl's life is full of deprivation and discrimination. This is reflected in the pathetic nutritional status, discriminatory food supply, higher morbidity and mortality (Ghosh, 1991). Parents often over indulge the male child at the cost of the female child. Also, parental occupation, eco-cultural context and aspects of socialization influence this situation. Discrimination in feeding, weaning and toilet training between 3-6 years old boys and girls has been reported (Bhogle, 1991). Age of sending to school, choice of academic curricular and future aspirations of the girl child also differ. In a nation-wide study Anandalakshmy (1994) has noted that "the birth of the girl child tends to be greeted with anaemic joy, if not grief, and that she continues to be treated within the family and outside as a second class citizen, (p. 43).

Conclusion

In conclusion it may be noted that poverty is a multifaceted phenomenon. It relates to unsatisfied needs and characterizes a condition of relative deprivation owing to unequal distribution of resources in a given societal context. The insufficient income does not allow poor to take care of basic needs. They are unable to undertake those activities and enjoy the facilities which are customary to the society to which they belong. It is being increasingly realized that poverty is not due to poor person's fate or *karma* or bad deeds but, as economic and social analyses have shown, is determined by the socio-political processes and arrangements in the society. The division of society into rich and poor categories is widespread in developed as well as developed part of the world. However, the specific factors underlying poverty in different countries may be different. At socetal level, poverty is caused and maintained by a variety of contextual factors incuding ecology, cultural traditions, economic policy as well as political orientation. At individual level, the processes of social comparison, aspiration and perception of options and possibilities to pursue alternative life courses mediate the experience of poverty. Of course ,the resources and constraints in the ecological settings delimit the choices of people in significant ways. In the Indian context poverty's association with social hierarchy and gender gives it a different meaning causing the phenomenon of social disadvantage. In addition, continuous migration of rural peopole to cities, introduction of labour saving gadgets, displacement of people due to various developmental projects, illiteracy, unemployment, unequal distribution of resources of production and centralization of capital and economic power have made many sections of population vulnerable.

It has been indicated that the policies, the beneficiaries and the mechanisms are often guided by the interest groups in power. In other words poverty is approached with the hidden agenda of the rich or the non-poor who are central to the decision making process. While assault on poverty has made certain provisions for the poor, the population explosion and increased standards of life have contributed to the increase in the number of the poor people. Eliminating poverty by bringing poor to a minimum standard of life requires not only the resources but also political commitment and a responsive bureaucracy to achieve equity in the distribution of income and a reorientation of the production process geared towards the goal of uplift of the poor.

3

Psychology and Poverty : A Fresh Look at the Researches

DURGANAND SINHA

Poverty is a widespread phenomenon in the world with approximately two-thirds of the population suffering from it in varying degrees. The problem is acute in the so-called developing countries. Though estimates have varied, well-over thirty per cent of the population of our country is below the poverty-line. In spite of the fact that it constitutes one of the most pressing problems, except during the short period following the depression and the Head Start years in U.S.A. in the sixties, the topic hardly found a place in the mainstream psychology. It is a matter of greater surprise that despite the problem being so pressing and acute in our country and the de-humanizing influence that poverty has on the people, psychologists in their research have for long ignored the phenomenon. It was only after Indira Gandhi's election slogan of *garibi hatao* (eradicate poverty) in early seventies and the various poverty alleviation programmes that were incorporated into the five-year development plan that the topic came on the agenda of psychologists. In fact, the ICSSR recognised it as one of the 'priority areas' for research. As far as psychology is concerned, it was for the first time taken up formally when I chose for my presidential address to the 13th annual conference of IAAP (Indian Academy of Applied Psychology) at the University of Karnatak, Dharwar, in the last week of December 1975 the theme "Study of Psychological Dimensions of Poverty : A Challenge and Necessity" (Sinha, 1976). It was more than mere coincidence that about a week later in the first week of January, 1976, Professor T.E. Shanmugam also had the theme "War on Poverty" for his presidential address to the Section of Psychology and Educational Sciences of the Indian Science Congress held in Andhra University, Waltair. This was an auspicious beginning and over the years psychologists in India have been actively engaged in analysing various psychological concomitants of poverty and trying to suggest remedial measures.

Many scholars of other social science disciplines do not generally consider the study of poverty as falling under the domain of psychology. In fact, the eminent economist and social scientist, late Professor V.K.R.V. Rao, who inaugurated the IAAP conference in Dharwar, expressed surprise when I mentioned to him the theme of my presidential address. The fact of the matter is that psychology does not deal with the causes of poverty, nor does it claim to solve the problem through psychological interventions and remedies. However, a psychologist feels somewhat impatient when inspite of endless discussions on the various nuances of the causes of poverty that have gone on for centuries, the problem continues to remain as acute as ever. When a person's eyes are burning due to the entry of a foreign particle, one does not wait for identifying the *real* cause that made the intrusion of the nauxious particle, but wisely seeks immediate remedies. It is more exasperating when even transcendental causes are advanced ascribing the condition of poverty to actions and deeds committed during past life (*karma*), or the doctrine of *maya* (illusion) is brought in to explain it away. It probably underlies the attitude of indifference that one finds in Indian people being immune to the most appalling condition of misery and squalor and displaying insensitivity to it and almost regarding it as inevitable.

A psychologist does not get lost in the endless controversies in defining poverty nor in high-level academic debates on its 'causes'. Neither does he lay any claims to solving the problem and eradicating it. His claim is modest. As a discipline, psychology deals with identifying its attendant conditions, analysing either singly or collectively their debilitating and deleterious impact upon the individual and his/her functioning that renders the person less capable of meeting the demands of the environment and thereby reduces the competency to combat the condition of poverty. At least implicitly, the goal of these studies is not merely academic. It is hoped that such exercises would yield results that are likely to be helpful in devising interventions and programmes for remedial actions for rendering the individual capable of overcoming the deficiencies caused by poverty. The approach mainly focuses on the *negative* aspects of poverty. In this context, the role of the individual as a self-regulating system cannot be underestimated. Some investigators have drawn attention to what has often been called the "lotus in the mud" phenomenon (L.B. Tripathi, 1986) and the so-called "strengths" displayed by people growing in poverty that have enabled them to survive for centuries and still have capacity to smile. Cohesiveness, group activity, interdependence, tolerance and informal structure that often characterize the poor have often been referred to as positive psychological qualities. Lapierre (1986, p. 56) while providing a graphic account of extreme poverty of Calcutta slums observed how every individual was linked to the rest of the social body by a network of incredibly diversified ties as a result of which nobody was completely isolated or abandoned. They, could still survive and smile despite all the misery and squalor. The poor have learned "despite incredible difficult odds, to survive, to share and to love" (p. ix). While these aspects do deserve to be analysed and studied carefully, they do not find a prominent place in psychological literature. The danger of focussing on the so-called "strengths" of the poor may lead to a "status quoist" attitude, and in a way provide justification of poverty.

The Domain of Psychological Research on Poverty

In psychological literature, poverty has many conceptual nuances and there is often confusion about the criterion/ criteria used to classify groups as poor. A psychologist avoids these controversies. Ignoring sophisticated measurement procedures, psychologists have preferred to work with categorical-level variables and with conditions that surround the condition of poverty. On the basis of these conditions, specific scales for assessing poverty like "deprivation index" (Whiteman & Deutsch, 1968), the Prolonged Deprivation Scale (Misra & Tripathi, 1978) and the like have been utilized.

Thus, psychologists have conceptualised poverty as a situation with a number of attendant conditions that individually or collectively influence the development of the person, rendering him less capable of overcoming poverty by personal efforts.

Poverty is associated with low income, low caste and class status, poor housing, overcrowding, lack of public amenities, various degrees of malnutrition and high susceptibility to disease. The poor is exposed to less stimulating environment, inadequate school facilities, lack of parental support, and the like. Some of these conditions belong to the immediate proximal environment (more visible layer) while others constitute the outer or the surrounding layer of the environment. The two layers do not operate independently but constantly interact with one another. Taking these aspects into consideration, an ecological framework for identifying the conditions and the psychological processes related to poverty and deprivation has been developed (Bronfenbrenner, 1974; Sinha, 1977). The model used by me (Sinha, 1977, 1982b) is illustrated in Figure 3.1.

The common psychological effects of poverty conditions acting singly or collectively are inappropriate cognitive functioning, attentional problems, learning disabilities, inadequate linguistic skills, stagnant or unrealistic aspirations, sense of helplessness, low self-esteem and health problems (including mental health). These, in turn, result in coping strategies that are dysfunctional in various life situations. The behaviour outcomes in the form of low competencies, low academic performance, high rate of wastage and dropout, low school attendance, failure, withdrawal, and apathy imply that the people are not able

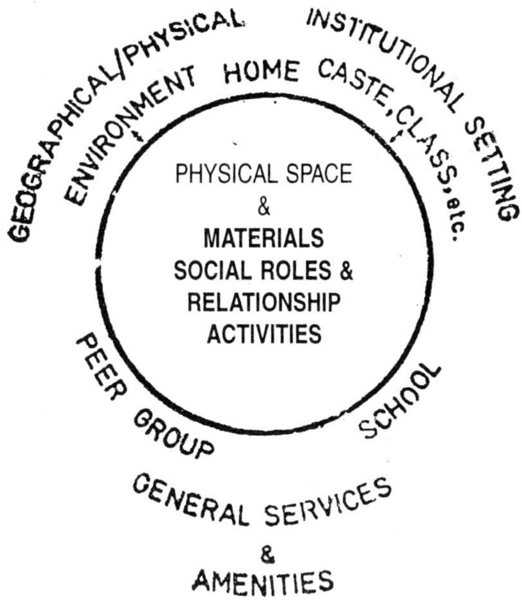

FIGURE 3.1 : *Ecological Perspective on Poverty*

to cope successfully with their problems. All these in turn accentuate the condition of poverty. In other words, psychological processes operate as mediators between the condition of poverty and its detrimental impact on behaviour. The sequence of processes representing the relationship between poverty and its psychological and behavioural consequences is illustrated in a schematic model (See Figure 3.2). It would be wrong to imply that one is poor because of the psychological limitations. But at the same time, it is also true that a life of poverty produces many psychological ill-effects rendering the individual less capable of overcoming the problem. A kind of vicious circle is created. What psychological researches imply is that rather than being its cause, psychological concomitants accentuate the situation of poverty. It is contended that understanding these psychological dimensions is likely to help in devising action programmes and policies for eradicating poverty. Further, ignoring psychological variables may lead ameliorative programmes

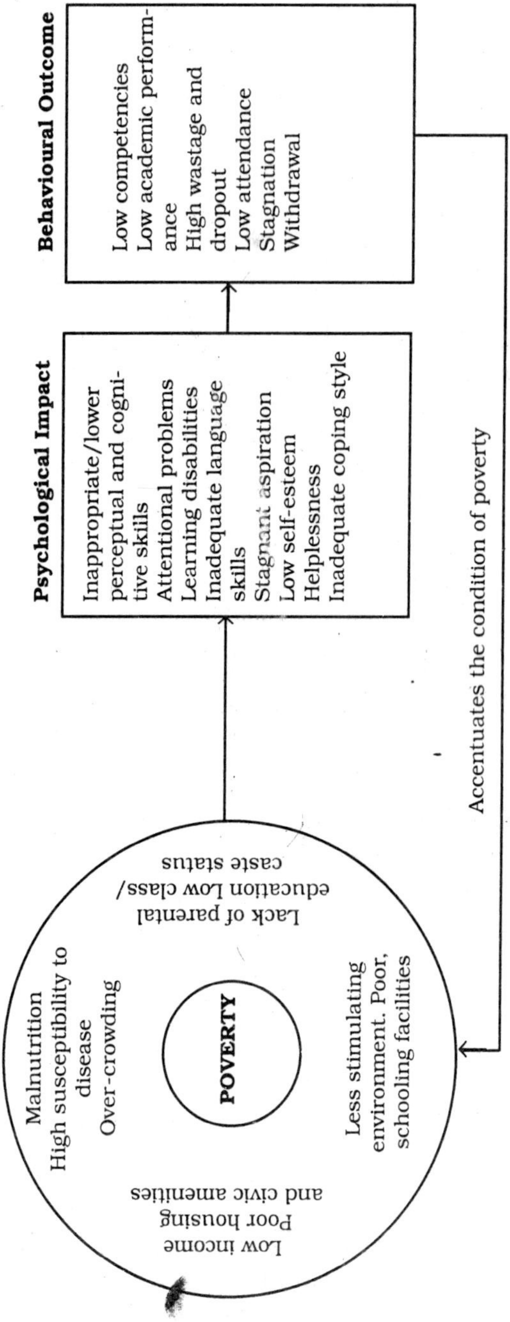

FIGURE 3.2 : *Schematic model of the relationship between poverty, its psychological consequences and their outcomes*

to unexpected and at times undesirable consequences. As I have observed (Sinha, 1990, p. 80), "Understanding the psychological characteristics of the poor is no less important than the analysis of the system that brought in the condition of poverty."

Psychological Research on Poverty and Deprivation

It is not possible to give a detailed account of the enormous volume of research conducted by psychologists in the country within the short period of just over two decades. A brief reference is only made to the aspects of poverty that have been commonly investigated, and highlight the main trends of the findings. Psychological studies have generally centred on the following aspects :

1. Psychological impact of malnutrition
2. Perceptual and cognitive domain
3. Impact on personality and motivation
4. Poverty and Rosenthal Effect
5. Attributional studies
6. Intervention studies

1. *Malnutrition and its Psychological Impact.* Malnutrition of various degrees is a condition most frequently associated with the population living in poverty and adverse socioeconomic circumstances. Although early and severe malnutrition occurs with considerable frequency in the poorer populations of developing countries (upto 20 per cent in some instances), the most widespread type of malnutrition is that of mild-to-moderate chronic undernutrition which is most readily noted in some retardation of physical growth as well as in psychological development. It is, therefore, but natural that most studies of psychological impact have been on mild-to-moderate chronic malnutrition.

Studies conducted in India and other parts of the developing world provide considerable evidence that physical development of children (especially height and weight) go hand in hand with development of other areas such as language and cognition, visual-motor coordination, intelligence, and immediate memory. The general finding seems to be that apart from physical growth, malnutrition adversely affects many psychological processes : apathy, withdrawal, responsiveness, reduced curiosity and exploratory behaviour, attentional deficiency and learning disabilities. Physical growth and development of cognitive and linguistic behaviour seem to go together. Undernourishment often shows itself in verbal reasoning, comprehension, conservation tasks, perceptual skills, inadequacies in social competence and communication. Evidence of the impact on I.Q. is somewhat ambiguous, though there is clear indication that the undernourished even with normal intelligence has poor academic performance.

Findings on the relative influence of malnutrition and social factors are not always consistent. However, there is strong evidence that unfavourable early child-care practices and dysfunctional patterns of caregiver-infant interaction contribute to the level of behavioural development. Suitable educational interventions on mothers bring about marked improvement in cognitive and language development (Murlidharan & Kaur, 1987). Importance of social influence and *enriched* enduring learning environment in counteracting the ill-effects has been brought out in several studies. Therefore, intervention has to be concerned both with nutritional supplementation and environmental enrichment of an enduring character. If the enrichment is temporary, it results in "*punarmusko bhaba*" phenomenon (go to the original state). Lastly, psychological and physical effects of malnutrition are generally not irreversible if appropriate measures are taken early. Potential long term effects of early malnutrition may be greatly attenuated and even eliminated by creating favourable environment for the child. On the other hand, effect may be compounded by less favourable environmental conditions.

2. *Impact on Cognitive Functioning.* Effects of poverty on cognitive domain have focused on intelligence, perceptual and cognitive skills, learning and mediational processes, memory, concept formation and Piagetian

conservation, language skills, and academic performance (for a summary, see Sinha, 1990, pp. 77-97). Though the findings are sometimes conflicting, there is strong indication of general impairment in cognitive functioning due to poverty conditions. Most of the cognitive processes that are adversely affected are highly relevant to school performance and any deficiency caused in them proves as impediment to the child. On language, effects of poverty result in discontinuity between the school and the child (see Sinha, 1990, pp. 83-85 for details).

As for the educational sphere, effect is reflected in very low enrolment, irregular attendance, high dropout rate and poor academic record. There is ample evidence for adverse effects on academic performance even when the factor of intelligence is controlled. Significant role of parental support and family in compensating for the adverse effects of poverty on school performance has been highlighted in many studies. Lastly, comparison between privileged and underprivileged children exposed to the

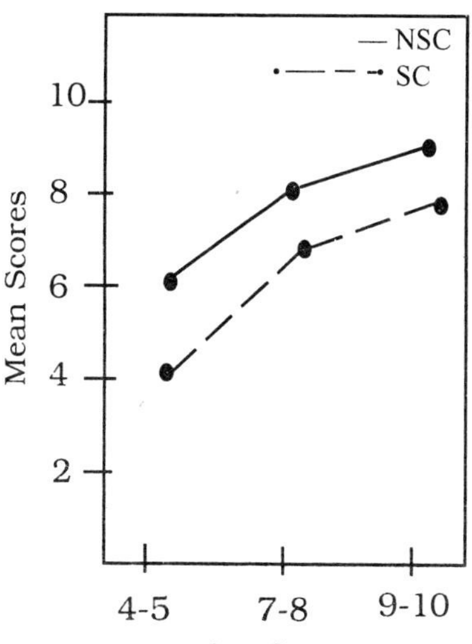

FIGURE 3.3 : *Pictorial Interpretation in Ordinary School*

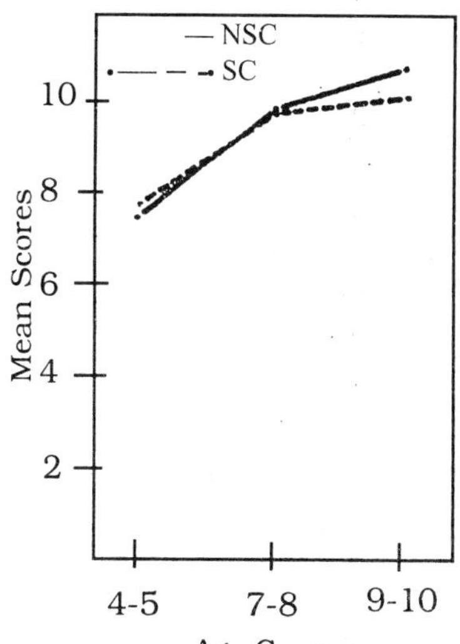

FIGURE 3.4 : *Pictorial Interpretation in Superior School*

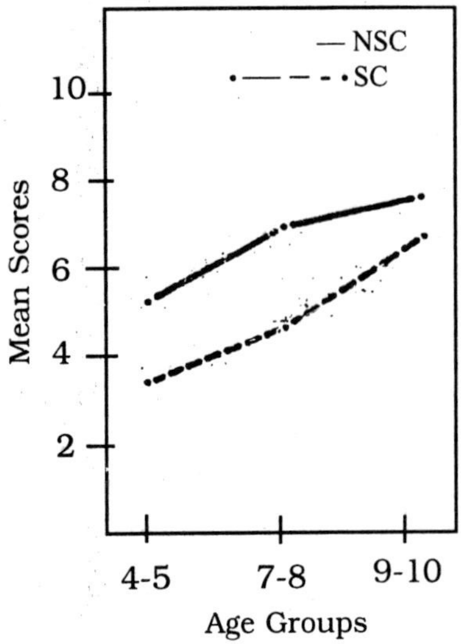

FIGURE 3.5 : *Sequential Perception in Ordinary School*

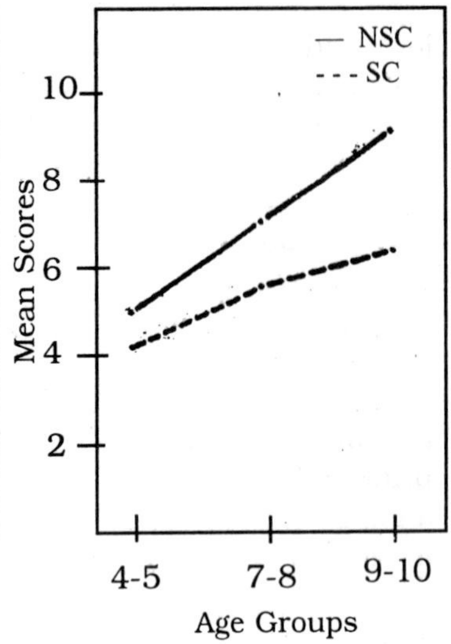

FIGURE 3.6 : *Sequential Perception in Superior School*

environment of 'superior' schools on their performance on perceptual and cognitive tasks of varying complexity has revealed an interesting but significant phenomenon called the "broomstick effect" (Sinha, 1977). As illustrated in the graphs (Figures 3.3-3.6), though better facilities of 'superior' schools do enhance the performance level of disadvantaged scheduled caste children (SC), the differential between advantaged non-scheduled caste (NSC) and the disadvantaged groups tends to get accentuated with increase in age and grade causing a kind of cumulative deficit.

3. *Personality and Motivation.* Impact on personality and motivation of individuals existing in deprived conditions has been analysed. Deprivation has been found to be associated with neuroticism and introversion, social maladjustment, immaturity, autism, alienation and withdrawal. The disadvantaged were more external and chance-oriented and displayed greater aggression.

Findings on motivational dimensions appear more significant and useful. The disadvantaged tend to have low and stagnant level of aspiration, display low goal-discrepancy index, greater fear of failure and absence of risk-taking. They possess low need for achievement, autonomy, lack of initiative and aggression, and greater need for affiliation, succorrance, abasement and nurturance. It has also been observed that they are low in decision-making, responsibility, emotional stability and friendliness, but high on anxiety. Deprivation has adverse effect on self-concept, and is negatively related to self-esteem.

Adverse effects on the motivation of deprived children are often associated with "socialisation of apathy and underachievement"—a projection of similar motivation among their parents. The disadvantage also gets reflected in time orientation, locus of control and reactions to success and failure.

4. *Poverty and Rosenthal Effect.* A very serious penomenon that is associated with the performance of the poor and deprived especially in the academic sphere is the "Rosenthal Effect" (Rosenthal & Jacobson, 1969) which is often referred to as "self-fulfilling prophecy" or "Pygmalion effect". It is a widespread phenomenon that teachers entertain expectations and beliefs about the abilities and performance of their pupils. In this respect, fixed labels like class, caste, and untouchability (Dusek & Joseph, 1983; Sharma & Tripathi, 1988) are frequently used in categorizing pupils. Depending on attitudes regarding these, certain expectations go along with the labelling, which in turn influence our thinking and behaviour vis-a-vis the pupils in a significant way (Panda, 1988, p. 298). The pupils in their turn perform according to the expectations of their teachers. In essence, teachers get less from the disadvantaged because they expect less. The labelling of the "poor" as lacking in abilities and expecting them to fare poorly in examinations make an unintended impact on teacher-behaviour and affect students' performance adversely (Rath, Dash & Dash, 1979, pp. 93-96).

The mechanism of how this expectation or *unintentioned bias* operates need not be discussed. But the phenomenon is there, and has serious implication for the academic behaviour of pupils of deprived groups.

5. *Attributional Studies.* Search for causal explanation of social and natural events is an indispensable part of human thinking process. Analyses of causal attribution of poverty in general reveal that low income people attribute it more to fate and luck than the high income ones. The former also tend to blame themselves more for their poverty (Y. Sinha, Jain & Pandey, 1980). Attribution of failure to self and success to external factors (Rath & Sircar, 1960), self-blame and low self-image were found to be strong among the disadvantaged. They attributed success more to luck, God and chance (i.e., externalise it) while the advantaged attributed failure to luck and other 'external' factors (Sinha, 1980). The most significant factor distinguishing the two groups was that of "controllability" (Misra & Jain, 1988). The opposite was the case with the disadvantaged who blamed themselves more for failure and at the same time took less credit for success which were attributed more to "uncontrollable" causes. Thus, the disadvantaged felt more self-pity, discouraged, and a sense of guilt thereby building a mechanism of self-discouragement (Sinha, 1980). Thus, in case of the poor, the reinforcing effect of success was not as much as it should have been because credit for it was not perceived to lie in oneself. On the other hand, failure was largely attributed to oneself, which was shattering and damaging to the self-esteem. The poor was a loser in both cases— a kind of a "no-win" situation.

Concluding Observations

There are other aspects of individual's functioning like health, incidence of mental-illness and social behaviour that have been found associated with conditions of poverty. But it is not possible to deal with them here in any detail.

By way of general observation of the studies as a whole, it may be stated that while the findings in themselves are interesting, they do not seem to have influenced very much the ongoing poverty-alleviation programmes, nor have made much impact on developing intervention strategies.

Theoretical and scientific concerns seem to dominate. Problems that are investigated are located and formulated more on the basis of one's reading of scientific literature than on their salience to the existential reality. Thus, the studies appear more academic as *research for prestige* rather than *research for policy*. Moreover, many of the findings are in no way novel, and they could easily be derived from sound commonsense without the elaborate and intricate procedures that a research usually involves. There is obviously need for "a fresh look" at the entire gamut of psychological studies on poverty. Methodologically, they display high scientific quality and sophistication. But the practical outcome does not seem to be commensurate with it. Further, a large volume of studies have taken the "extreme groups" comparison approach and confined themselves to convenient samples. There is need to expand the sphere by having more studies on rural poor, landless, homeless, slum dwellers, rural migrants and what I would call "the poorest of the poor".

A drawback which probably is responsible for the limited impact these studies have made on the policy and programme for poverty alleviation is the microcosmic, individualistic, and intra-individual perspective that characterize the psychologists' approach. Systemic and structural variables are largely ignored—the main concern being subjective and experiential aspects of poverty. There is need to go beyond and adopt a more macrocosmic approach and make an effort to incorporate structural variables in the very design of these investigations. Poverty after all is a phenomenon of multiple determinants in which structural factors have a dominant place. If psychological studies on poverty and deprivation are going to make a vital impact on policy and formulation of intervention programmes, they have not only to expand their methodological repertoire and go beyond factors whose locus is not only in the individual but the social system as a whole. A fresh look at these investigations is essential.

4

Perception of Poverty : Socio-Psychological Dimensions[1]

JANAK PANDEY

The Euro-American psychology has traditionally been person or individual centered and as such has been decontextual in its approach to the study of behavioural phenomena. As a result, problems like poverty, deprivation and disadvantage could not catch the attention of researchers. However, in the context of developing countries like India, the socio-economic variations constitute a relevant class of variables influencing behaviour at individual as well as collective levels. The present paper analyzes the different ways in which poverty has been treated in various social sciences including psychology. It begins with an analysis of various measures of socio-economic condition and proposes a comprehensive perspective on poverty and demonstrates its efficacy. Finally, the subjective perception of poverty is examined and its implications are presented.

The socio-economic variables have not received the prominent place they deserve in psychological research. The most frequently used measure to assess the socio-economic level has been the Socio-Economic Scale (SES) consisting of items related to income, education, rural-urban background, social and racial categories (e.g. race, caste, class), and some other socio-demographic variables.

1. The paper is based on an invited lecture delivered at the 12th Congress of the International Association for Cross-Cultural Psychology (IACCP) Pamplona, Spain, July 24-27, 1994.

For example, one most frequently used scale in India, was developed by Kuppuswamy (1982). The social science researchers have also used a number of economic, health, nutritional, social and educational indicators as measures of socio-economic level and poverty. Some of the most frequently used indicators in social-science research are briefly reviewed.

Poverty Indicators used in Social Sciences

Economic Indicators : Economists have built a research tradition around income distribution as an indicator of poverty. They consider various measures of income such as individual income, total family income, and per-capita income. The International Labour Organization (ILO) considers the number of hours in paid employment and capacity to buy certain goods as measures of poverty.

Human Development and Health Status Indicators : The medical profession, the WHO and some others prefer health status indicators as powerful measures for international comparison of poverty. Some of the health status indicators are : mortality, resistance to disease, calorie intake, and nutritional level of food. A recent innovation has been construction of a Human Development Index combining income, health status, with additional social indicators, such as adult literacy and life expectancy (UNDP report, 1991).

The Administrative Definition : Generally, the welfare states single out certain groups, such as certain castes, tribes, the elderly, disabled, the unemployed, single mothers, as low income poor groups to provide welfare or extend certain benefits. Thus, welfare states identify certain sections of population for poverty related programmes. The administrators, frequently use some popular phrases for poor to generate public support for political advantages of politicians.

The Visible Definition of Poverty : According to the visible definition, the poor constitute ". . . an identifiable group or category of people whose total life situation displays such features that they are intuitively labelled as poor" (Oyen, 1992; p. 620). Lewis' (1966) conceptualization of "poverty culture" and Wilson's (1987) idea of the "urban underclass" are examples of the visible definition approach.

In the 1960s and 1970s the *culture of poverty* perspective influenced to a large extent research and policies on poverty in the west and particularly in the United States. A number of questions related to the validity of distinguishing poor from non-poor as a separate cultural group on the basis of certain dimensions like attitudes, values, family, nature of slum/neighbourhood, and relationship with the larger society (Leacock, 1971), were raised. The emphasis that very poor in all countries, and in all ethnic groups, are different in life style from the affluent group did not receive consistent empirical support even in the United States (Coward, Feagin & Williams, 1974). It is unfortunate that the 'culture of poverty' came to be accepted as a fact without empirical analysis of the attitudes, behaviours, and actions of the poor and non-poor.

The above mentioned measures either independently or in various combinations have been used as the criteria to determine socio-economic level and poverty line. These measures are also mostly products of the western socio-cultural and economic context and some of them may not even be either intuitively or practically useful for research purposes in the context of certain sections of the developing societies.

Social-Psychological Measures of Poverty

The measures described above do not consider the way an individual perceives his/her own economic condition. A category of people may look homogeneous on certain economic, social and educational indicators, but they may show an extremely heterogeneous picture on psychological dimensions (Allen, 1970). To label the low income group as a separate cultural group is obviously wrong and inappropriate (Coward *et al.*, 1974). There has been a gradual shift in the definition of poverty line. The economists, who used to rely only on crude income figures to define poverty level, tend to recognize non-economic factors. For example, family size, subjective feelings of the respondents to income, minimum subsistence level, and other considerations are now included by the economists in analysis of poverty level (Goedhart, Halberstadt, Kapteyn & Praag, 1977; Stanovnik, 1992).

In addition, it is difficult to know the exact income level of people due to several factors. People hide their income due to a variety of motivations. People who live in societies with high unemployment rate, may not have a stable income. In many rural, and in traditional societies, cash is not the major basis of economic transactions. In such a situation, people fail to report their income in figures. Thus, cash income as a criterion could be only useful in a limited way to determine real economic level of an individual or a family.

An Integrated Approach to Poverty

It appears that individual's perception of his/her economic condition both in absolute and relative terms is important. Perceived poverty has greater psychological meaning for the perceiver. Our efforts have been to develop an integrated approach by including objective and subjective criteria of poverty. Different aspects of this integrated measure developed by us are described below.

Perceived Poverty. We have conceptualized 'perceived poverty' as an individual's subjective assessment of : 1. income in relation to household expenditure, 2. dissatisfaction with economic condition, property, standard of housing, food, clothing, and, 3. anxiety concerning resources for essential expenses (e.g., festivals, marriage, rituals) and unexpected events such as illness, accidents, and death (Pandey & Singh, 1985). The original questionnaire (Pandey & Singh, 1985) consisted of eight items, each with 5-point rating scale. Later, some revisions were made in the scale (Nanda-Biswas & Pandey, 1996). We have found that perceived poverty correlates positively with per-capita income (r = .67) and quality of living conditions (r = .69) implying that the perceived poverty which represents constructed social-psychological reality of economic condition is partly based on the perceiver's objective, economic, and living condition. However, perceived poverty in comparison to objective indicators has been consistently found to be a stronger predictor of an individual's reactions to poverty, in terms of coping and adaptation (Pandey & Singh, 1985).

In a study of perception of poverty and income satisfaction of Slovenia household, Stanovnik (1992) has argued in favour of the subjective poverty line. In this study, the respondents were asked to evaluate their family's income in relation to their living costs on a 4-point scale ranging from "very insufficient" to "amply sufficient".

Relative Poverty : Poverty is also relative. We perceive our economic condition relative to some other individual or other group of individuals. Perception of one self as poor or affluent is dependent on one's own economic status relative to others whom one selects for comparison. The relative poverty scale consists of eight-items, each with a 5-point scale, to assess the respondents' relative feelings about own level of poverty relative to other members of their community.

Perceived Social Status : Traditionally, social class, occupation, caste, and other factors have been considered by social scientists as determinants of individual's social status. In the developed societies, occupation, education, standard of living and position in the production system are generally regarded as determinants of social status of a person. However, in developing societies, some additional factors such as caste, specially in rural India, play a significant role in the social status of a person. The perceived social status measure consists of three items, with 3-point scale related to perceived caste/tribe status, social status, and perceived occupational status. The total score ranges from 3 to 9 with internal consistency measured by Cronbach *alpha* of .88.

Measures of Socio-Economic Mobility : The socio-economic mobility or lack of it by an individual or of groups of individuals indicates the process and extent of change.

Mobility was conceptualized as improvement in the educational, occupational, and income status of the respondents in comparison to the status of their parents. To measure the inter-generational socio-economic mobility, (1) growth in income, (2) growth in educational status, and (3) growth in occupational status are critically important.

The items were designed to assess income, education and occupation of the respondents and of their same sex parent. Respondents are asked to report their income, education (7-point scale) and occupation (6-point scale) as well as of their same gender parent's past status on these dimensions, generally twenty years back. Discrepancy scores for each item (difference between parent and respondent) and total discrepancy scores are computed to determine the degree of mobility of a respondent.

Rated Quality of Living Condition : To assess the quality or standard of living in home and its neighbourhood, a ten item check-list with 5-point rating scale (score range 10 to 50, higher the score, better the quality) was developed. The internal consistency in terms of Cronbach *alpha* was found to be .99.

The rating scale was particularly developed with a concern that certain poor sections of society fail to report their poverty level due to their accommodation or acquiescence to a constraining reality (Katona & Strumpel, 1978). The rating scale is completed by the interviewer for each respondent during his/her actual visit of the respondent's household. Considerable direct experience and knowledge of the community and the context are essential for the interviewer-rater. It also requires on-site training to acquire efficiency and objectivity in rating.

Some Research Findings

The findings reported here are based on a recently completed study in the tribal belt of Orissa. The respondents were 274 males belonging to three social groups, namely Scheduled Tribe (ST) (n = 94), Scheduled Caste (SC) (n = 92), and Upper Caste (UP) (n = 88). The mean age of respondents was 34.6 years. Half of the respondents were socio-economically mobile (prosperous) in comparison to their parents and the other half were economically stagnant, similar to their parent's status. The immobile respondents were mostly manual casual labourers, whereas, with an exception of six respondents employed in their own business, all other mobile respondents had jobs in governmental organizations. The scheduled tribe respondents belonged to *Kond* and *Oraon* tribal groups. The scheduled tribe and caste groups differ in an unique way. The tribal groups are not generally part of the caste hierarchy system. Each tribal community has its own unique social structure, outside the dominant caste-system. Thus, the scheduled caste people are lowest in the caste hierarchy. The scheduled tribes, on the other hand, are deprived due to their social isolation, and other forms of exploitation.

Table 4.1, presents the mean scores of the respondents and of their fathers for education, occupation, and income for the immobile and mobile groups. The mean discrepancy scores for education, occupation, and income of the immobile and mobile groups were significantly different.

Table 4.2 presents means with *F*-ratios of perceived economic condition, relative poverty, perceived status, and rated quality of living condition for the three social groups (scheduled tribe, scheduled caste, and upper caste) and also of mobile and immobile groups.

The main effects of mobility reveal that the mobile respondents perceived their economic condition and social status significantly higher than the immobile respondents. The mobile group rated their relative poverty significantly lower than the immobile group. The quality of living condition of the mobile group was rated to be significantly better than the immobile group.

The main effect of caste was significant for perceived status and rated quality of living condition. The results indicate that the SC respondents rated their social status significantly lower than the ST and the upper caste respondents. The rated quality of living condition of the ST group was however, significantly lower than the

TABLE 4.1 : *Means and discrepancy scores of inter-generational socio-economic mobility*

Variables	Immobile			Mobile		
	Parents'	Respondents'	Discrepancy	Parents'	Respondents'	Discrepancy
Education	1.05	1.66	.61	1.29	4.91	3.67
Occupation	2.01	2.03	.02	2.08	4.42	2.35
Income (in Rs.)	134.54	363.68	229.14	211.47	2603.48	2392.01

TABLE 4.2 : *Means and 'F' ratios for the main effects of caste and mobility on poverty related variables*

Variables	Main effect of caste				Main effect of mobility		
	ST (n = 95)	SC (n = 92)	UC (n = 88)	F (2,266)	Immobile (n = 138)	Mobile (n = 137)	F (1,266)
Perceived Poverty	18.69	18.16	19.57	2.68	16.91	20.78	61.63**
Relative Poverty	24.53	24.22	25.17	0.75	27.30	21.85	69.57**
Perceived Status	6.33^{b}	5.00^{a}	6.89^{b}	45.66**	5.44	6.03	10.57**
Rated Quality of Living Condition	24.20^{a}	27.95^{b}	29.77^{b}	51.71**	14.40	40.64	4544.88**

Note : ST = Scheduled Tribe, SC = Scheduled Caste, UC = Upper Caste
Means with common subscripts do not differ at .05 level (Newman-Keuls test)
** $p < .01$

scheduled and upper castes. The upper castes were rated to be highest in terms of quality of living conditions, but they did not differ significantly from the SC group.

Figure 4.1 presents the means of the caste × mobility interaction effect on perceived poverty (economic condition). The internal means comparison revealed that immobile respondents of the three social groups did not differ significantly. However, the mobile respondents of the three

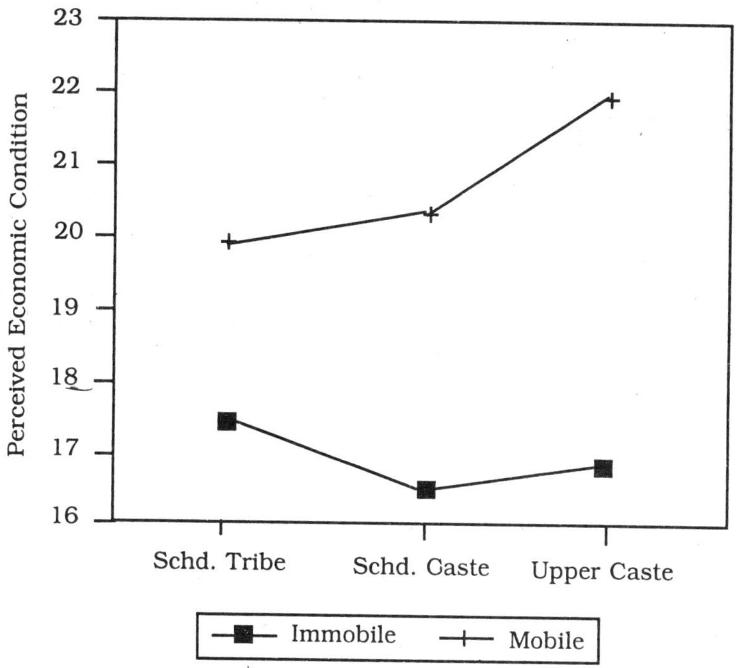

FIGURE 4.1 : *Perceived economic condition as a function of interaction of caste and mobility*

social groups differed. The upper caste respondents perceived their economic condition significantly higher (22.16) than the ST (19.91), and SC (20.17).

Figure 4.2 presents perception of relative poverty as a function of interaction of social groups and mobility. Each immobile social group perceived significantly more relative poverty than the counterpart mobile group. The upper caste immobile respondents, however, perceived maximum

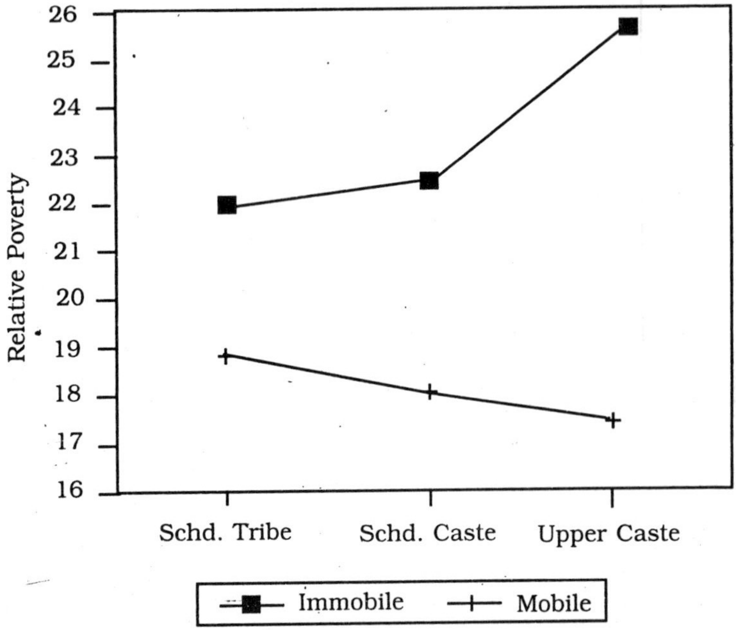

FIGURE 4.2 : *Relative poverty as a function of interaction of caste and mobility*

(25.51) and the mobile respondents perceived minimum (16.93) of the relative poverty. The SC and ST respondents did not differ significantly in the mobility or in the immobility condition.

Figure 4.3 shows that perception of status was significantly influenced by social group and the mobility factors. The interaction effect was not significant. To understand the relationship between perceived social status and poverty (economic condition), mean scores on these two variables for the six subgroups based on caste and mobility are presented in Figure 4.3.

The six subgroups fall into the four quadrants. The immobile ST and immobile SC groups which cluster in quadrant 1, are characterized by lower perception of economic condition as well as lower perception of social status. This result is in congruence with the expected trend. People of this category who have not moved up

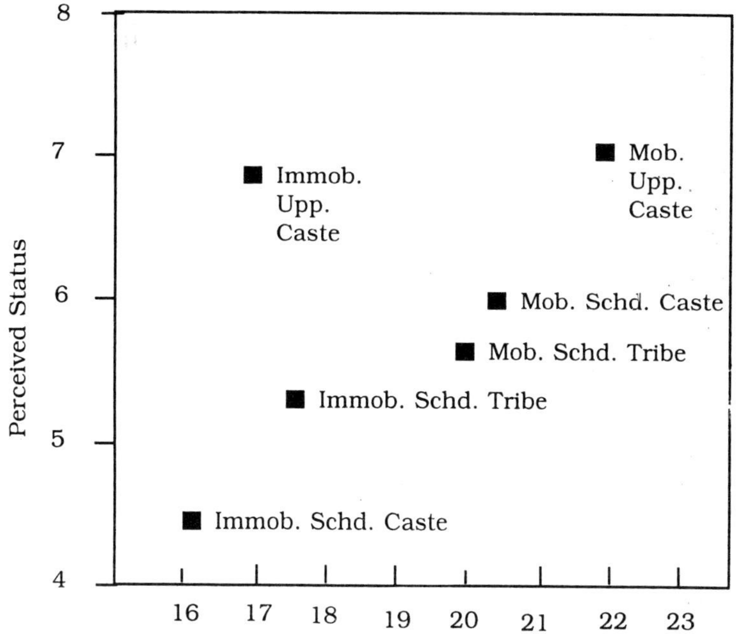

FIGURE 4.3 : *Plots of group means of perceived status*

socio-economically would perceive themselves poor as well as lower in social status. In the second quadrant, the mobile SC and ST groups are located, showing that even though they perceive their economic condition higher, they perceive their social status lower. Socio-economically mobile upper caste falls in quadrant 3, which represents perception of higher economic condition as well as perception of higher social status. For the mobile upper caste people, perception of social status is in congruence with their mobility and perceived economic condition. Quadrant 4, represents upper caste immobile group respondents who perceive their social status higher in spite of their stagnated economic condition. But their perception of poverty (economic condition) is in congruence with their objective economic condition.

Explaining the Causes of Poverty

Only a few studies have examined perceptions of the

causes of poverty and laypersons' beliefs about why people are poor. We do have, however, examples of such research carried out in different parts of the world such as in Australia, West Indian Islands—Barbados and Dominica, Europe, India and the United States.

Feagin (1972, 1975) developed a list of 11 causes of poverty which he categorized into three types : (a) individualistic explanations such as laziness, by implication, blaming the poor themselves for poverty; (b) structural explanations, holding socio-economic factors responsible; and (c) fatalistic explanations. Feagin (1972) in his large representative national survey found that most Americans ascribe poverty to individualistic factors. The older, White, middle-income Protestants tended to be most individualistic in their explanations.

In the mid-1970s, using an Australian sample, Feather (1974) found evidence for the three types of causes and also reported that the Australians were generally less likely to blame poverty on the poor themselves than were the Americans. Feather (1974) has argued that values and beliefs as well as macro-economic factors should be considered in attempting to predict people's explanations of the causes of behaviour.

The findings of a very extensive study on the perception of poverty in Europe (Commission of the European Communities, 1977) showed that, in rank order, the most common causes of poverty were believed to be poor luck, laziness, lack of willpower and injustice in society. However, some significant national differences were found, with the Italians and French blaming the societal factors; the British and Irish blaming the victims of poverty; and the Danes blaming the fate. In general, those highly educated and economically well off, mostly blamed social injustice; but the less educated and economically less well off, blamed the victims more. In a British study, Furnham (1982a, b) found that English public-school boys considered individualistic explanations for poverty more important than the poor school boys who found societal explanations more important.

Pyne and Furnham (1985) in their study compared

the explanations adolescents gave for poverty in the relatively wealthy island of Barbados and relatively poor island of Dominica. The Barbadian adolescents showed more concern than their Dominican peers about social inequalities and injustices. The West Indian adolescents in general gave societal explanations to be primarily responsible for the cause and persistence of poverty in the Caribbean region.

In our research (Sinha, Jain & Pandey, 1980) we found that individuals in India may differ in perception of the causes of poverty in relation to their varied socio-economic status and political ideologies. Urban rickshaw-pullers rated the role of self-characteristics (ability and effort of the poor), fate and luck of the poor, government, and dominance of a few as causes of poverty in Indian society. The results revealed that the rickshaw-pullers who did not own rickshaws blamed the government and a dominant few as causes of poverty significantly more than the rickshaw-pullers who owned their own rickshaws (Sinha, Jain & Pandey, 1980). It implies that even at the lower class level also ownership status influences attribution of causality to poverty.

In another study (Pandey, Sinha, Prakash, & Tripathi, 1982), we examined the role of right and left political ideologies on attribution of the causes to poverty. College students belonging either to left or right wing political organizations and neutral students not belonging to any political organization were the respondents. The findings have been summarised in Table 4.3. The left respondents were significantly more radical in their views towards the present state of the society, the process of change, and the goal of change in comparison to the right and neutral respondents. In general, there were greater attributions by all respondents to governmental policies and economic dominance of a few as the causes of poverty. The results further revealed that the neutral and right respondents attributed significantly more to self (ability of the poor), and fate of the poor as causes of poverty than the left respondents. The left resondents, attributed significantly more to governmental policies and to economic dominance

TABLE 4.3 : *Means of attribution of causes to poverty by the Neutral, Right and Left politically affiliated subjects*

Perceived causes of poverty	Neutral	Right	Left	F (2, 87)
Self	5.63a	5.76a	3.96b	6.26*
Fate	4.40a	4.86a	2.96b	7.85*
Government's policies	6.50a	7.26a	8.56b	9.07*
Economic dominance	7.23a	6.76a	8.96b	9.33*

*p <0.01.

Note : Means with common subscripts do not differ significantly.

of a few in the society as causes of the poverty than the rightists and neutrals.

The functional nature of poverty is commonly observed. Poor people perform a number of functions which well to do people would not like to do. For example, generally, the poor do dirty jobs. They utilize used consumer goods and provide status feeling to the rich. They serve as recipients of charity and donations in their society and provide feeling of benevolence to the donors. In order to study the functional perception of poverty (Pandey, Kakkar & Bohra, 1982), a questionnaire consisting of seven statements (e.g., "the presence of the poor helps the society to get dirty jobs done") with 5-point scale related to the functional nature of poverty was developed in Hindi. The range of total score was 7 to 35 with a high score indicating a greater functional nature of poverty. The respondents were again non-student middle class males and females from rural and urban areas in Northern India. The means of four groups ranged from 24.20 to 27.13 indicating that all the four groups perceived poverty as functional. There was significant gender difference with female (M=27.13) perceiving poverty as more functional than males (M=24.2).

Conclusions

It is difficult to compare findings of independent studies carried in varied socio-economic political contexts. However, the findings suggest the variability in beliefs about the causes of poverty. The research findings provide some answers to the question concerning the antecedents of the causal opinions related to poverty. For example, the White, middle income Protestants in U.S.A. (Feagin, 1975), English-public-school boys, and conservatives of U.K. (Furnham, 1982a, 1982b), and right wing political ideology oriented Indian college students (Pandey *et al.*, 1982) tend to give most individualistic causal explanations of poverty. On the other hand, the poor shcool boys of U.K. (Furnham, 1982a, b) the Barbadian and Dominican adolescents (Pyne & Furnham, 1985), and left wing political ideology oriented Indian college students (Pandey, *et al.*, 1982) tend to endorse societal explanation. It is obvious that political ideology and socio-economic class background of persons are sources of variability in beliefs about the causes of poverty. In addition, economic system, public awareness and involvement in political and economic affairs may influence causal opinions. The findings reported by Pyne and Frunham (1985) that the Barbadian adolescents were more concerned than their Dominican peers about social and economic injustices support this contention. The Barbadians were more knowledgeable about the social issues and more exposed to economic inequalities than the Dominicans. Probably, sensitivity to socio-economic issues increases with the visibility of economic progress.

One might ask what are the consequences of causal beliefs related to poverty? There have been some attempts to answer this question. Feagin (1975) has argued that individualization of social and economic problems makes it impossible to attempt a redistributive reform. He has commented that individualistic explanations and beliefs of poverty reflect"...false consciousness and mesh well with establishment's attempts to maintain the *status quo* whereas the structural interpretations lend themselves to attempts at counter-ideologies and at structural reforms..." (p. 126). Thus, explanations of poverty are systematically linked to attitudes to welfare or to poverty eradication measures. The obvious implications are: "... People hold coherent theories about both the causes of, and cures for poverty" (Paynes & Furnham, 1985, p. 216). For example, the people who tend to endorse individualistic causes also show resistance to social change.

These studies on poverty draw our attention toward some issues of special importance for the developing societies. The emergence of cultural perspective in psychology in the post-colonial era in the late 1960s and early 1970s and growing emphasis on socially relevant research led to certain expectations that issues and problems of developing countries such as poverty and disadvantage will receive some special attention from psychologists. However, the colonial trend to treat non-Euro-American societies as fertile soil for merely testing theoretical validation and generalization continues. It is our hope that attention of psychologists particularly of the developing countries like India would shift more to study of problems of their own developing societies, including poverty.

5

Psychological Research on Poverty : A Social Constructionist View

UDAY JAIN AND TARA SINGH

Since long, the condition of poverty has remained an inevitable part of the Indian society. The processes of social stratification based on the concept of '*varna*' and theory of '*karma*' have been cited as explanations of poverty. Poverty has also been considered as a state of suffering (Lam & Palsane 1997), sometimes, 'good' for the sufferer for transcending the same by good deeds and devotion to God. In folk tales one can easily find many instances of glorification of poverty. However, in modern political and social context poverty is considered as an undesirable state to be reduced or eliminated (Sinha, 1988).

Although, a number of rational, metaphysical, philosophical and religious explanations exist within the Indian culture, no Indian religion or philosophy has ever explicitly advocated the removal of poverty (Chatterjee, 1982). There are many suggestions about coping with poverty, often even legitimizing poverty, but none about its removal. Poverty was not seen as necessarily 'bad' or 'evil'. The desire and the need to remove poverty could easily be traced to the humanistic liberal traditions of the West and the nationalism of the 19th century. This call for removing poverty has made poverty a disease, a curse, an 'evil', the removal of which is necessary for the well-being and happiness of the people in modern India. Hence, the causes of poverty are seen as negative forces and carry the stigma of blame. No single institution or group of people likes to be held responsible for poverty, rather such groups try to defend against being blamed for poverty (Sinha, 1988).

For the last two decades, academicians, policy makers and many other government and non-government organizations have devoted increasingly greater attention to the various aspects of poverty and deprivation. The present critique attempts to seek an understanding of poverty, as a complex social problem, by analyzing the psychological theories, research findings and explanations based on Indian studies on poverty and looking at the relevance of social constructionist view for understanding social processes underlying the condition of poverty.

Following the dominant paradigms of research, psychologists have conducted their investigations by listing variables as antecedents and consequents of poverty or disadvantage in terms of social status, caste groups, income, so on and so forth. The researchers were interested in identification of groups which were further tested on various psychological and behavioural measures. The obtained scores were subjected to appropriate statistical tests to find out the significance of differences between the groups, or correlations between variables, or predictions of some variables of interest on the basis of other selected variables.

Deficiency vs. Difference

Diverse types of presumed deficiency conditions of stimulation are considered mainly in terms of childhood "deprivation" (Gewirtz, 1972). Effects of such deficiency conditions are taken to involve deviations from the supposed course of 'normal' child development patterns. Such deviations include a lack of alertness to environmental stimulation, poor adaptive behaviour patterns in social situations, intellectual and personality defects, and other conditions of incompetence. During 1960s, deficiency conception was also applied to life conditions of various subcultural groups which have been uniformly subjected to extreme disadvantages (e.g., extreme poverty). It has focused on the defined limitations or inadequacies in behaviour/outcome patterns presumed to result from "deficient" experiences shared by members of the cultural groups, rather than on the individual's personal experiences and behaviours.

Drawing mainly on the early animal studies on the effects of stimulus deprivation on psychological functions, various indices have been proposed to consider poverty as a state of deprivation of stimulus conditions or experiences essential for the normal growth and development of the individual. Deprived groups in comparison to non-deprived groups are found to be lower on almost all positive attributes essential for leading a better quality of life (e.g., n-ach, aspirations, cognitive and perceptual skills, scholastic achievement, low self-esteem, etc.). To add to their plight, studies have also indicated that high-deprived individuals exhibit high anxiety, alienation, helplessness, neuroticism, insecurity etc. The gap between high and low deprived people is reported to accentuate with advancing age.

Researchers have explained these results primarily in terms of lack of or limited experiences resulting from impoverished environmental conditions. Initially, such findings and their explanations appear to 'blame the victim'. Psychologically speaking, the poor lack the adequate experiences in their environment which cause psychological deficits resulting in an inadequate coping strategies to overcome the poverty situation (Sinha, 1994).

Justifications for the failure of poverty alleviation programmes given by elite in the society are partly in line with psychological research findings and explanations such as the lack of motivation of the poor, deficits in cognitive skills and abilities, and bad habits rendering poor people less capable, or sometimes unable, to overcome poverty. Psychological interventions have usually focused on individual level. NGOs and bureaucrats often are impressed with training programmes aimed at the enhancement of motivation, skills and abilities of the poor. Psychologists are ready to come up with packages of services with regard to alleviation of the negative effects of deprivation

(Krishnan, 1990). Such programmes may have temporary effects on the individual but their long-term success in the absence of structural changes in the society, is suspected. If one accepts the ecological model and its stated attendant conditions of poverty, one may realize the necessity of removing these conditions, by any poverty alleviation programme. If we extend this logic, probably the need of removing the so called 'psychological deficits' may not arise since 'enriched environment' itself, in this logic, is supposed to take care of such 'deficits'.

Culturally sensitive psychological studies have opted for a 'difference hypothesis' stating that the poor differ in areas of competence, ability, cognitive schema, attributional style, life styles, cultural norms, etc. A closer look at the stated differences between high- and low-deprived, disadvantaged groups indicates low level of attainment in the deprived groups in comparison to low or non-deprived ones.

Psychology often reflects aspects of social reality that conform to the view of power groups in developed societies and socio-historical and cultural factors that constitute social reality are largely ignored (Moghaddam, 1990).

The research findings suggest that poverty is a state of impoverished environment where the individual lacks enriched experiences and therefore psychological deficient are inevitable (Pareek, 1970). Taking this argument as valid poses a paradox. If prolonged experiences (Misra, & Tripathi, 1980) in such an environment. (i.e., deficient environment) leads to any deficit(s) then how can short-term training of linguistic skills (see Mohanty, 1999) or cognitive competence (Mishra, 1990b) remove the effects of prolonged deprivation? This is a historical fact in Indian conditions that families have suffered deprivations for many generations and thus entered in the so called "vicious circle" of psychological and social deficits.

Construction of Poverty in Psychological Research

Indian research on poverty is impressive. In this section, we will reexamine the findings of Indian research on poverty and show how these findings have shaped the construction of reality of poverty.

The measurement of poverty entails several problems of conceptual and practical nature. There is a need to identify with poverty, minimal subsistence, destitution, deprivation and the host of terms which have proliferated to suit various approaches and priorities of politicians as well as the students of social and economic stratification. In general, two approaches have been widely used in psychological research for establishing cut off points: *absolute* (some definite point on the income scale), and *relative* (some percentile or porportion of the total range to differentiate the standard of living). However, both these measures have their own problems. With regard to the concept of 'absolute' poverty, there is lack of consensus among the various disciplines. For the concept of 'relative' poverty, for practical purposes, the standards become so fluid that no definition of need is possible, no matter how broad or satisfied are the ever changing expectations of modern life. Increase in perceived poverty is a phenomenon particularly characteristic of American life during periods of so called prosperity.

"To deprive" means to dispossess or strip (a person or an object) and implies a 'felt loss' (Sinha, 1982b). According to Sinha (1982b) deprivation suggests certain deficiencies in the environment which are not only there but are also experienced by the individual. It relates to certain features or aspects of the environment that are absent or inadequate in certain degree and have an impact on the functioning of the individual. An individual's psychological processes can have meaning only if they are conceived in their proper setting or viewed in terms of their interactions with environment. Sinha (1982b) has emphasized that behaviour is to be viewed not in simple terms of individual factors, nor the environmental factors as having isolated impact on the individual, but in the entire '*individual environmental complex*' as a constant two-way interplay.

There exists a running dispute about the extent of poverty. However, three alternative conceptions of poverty have been presented. (1) *Subsistence* (Rowntree, 1901), an income below that 'sufficient to obtain the minimum necessaries for the maintenance of merely physical efficiency' (p. 86). The necessaries include clothes, fuel, and some other items but had mainly to do with a basic diet. (2) *Basic needs*, (International Labour Office, 1976), specified two components: 'minimum requirements of a family for private consumption' (food, shelter, clothing and some furniture and equipment) and 'essential services provided by and for the community at large, such as safe drinking water, sanitation, public transport and health, education and cultural facilities' (pp. 24-25). (3) Social conception in terms of '*relative deprivation*' as 'the only way poverty can be defined objectively and applied consistently' (Townsend, 1979). People are 'relatively deprived' if their resources do not let them meet the social demands of membership of their society—expectations which are then translated into an income threshold required for meeting them. These three conceptions have different implications for what counts as poverty and what policy should be adopted to overcome it. If poverty is a matter of relative deprivation, then the nutritional aspect of people's diet is only part of what must be reckoned with. There is more to food than calories, since what one eats, how it is cooked, where and with whom it is eaten are deeply part of oneself and one's social identity.

The Problem in Defining Poverty

Although the task of defining poverty has been a major problem for academicians and policy makers, the logic underlying the process of defining poverty as well as offered definitions have their own consequences. In many ways the offered definitions determine the entire process of dealing with poverty, ranging from understanding poverty to the implementation of poverty alleviation programmes. Success or failure of any programme depends on the definition of poverty. Let us examine this problem in some detail.

Today, there is considerable encouragement, support, and pressure on behavioural scientists to engage in work with social utility. Those of us who feel that the social sciences have not met their social responsibility welcome this upsurge of interest in the problems of society.

Actions about poverty depend on how it is defined. The way poverty is defined determines the attempts at remediations, the foci and the techniques of intervention. The definitions of poverty are based on assumptions about the causes or sources of poverty. If poverty is defined in person-centered terms, then it would be logical to initiate person-change techniques and intervention strategies to deal with the problem. On the other hand, if the explanations of poverty are situation-centered, then efforts toward alleviation or reduction of poverty and its effects would logically have a system-change orientation.

Once the definitions are legitimized, they tend to locate the problem. Programme administrators and change agents develop a vested interest in maintaining the established definitions since their very jobs, status, power, and the employment of subordinates may depend on those definitions being accepted as correct. If intervention fails, the problem definition and the delivery system are seldom held responsible. The responsibility for the failure is located in the target group. They interpret failure of the programme as a sign of the seriousness of the problem.

While defining a problem in the context of social policy, the social scientists are expected to provide expert and unbiased knowledge. But, the meaning of 'unbiased' is not identical for the consumers and the producers of social science knowledge. To the knowledge user, it may mean (a) that the problem will be viewed from all vantage points and that the interpretation offered will depend on the assessment of a sufficient variety of competing hypotheses that reflect the complexity of the issues, and/or (b) that the new information does not challenge the established definitions.

Social scientists define "unbiased" in terms of the canons of scientific methodology. However, psychology focuses on person-centered variables and this results in a definite bias on the inferential potential of the findings when used as a premise on which to base the actions for the corrective change. Psychologists study individuals and in particular their mental states—their thoughts, attitudes, motives, etc. and prefer to view these constructs as independent variables, i.e., antecedent and causal in relation to behaviour. However, they pay little attention to the contextual factors influencing behaviour.

Preoccupation with person-centered variables is also related to career gains. It is more likely to enhance one's own position among colleagues by conducting so called 'relevant' research and offering explanations and solutions within the dominant paradigm of the discipline. It is the goodwill and approval of peers in the scientific community, not that of the target population, that get us ahead. However, what is good for science and the individual scientist may not be good for those on whom the research is based. The view of the world they inspire or perpetuate, may seem like epiphenomena to us, but they are often painfully real for those affected by them. Thus, psychology as a profession has a special reason to consider a more balanced approach in selecting variables for the study of poverty. Any discipline-bound approach to social problems such as poverty or deprivation can be only partially correct. Person-blame explanations of social problems, whether valid or not, hold the potential for reinforcing the established stereotypes and thereby perpetuating the conditions of the poor.

Social scientists seldom question the established definitions of poverty or wisdom behind the process that leads to identification of poverty. Why does one kind of poverty concerns us, and another does not? Why do we constantly study the poor rather than the non-poor in order to understand the origins of poverty? Why do we study nonachievement among poor or disadvantaged as an undesirable behaviour, but do not study exaggerated profit motive among the successful businessmen as a form of deviance? These questions are rarely raised. Yet a social scientist must understand that by his or her involvement *qua* scientific authority in research operation(s)he has, consciously or unconsciously, explicitly or implicitly, lent credibility and legitimacy to a given view of poverty.

When person-centered attributional bias is applied to poverty, it favours explanations in terms of personal characteristics of the poor and disadvantaged, while disregarding the possible influence of external forces. However, there are many latent functions of person-blame interpretations of poverty. They offer a convenient apology for freeing the government and social institutions from blame for the poverty condition. Since those institutions are apparently not the cause of poverty, it may be legitimately contended that they cannot be held responsible for poverty amelioration. If they do provide such help, they are credited with being exceedingly humane, while gaining control over those being helped, through the manipulation of definition of poverty. Such interpretations provide and legitimatise the right to initiate person-change rather than system-change treatment programmes. For Caplan and Nelson (1973), this in turn, has the following functions: (a) it serves as a publicly acceptable device to control troublesome segments of the population; (b) it distracts attention from possible systemic causes; and (c) it discredits system-oriented criticism. Thus, the person-blame interpretations are in everyone's interest, except those subjected to analysis. These interpretations also produce enormous political benefits.

Contextual Concerns in the Explanation of Poverty

An alternate effort to understand poverty (as opposed to person-centered or person-blame approach) has been made by researchers seeking to understand poverty in its total context. Some of these efforts merit brief mention.

An alternative hypothesis explaining poverty and its consequences has been advanced in terms of the characteristics of environment. Stone and Church (1972) refer to "intelligent life spaces" or "intelligent environments". There are "competent environments" capable of offering a sense of mastery to people of varying ability levels and differential endowments. Vance (1973) has suggested that "the extent of poverty in the urban settings, is the single greatest disabling factor in competence and is developmentally operative prior to all other variables investigated" (p. 501). Externality is more of a characteristic of the culturally alienated and of lower socio-economic group, than of middle and upper socio-economic groups.

In an attempt to understand the psychology of poverty and its dynamics by adopting an environmental perspective, two Indian studies (Anandlakshmy, 1975; Saraswathi & Dutta, 1990) suggest solutions to overcome some of the difficulties encountered by psychologists while dealing with the explanations of poverty and its effects. In her study on the socialization of competence in children (Anandlakshmy & Bajaj, 1981) and abilities and skill development in disadvantaged children, Anandlakshmy (1975) suggested that "not only is competence a trait of individuals, it could also be described as a trait of environments".

While studying the socialization of girls among the urban and rural poor, Saraswathi and Dutta (1990) examined some of the environmental potentials and constraints that operate in the process of socialization of children in the urban and rural poverty settings. An ecological perspective (See Barker & Wright, 1954; Lewin, 1951) was adopted for interpreting the process of socialization with the assumption that it is the broader environmental context which gets filtered to the children through the parent's beliefs, practices, hopes, and aspirations. It is this context that determines the constraints and the facilitating factors which in turn influence the goals of socialization. By adopting Bronfenbrenner's (1974, 1979) model, they have argued that poverty is a macro-level phenomenon common to the rural and urban poor, and continues to exist on a nationwide scale regardless of the debates on what constitutes an index of poverty level, and consequently, how pervasive it is. Saraswathi and Dutta (1990) have argued that socialization of children in any community setting forms the dynamic link in the fluid chain of past, present, and the future.

Himmelweit (1990), while describing implications and

scope of societal psychology, argued that, in the past 40 years, mainstream social psychology's concentration has been on the study of the individual's thoughts, feelings, and actions, while paying little attention to the study of environment, its culture, and its institutions. The cost of the restricted vision of psychology and neglecting the environment has also been evaluated and described by Gergen (1973, 1985), Moscovici (1976), Rosnow (1981), and Rosnow and Georgoudi (1985). Urging psychologists not to neglect the study of environment has a long and distinguished tradition (Brunswick, 1952; Lewin, 1951). More recently, Doise (1978) has distinguished four levels of explanation in social psychology. He makes a convincing case that his first two levels, the interpersonal and the intergroup, are incomplete unless one relates them to the other levels largely ignored by social psychology : the social structural and institutional, and the ideological.

Social Constructionist View of Poverty

The focus of psychology on the 'individual' is an outcome of historical circumstances (e.g., see Danzinger, 1990, for details). 'Methodological individualism' is also prevalent in other social sciences. The focus on individual's characteristics as causes of social phenomena has a long history in Western thought. Hobbs, for example emphasized on the understanding of "constitutive causes" for understanding compound and for J.S. Mill, "the laws of the phenomena of society" are, and can be, nothing but the actions and passions of human beings. On the other hand, many thinkers in early 19th century emphasized collective phenomena for understanding social life. This debate continues among sociologists, social scientists and psychologists. Psychologists along with other social scientists argue that society, groups and institutions all consist of people plus rules, roles and norms. The facts about society and social phenomena are to be explained solely in terms of facts about individuals. This is the doctrine of methodological individualism (Lukes, 1973). Such a theory entails that social phenomena are constructions of the mind and do not exist in reality.

A number of objections can be raised against the above thesis. First of all, the argument that in the social world only individuals are observable, is false. Many social phenomena are observable (e.g., procedures of court) while many features of individuals are not (e.g., intentions). In fact, both individual and social phenomena are observable and non-observable.

Thus, it appears that the thesis of 'methodological individualism' does not have any compelling ground to claim its separate identity in understanding social phenomena through individual characteristics. On the contrary, such phenomena have to be understood by socio-historical processes operating on the present institutions and individuals. Mead (1958) has extensively argued that minds and selves are essentially social products, and hence social processes are to be analyzed for understanding human experiences. Mead writes, "the behaviour of all living organisms has a basically social aspect; the fundamental biological or physiological impulses and needs which lie at the basis of such behaviour, especially those of hunger and sex, those connected with nutrition and reproduction, are impulses and needs, which in the broadest sense, are social in character or have social implications, since they involve or reqtuire social situations and relations for their satisfaction by any given individual organism" (pp. 227-228).

In recent years, a growing body of knowledge has challenged the basic assumptions of traditional psychological research conducted in the Western scientific tradition. The focus on the individual's internal characteristics and mechanisms as the basis of behaviour devoid of social processes has been challenged. It has been argued that the concept of 'self-contained individual' and attempts at 'objective', 'authoritative' knowledge about it is an 'artifact' and constructed by a community of scientists'. Once such knowledge is constructed its claim as 'factual' is protected and popularized. Social constructionists view psychological phenomena within the shared systems of intelligibility usually through the spoken or written language. Hence, independent of observers, the study of psychological phenomena is neither possible nor desirable as our understanding is primarily interdependent and relational. The 'reality' emerges through interactions of related individuals and the social context in which the phenomenon is discussed, disputed and agreed upon. The study of any social problem (in this case, poverty), therefore, cannot be based on the individuals' inner mechanisms. This has already been done by social psychologists who study individuals' behaviour in social situations (stimuli) where 'social' phenomena are reduced to the individual level (Jain & Misra, 1994).

Following the social constructionist approach, the study of poverty may be conducted by taking into account the various discourses on poverty prevalent in a society, culture or community. In this context, mass-media, literature, political meetings, deliberations in the seminars, government reports on poverty, and last but not the least, research by social scientists including psychologists may provide the raw data for understanding the concept of poverty practiced in the Indian society.

Human reality is created through social practices. Its meaning, therefore, is derived from a given socio-cultural context. Social behaviour is largely intentional and, therefore, the meaning attached to the phenomena and the relationship amongst people provides context for human acts. Social behaviours (except the routine and repetitive ones) are esentially dynamic and developing in nature. They unfold in the course of time.

It is argued that knowledge systems are fundamentally linguistic systems, sounds or markings that are used by people in relationships. In this respect knowledge would appear vitally dependent on social negotiations. Its constraints would not essentially be experiential but social. From this standpoint, the concepts of poverty, deprivation, social class, and the like are not matters of ontological significance; statements about them are not subject to empirical test. The statements employing such terms may or may not be supported by observation depending on how one chooses to relate such terms to observation.

Typically, such relationships mainly depend on the usage of the terms within social interchange. Since, such usage depends on coordinated actions among people, or "joint action" in Shotter's (1980) terms, knowledge in its linguistic sense can be viewed fundamentally as a social product.

Thus, if poverty is assumed to be under human control, the causal power of environment (stimulus or reinforcement) within the traditional exogenic framework is thereby diminished. The, theorist is granted broad scope with respect to explanation of poverty, i.e., where causal power is placed and how it is to be understood. The contemporary social psychology is based almost entirely on a logic of efficient cause; it searches for the immediate antecedents, both necessary and sufficient, for a given action. This is true in case of poverty and deprivation also. Yet poverty may be understood in terms of its place in a historical process, both with respect to the individual and the culture. How and why a given pattern of social class or poverty developed in the life of the individual or within the society? What transformations have such patterns undergone over time, and what functions have these transformations served? Such questions open an exciting range of possibilities.

Conclusion

In conclusion it may be said that an adequate approach to the study of poor and disadvantaged and use of this knowledge in practice cannot ignore the real circumstances within which we find ourselves. How are we to act in accordance with our scientific principles and avoid being a part of the problem rather than the solution? In this regard, gaining an understanding of a true and meaningful conception of culture, as well as of poverty, will be particularly helpful as the modern concept of culture refers to the process of helping things grow, a characterization of what society expects.

If we accept the argument for a socially constructed order of poverty and grant a functional link between the practices of the culture then alteration in practices have implications for any social order. In this way social psychological theory acquires an agentive role in social life. It can serve as a tool to be employed by the theorist, researcher, or others to strengthen, sustain or obliterate poverty or other forms of disadvantaged social life.

However, there are problems of value. What forms of social life are to be favoured, which are to be discouraged? The language of theoretical description and explanation should carry with them implications for action. To describe is inherently to prescribe. It is the theoretical interpretation of experience that has the capacity to transform social life, and not the empirical evidence itself. The data themselves are mute. Research may be viewed as a means of enhancing the efficacy of communication.

6

Perpetuating Inequality : The Disadvantage of Language, Minority Mother Tongues and Related Issues[1]

AJIT K. MOHANTY

Amid all the enthusiasm generated by the National Policy on Education (Govt. of India, 1986), its subsequent revision, the programme of *Education for All, Universalisation of Elementary Education, Anandamaya Siksha* and now the DPEP and what not, let me take you for a moment to a young Kandha child in class II of a primary school in a remote village in Raikia block of Phulbani/Kondmal district of Orissa. The Child, who has left behind many other children of her age who never came to school, is present in the class with wide-eyed curiosity trying to figure out what is going on. Despite all the pious programmes, improved curricula, operation black board and many such efforts, she just doesn't learn to read and write. She is not alone; there are many other such children from Kond families who also do not learn. They are all in each other's comforting company; days pass by but they do not learn. Examinations they may or may not pass but they are certainly passing time. An educational psychologist does not have to look far for the causes of learning failure, for any common person can tell you that she does not learn because she does not understand the

1. An earlier version of this paper was presented at the presidential address in the VIIIth Congress of the National Academy of Psychology (India), held at Bhubaneswar, December 18-20, 1997.

teacher, the texts and the curricula all of which use a language she does not know; it is not the language of her family, not the human resource with which she has ventured to come to school. The reasons of learning failure are simple, obvious and glaring. But strangely, it continues to elude the planners of our early education who are trying to provide equality of educational opportunity through EFA, DPEP, Operation Blackboard and many such expensive programmes, while fundamentally they have missed the point. Equality of educational opportunity through a standardised dominant language instruction to every one in complete disregard for their mother tongues is like a democratic doctor who uniformly prescribes the same higher antibiotics to all his patients ignoring the differences in their diseases and symptoms. In this country, preferential treatment of some languages as media of instruction and for other purposes linked with social mobility and status of advantage for some is one of many ways of perpetuating inequality and relegating many others to a position of disadvantage.

The mismatch between the home language or mother-tongue and the dominant or majority languages used as language of formal instruction in our schools is perhaps the most pressing educational issue for linguistic minorities in multi-lingual setting (Spolsky, 1986). In India, the 1961 census identified 1652 major mother tongues and an NCERT survey in 1981 revealed that only 47 of these were used as media of instruction in our schools (Chaturvedi & Singh, 1981). In other words, speakers of over 1600 mother tongues in our country do not have schooling in languages of their family, their culture. Less than 1 per cent of the ST children in India have education in their own language.

There are two reactions to such neglect of minority mother tongues. Some brush them aside as impoverished languages, languages of poverty and disadvantage. A very respected psychologist in India was firmly of the opinion that tribal languages are inadequate for dealing with abstract and scientific concepts and, hence, these mother tongues could not be used as languages of formal instruction. This argument typically smacks of a Whorfian position of linguistic relativity which, furthered by a misinterpretation of the Bernsteinian distinction between "elaborated" and "restricted" code, made language the main pillar of the deprivation position attributing educational failure of the disadvantaged children to the poverty of their languages (Mohanty, 1990 a). Studies motivated by such a position unfortunately promoted a linguistic-deficit view which characterised the speech of the lower class, the poor, the minority and the disadvantaged as deficient and inadequate for fostering educational and cognitive development. Without going into a critical analysis of this position, one can sum up with Edwards (1979) that the very idea of linguistic deficit is ill conceived and "saturated with middle class bias" (p. 48). Verbal deprivation of children in poverty and in social disadvantage is better understood as artifacts of methodological problems in testing such children and the imposition of dominant group norms on the less powerful minorities and disadvantaged groups. What is often forgotten in the parochial vision of linguicism is that language varieties are simply different symbol systems with their own logical bases and, therefore, the languages of the minority mother tongue speakers, of the poor and the disadvantaged are not deficient; they are only different.

Languages may differ in their form and structure but they are all equally functional in the cultural context of their use. "The differences in certain aspects of languages such as their complexity, ability to express specific experiences and the size of the vocabulary etc. are only superficial differences based on conventions and functional requirements; no language is inherently deficient, illogical or primitive" (Mohanty, 1990 a, p. 4). Work of Labov (1973) and many other linguists has made it amply clear that "a nonstandard variety is not a substandard variety". It is quite clear that "the view of linguistic deficit of the disadvantaged doesn't stand to critical scrutiny. . . languages do not vary in respect of the degree to which they facilitate or hinder cognitive functioning. However, this is not to deny that, for some, their speech is a liability.

No language (*qua* language) creates any cognitive or linguistic disability; the disabilities are social in origin resulting from the fact that, in our societies, languages (which are inherently equal) are treated in unequal manners. The language of poverty, therefore, does not entail poverty of language" (Mohanty, 1990a, p. 5). Inequalities are rooted in differential functional allocation of languages and speech varieties through social conventions which ensure negative evaluation of the speech of the disadvantaged as well as minority languages. Shukla (1989) has shown that stylistic and functional differences in speech use as well as children's communication are affected by maternal styles of speech. In a much more indigenous study of individual differences in language use, conducted under the guidance of Professor D. Sinha, Anjali Singh (1987) has found significant influence of grand parents in development of language.

Thus, the process of language socialisation is important in transmitting the conventional allocation of speech styles and speech varieties to different domains of social activity. However, in respect of functional differences and patterns of language use, differences within social class may be much more than differences across social classes. The association between poverty and deprivation and the so called disadvantaged speech styles seems to be grossly misplaced and misconceived. "There is no inherent cognitive deficiency associated with the language of the otherwise deprived; language is a product of certain socio-cultural factors which propagate a view of some varieties of language use as disadvantaged. The real disadvantage of the language of the disadvantaged, therefore, is attitudinal, and schools, unfortunately, represent such social attitudes" (Mohanty, 1990a, p. 6). Children in poverty and disadvantage may have other deficiencies — health, nutrition, housing etc. and the social attitudes towards the language and culture of the poor, the minority and the disadvantaged seem to augment the negative impacts perpetuating the myth of deficient or substandard language. In India, the underlying continuity between the hypothetical standard variety of languages and the nonstandard regional/local varieties is ignored in text books and in other educational use of languages. The "standard" form of a language in India is often judged in terms of the degree of *Sanskritization* and *Anglicization* of language perpetuated by an elitist bias in language use and communication. This has resulted in an artificial hiatus between standard and nonstandard forms marked in the obsolence of the top down approach to translation of technical and scientific terms into regional languages. Unfortunately, when such terms in educational use are prevented from growing up from popular speech use, the disadvantage of vernacular varieties necessarily follows, at least, partially. In any case, one has to agree with Edwards (1979) that the sharp discontinuity between home language and language of schools is "an integral part of the very definition of disadvantage" (p. 100).

The problem, therefore, is not of the language of the disadvantaged but of the disadvantage of language, the language of the minor, minority and non-standard speakers. This brings me to the second reaction to the minority mother tongues. The multiplicity and diversity of so many mother tongues is appalling in its complexity. The challenge is often passed by in favour of unity and homogenization. The result is an increasing pressure on the non-dominant mother tongues, their displacement, language shift, loss of diversity and above all, shame to minority language users. "When education goes under the banner of human resource development but, at the same time, ignores the most complete and complex form of resource with which a child joins school — human language — the inherent contradiction is too compelling to pass off, because, for millions of children who are forced to seek formal education in schools where curriculum and language of instruction has no relationship with their home language, this neglect of mother tongue spells their destiny. In the name of unity, standardization, integration, modernization and homogenization, so many people are stripped of their cultural rootedness and their primordial pride through loss of one of their primary identity tags — their mother tongue — and, in the process, kept out of the privileges of a majority dominated elitist society, that equality of opportunity remains a vague slogan" (Mohanty, 1990 *b*, p. 54). Elsewhere (Mohanty, 1990c), I have analysed the social psychological aspects of the Indian languages in contact to show that in a multilingual country like India, the issue of language planning cannot be viewed from the dominant monolingual perspective of the west. To quote a leading Indian linguist, Pattanayak (1984), "the dominant monolingual orientation is cultivated in the developed world and consequently two languages are considered a nuisance, three languages un-economic and many languages absurd. In multilingual countries, many languages are facts of life; any restriction on the choice of language use is a nuisance; and one language is not only uneconomic, it is absurd" (p. 82). It follows then that the problems of maintenance of minority mother tongues and their educational use have to be addressed strictly on indigenous considerations; imported models may be alluring but they simply would not work, as is true in all other areas of psychological research in the Indian setting. In this context multilingualism in India raises some very significant questions. Is mother tongue maintenance a barrier to socioeconomic and educational mobility of the linguistic minorities such as the tribes in Orissa? Does loss of minority languages through their assimilation into the dominant contact languages resulting in a loss of diversity, lead to social integration as is commonly believed?

In several studies over the last couple of decades, I have sought to address these issues from an indigenous framework (Mohanty, 1994 a) conceptualising Indian bilingualism as the first incremental step in the direction of societal multilingualism, bringing in a sharp contrast between the monolingual and multilingual perspectives. While the early studies of bilingualism gave rise to negative view of bilinguals as persons whose mental capacity was divided between two languages, a recent review (Mohanty & Perregaux, 1997) shows "the emergence of a positive perspective in bilingualism research" (p. 232). Our Indian studies have significantly contributed to this perspective. Let me point out that these studies have a distinct methodological advantage because, in the context of India's linguistic diversity and complex sociolinguistic realities, it has been possible to draw comparison samples of bilinguals and monolinguals from within the same sociocultural groups avoiding the confouding of bilingualism with cultrual differences characteristic of the western studies. Our studies (see Mohanty, 1990 *b*, 1992, 1994 *a*, *b* for details) in Phulbani have drawn comparable samples of Kui-Oriya bilinguals and Oriya monolinguals from among the Konds made possible by a sort of frozen language shift which has resulted in a complete language shift from Kui to Oriya in a part of the district and a stable form of Kui-Oriya contact bilingualism in the remaining areas. In a number of studies conducted within a period of about fifteen years, it has been clearly shown that the bilingual children, schooled as well as unschooled, have a distinct edge over their monolingual counterparts in terms of their cognitive and intellectual skills, metalinguistic and metacognitive task performance and educational achievement (in case of schooled children). Further, the Kui-Oriya bilingual children in their later grades (i.e. the high school grades) were found to perform in Oriya language tasks at the same level as the Oriya-only monolingual children. Other Indian studies have also shown positive consequences of bilingualism on educational and cognitive performance (e.g. Southworth, 1980, study in Kerala).

The Kond studies have led to development of an integrated model of the relationship between bilingualism, metacognitive process and cognitive skills in the context of Indian pluralism (Mohanty, 1992, 1994 *a*, *b*). "Ability to communicate using more than one language code seems to foster metalinguistic and metacognitive development. Bilingualism enables children to develop some degree of flexibility in cognitive operations, an analytic and objective orientation to language and an increased sensitivity to messages. It endows them with the ability to use language also as an object of thought and to efficiently utilize the various linguistic and paralinguistic cues for effective communication which involves much more than simple application of the rules of language" (Mohanty, 1994, *b*, pp. 10-11).

The metaliguistic and metacognitive hypothesis of bilinguals' intellectual and scholastic advantage has been widely supported in many studies — Indian as well as western. However, "it would be too simplistic to assume that the relationship is independent of the cultural context of bilingualism" (Mohanty & Perregaux, 1997, p. 235). The context of Indian bilingualism is its multilingualism. "A fundamental difference between bilingualism in the context of dominant monolingual and multilingual societies is that the former is transitional in nature whereas the latter is stable and maintenance oriented. In the west, bilingualism is the road from monolingualism (in the native language) to monolingualism (in the dominant/majority language). In the U.S., for example, the first generation of immigrants is usually monolingual in the native mother tongue, the second generation is bilingual in English and the native mother tongue, and the third generation is monolingual in English. In India, on the other hand, the immigrant communities remain native mother tongue (MT) users not by rejecting the language of the host society but by adapting it within a generation or two, as a second language in addition to other language(s) required..... In such a context, a child grows up with bilingualism as a first language or as a total bilingual person" (Mohanty, 1994 *b*, p. 2). Our studies on language socialization of children growing up in multilingual contexts (Mohanty, 1994 *c*; Mohanty, Panda & Mishra, 1999) have shown that Indian children pass through three periods of multilingual socialization, viz., period of language differentiation, period of awareness of languages and period of multilingual functioning, showing differentiation between languages as early as 3 years of age. Thus, the Indian life style, socialization and communication norms make multilingualism an accepted and positive phenomenon. As a result, "when other factors are controlled, social psychological and cognitive consequences of bilingualism can be expected to be positive in pluralistic and multilingual cultures" (Mohanty & Perregaux, 1997, p. 236).

Social psychological analysis of intergroup relation in bilingual contact situations also reveals an interesting picture. Berry (1990) has analysed the acculturation attitude of individuals or groups in contact along two dimensions: maintenance of one's own identity, culture, language etc. and establishing a relationship with the other group. Four outcomes of cultural/linguistic contact have been identified, depending upon positive and negative choices in respect of the two dimensions. These outcomes are assimilation, integration, separation and marginalization. In a sociolinguistic survey (Mohanty, 1987) of 25 to 50-year old adult Kond and non-tribal villagers from bilingual and monolingual areas in Phulbani, "the tribals were found to be displaying integrative orientation by a positive evaluation of the maintenance of their own language (Kui) and culture, and by viewing favourably the language (Oriya) and culture of the non-tribals. Within the tribal group, the bilinguals displayed greater integrative tendency compared to the monolinguals ..... Within the sample of nontribals, the bilinguals were less segregation oriented compared to the monolinguals". A repeat survey (Mohanty & Parida, 1993) essentially arrived at the same findings; tribals and nontribals in bilingual contact areas displayed assimilation orientation and the nontribals a segregation attitude.

Thus, bilingualism seems to promote integration defined as positive self/ingroup identity along with positive other/outergroup identification. Permitting a little digression, it may be recalled that nearly 7 years after our first survey and eight months after the second, there was tension in April 1994, for the first time in the District, between the Konds and a particular class of non-tribals involving large scale violence, armed conflicts and riots. The conflict not only originated from a monolingual village but also continued for nearly three months without spreading at all to bilingual areas. One would perhaps have predicted otherwise, with linguistic divergence more prominent in bilingual areas where organised linguistic and cultural movements are also more active. But the actual turn of events confirmed the findings of the two sociolinguistic surveys that bilingualism in contact situations promotes better social integration whereas, in situations in which the minority/minor group is linguistically assimilated, there is disintegration. Implications of these intergroup relationship studies merit a mention. Given the existing relationship, forces towards promotion of cultural identity of the Konds and maintenance of Kui language can be expected to foster integration whereas, all forces tending towards shift of Kui language, acculturation, or rather, deculturation of the Konds and imposition of Oriya, are likely to move the contact outcome in the direction of assimilation, loss of Kui and of cultural diversity. Apart from other benefits of bilingualism, maintenance of Kui seems to be a better option for the sake of cultural pluralism and social integration.

To return, briefly, to the two questions raised earlier about the role of mother tongue maintenance in social and educational development and upward mobility of the disadvantaged linguistic minorities and about the consequences of assimilation, it can be pointed out that the Kond studies are quite unequivocal in suggesting that there are considerable advantages of mother tongue maintenance for socioeconomic mobility through psycho-educational development and for social integration of the linguistic minorities like the tribals in India. "Denial of the rights of the minority groups to maintain their indigenous mother tongue, to develop a sense of pride in the linguistic identity and to maximally utilize their cultural resources by educational use of their mother tongue is clearly a denial of equality of opportunity to these minorities in a multilingual multicultural society like that of India" (Mohanty, 1990 *c*, p. 63). The question of unequal treatment of languages (and cultures) putting some groups at an advantage is, thus, linked with the perpetuation of disadvantage among others who are rendered powerless by social design.

This leads to the question of mother tongue education. It is quite clear from the empirical examination of the issues as well as from ideological perspectives that mother tongue education must be considered children's "linguistic human rights" which Skutnabb-Kangas (1986, p. 160, 1988, p. 19) would have declared as follows:

1. Every child should have the right to identify positively with her original mother tongue(s) and have her identification accepted and respected by others.
2. Every child should have the right to learn the mother tongue(s) fully.
3. Every child should have the right to choose when she/he wants to use the mother tongue(s) in all official situations.

In several of her writings, Skutnabb-Kangas has sought to expose the double standard in multilingual societies in which the linguistic human rights are realized to a large extent for the majority children whereas the minority mother tongue children do not enjoy the same rights. "Groups defined on the basis of their mother tongues thus have unequal access to educational resources, i.e. these educational systems reflect linguicism" (Skutnab-Kangas, 1988, p. 20). Linguicism promotes linguistic as well as sociocultural disadvantage.

The Kond studies demonstrate the cognitive and social psychological cost of imposed monolingualism. Like the Kond children, millions of linguistic minority children in India are forced to suffer through an unsympathetic discriminatory educational system that does not even recognise their only genuine resource — their mother tongue. In such a scenario, minority and disadvantaged children do not '*drop out*' they are '*pushed out*'. The problem of language of instruction, therefore, cannot be viewed from a typically monolingual perspective that treats languages as unequal. The role of multiple languages for local, regional, national and wider levels of communication cannot be denied in the Indian context. Therefore, our education must be multilingual in the true sense of the term. "Pluralism cannot be sustained without an active policy of multilingualism at a broader national level and such a multilingual policy is bound to be ineffective unless it is supported by a policy that promotes bilingualism at the individual, community, educational and other institutional levels. The idea of accommodating to the hierarchical pattern of language use has to be built into the educational system in particular because education cannot afford to persist with a model that is multilingual at the surface level and monolingual in the underlying level" (Mohanty, 1994 *b*, p. 22). Before we blame the victims of inequality for their disadvantage, we must examine how social policies and institutions lead to the psychological conditions often associated with disadvantage. Education is an important social instrument which perpetuates inequality.

A rationale for multilingual education with emphasis on mother tongue instruction must be, atleast briefly discussed; lest the suggestions might sound impractical, vacuous and idealistic. While the efficacy of mother tongue education in promoting conceptual learning has been amply demonstrated in several studies (see for review Mohanty, 1994 *a, b;* Mohanty & Perregaux, 1997 etc.) a monolingual programme of mother tongue education is not enough for linguistic minority children nor for the children from major or dominant languages in Indian context. True bilingual/multilingual programmes of education, in which different languages are used as languages of instruction either synchronously or at different points in education, are necessary. It must be pointed out here that promotion of mother tongue proficiency beyond the level of basic interpersonal communication skills (BICS) to the level of using language for cognitive activities in academic settings i.e. the cognitive academic language proficiency (CALP) is a necessary condition for subsequent promotion of second, third or fourth languages (Cummins, 1979, 1984 etc.). Therefore, initial years of mother tongue medium instruction need not be seen as wasted for a child who may have to learn major languages later on. In fact, the linguistic interdependence hypothesis (Cummins, 1979) suggests that, unless a child's proficiency in her first language, L_1 is sufficiently developed in the school context, instruction in L_2 or other languages is likely to become ineffective. It should also be pointed out here that the same principle applies to the English medium schools which, because of the prestige and instructional values attached to English in India, are becoming increasingly popular. Studies by Swati Patra (in press) and others at the Centre of Advanced Study in Psychology at Utkal are beginning to expose the myth of the English medium superiority. Despite the advantages in terms of quality of schooling, learner motivation and other positive socioeconomic conditions, matched-sample comparisons from English and regional language medium schools show little differences or differences in favour of the regional language medium children in their arithmetic, science and aspects of language achievement.

Turning back to the bilingual education programmes, of the several models available only some are suitable (see Mohanty, 1990 *d*, 1994 *a* etc. for reviews based on theoretical formulations of Skutnab Kangas, 1986). Empirical and theoretical support exists for a bilingual educational programme for the minority language children which seeks to start their school instruction in the mother tongue medium and to develop their L_1 competence so that it can be used as a base for fostering L_2 competence at a later stage in the primary grades. Such programmes have been shown to be more effective in the long run in promoting L_2 proficiency as well as proficiency in other languages later in schools moving towards gradual sharing of instructional time by multiple languages as media of instruction. In other words, a language shelter type mother tongue maintenance programme of bilingual education seems to be ideal for linguistic minority children in the context of Indian multilingualism. The preceding discussion has sought to show that by denial of such education and rights to use the mother tongue, linguistic groups are put at a position of disadvantage which then is used to justify social neglect of their language pushing them into a vicious cycle of disadvantage.

However, as long as languages are treated with neglect and denied equality of status in a society like ours, bilingual education programmes are likely to draw scepticism until their efficacy is convincingly demonstrated in face of several myths surrounding English and majority/ dominant language medium programmes of education. By the time we realize the hidden cost of such programmes, it may be too late.

To conclude, I must go back to the issue of the disadvantage of language, by quoting from an earlier writing (Mohanty, 1990 *a*):

".....the real disadvantage lies not in the fact that some languages are poorer or deficient but in that the speakers of some languages, dialects or varieties are rendered powerless by various modes of neglect, social discrimination and prejudice which they are subjected to. It is not the language of the disadvantaged but the disadvantage of some languages and their speakers that deprives them of equality of educational and social opportunities. This perpetuates a vicious circle in which languages are weakened and put to disadvantage by educational neglect and social discrimination which, in turn, are sought to be justified on the grounds of the so called weaknesses of the disadvantaged language. The result is an agony best described in the words of Mowbray in Shakespear's Richard II (1.3):

"*What is thy sentence, then, but speechless death, which robs my tongue from breathing native breath?*"

Or, as they would say in Kui language: *Nanda ra aa bangasi kritaraja Nai kattadi nimbaselu ki sabeselu paheri tastam.* "Do not cut my tongue, let me live and die with my language".

SECTION-II

CONCOMITANTS OF POVERTY AND DISADVANTAGE

7

Consequences of Poverty and Disadvantage : A Review of Indian Studies

GIRISHWAR MISRA AND AJIT K. MOHANTY

Poverty and disadvantage are processes as well as products of a complex set of interacting conditions — physical and economic, social and cultural, individual and psychological. Together they constitute the total context within which one can attempt to understand these phenomena. In speaking of poverty and disadvantage two dominant dimensions are implicitly referred to — a set of physical and economic conditions which are visible and another set of less visible conditions. The latter includes cultural, social and psychological conditions such as the cultural norms about hierarchization or stratification of the society into layers, allocation of resources and privileges, practices of discrimination tending to limit the growth and development of groups of individuals, and socialization processes through which expectations, aspirations and atitudes are transmitted. Along with the physical and economic conditions including the home environment, the psychosocial context of the poor and disadvantaged are often branded as the 'culture of poverty' the *deficiencies* of which are held as explanations of poor performance of those belonging to such cultures, thus blaming the victims of poverty and disadvantage. But, it cannot be denied that the contextual conditions of poverty and disadvantage have psychological consequences for the individual affecting some basic processes which are reflected in performance in task and test situations, scholastic achievement, classroom and other social situations. In Chapter 3, Sinha has presented a model of the relationship between poverty, its psychological consequences and their outcomes (Fig. 3.2). The total context of poverty, according to Sinha, has a set of psychological consequences leading to some behavioural manifestations which are commonly observed among the poor. The behavioural outcomes accentuate the condition of poverty giving rise to a vicious circle in which poverty is viewed as a cause and consequence of certain psychological characteristics. Thus it is important to understand the nature of relationship between aspects of the total condition of poverty and disadvantage and their psychological and behavioural manifestations. Studies exploring such a relationship have become quite numerous over the years in Indian psychological research. Here an attempt is made to locate the major trends in Indian research focusing on recent research without getting into an exhaustive review of studies. Here, we seek to analyze (a) more direct and visible impacts of poverty and disadvantage in terms of health, nutrition and development of those living under conditions of economic and physical impoverishment, (b) underlying psychological processes such as socialization, personality and motivational dynamics associated with growing up in poverty, and (c) cognitive and behavioural outcomes as concomitant of poverty and disadvantage. Finally, we have also briefly examined the explanations of the relationship of poverty and disadvantage with their outcomes. Some methodological and conceptual issues in the Indian studies have also been discussed while analyzing the studies and their implications.

Health, Nutrition and Development

Lack of economic resources of the poor restrict the quality and quantity of their nutritional intake, particularly affecting the mothers and children in poverty. This adversely affects cognitive functioning and basic cognitive processes such as attention, and increases the chances of poor health and lack of immunity. Protein energy malnutrition (PEM) is commonly found among people in extreme poverty. The reversibility of the effects of severe malnutrition is a debatable issue, but it is generally agreed that the earlier such malnutrition occurs among children, the more damaging its effects. Social class differences in intake of nutritive food are quite evident. Conditions of nutrition are associated with birth weight which averages around 3200 gms. for high SES and 2800 gms. for low SES samples. In some Indian studies (e.g., Kaul *et al.*, 1982) low birth weight has been associated with later physical growth and development. Low SES children also show lower body weight and height and delayed onset of puberty. Gupta *et al.* (1985) have reported lower growth standard for slum children in the 0-15 years age range. Mothers' SES and children's nutritional well-being are also found to be positively correlated (Vazir, Bhogle & Naidu, 1988). In a longitudinal study of children's growth from birth to 14 years, Dutta Banik (1982) found that height and weight measures were related with SES.

Many studies in India show a positive relationship between children's nutritional status and their general development including cognitive and motor functions although a causal rlationship has not been established. In fact, it has been argued that malnutrition as well as poor cognitive performance may both be related to poor social environment (Agarwal, Agarwal & Upadhyaya, 1987). In their large scale study on 6 to 8 years old rural children in Varanasi, Agarwal *et al.* (1987) found that the adverse effect of malnutrition on intelligence increased with its severity. Besids intelligence, verbal reasoning, short term memory, comprehension, scholastic achievement, perceptual and spatial skills and fine motor coordination were also found to be affected by malnutrition. Further, when malnutrition was associated with stunted growth, with children attaining less than 90% of the expected height for their age, the effects of malnutrition on all the functions was even more severe. Negative effects of malnutrition have also been reported in a number of other studies for a variety of cognitive and other tasks — fine motor and gross motor skills and personal-social and language tasks (Rastogi, Srivastava, Dutt & Singh, 1987) and various other measures of intellectual functioning (Kaur, Singh & Malhotra, 1985; Singh, Kaur & Dubey, 1986). Similar findings have been reported relating to infants' mental and motor development and social maturity (Phatak, Ranganathan & Deshpande, 1993, 1994; Upadhyaya, *et al.*, 1992). However, some researchers have suggested that these negative effects of malnutrition can be reversed by nutritional and environmental enrichment (Agarwal *et al*, 1987). For example, dietary supplementation was found to elevate intelligence in *kwashiorkor* children (Singh & Aggarwal, 1987).

Despite the large number of studies reporting a negative relationship between malnutrition and developmental competence, a clear causal link has not been unequivocally established. Anandalakshmy (1985), in her study of 6- to 24-month old infants from Delhi, did not find a direct relationship between their mental development and nutritional status. Motor development, however, was significantly related to nutrition. It was noted that nutritional insufficiency was largely due to lack of semi-solids and it generally occurred around the birth of a sibling or mother's next pregnancy which may also indicate lack of maternal attention to the child being tested. Another study conducted by the National Institute of Nutrition (ICMR, 1992) showed that childhood nutritional status did not influence adult intelligence although SES and adult intelligence were related. It seems, malnutrition is one of the dimensions of adverse environment which affects intelligence and cognitive growth.

On the whole, it can be said that the relationship between maluntrition and general intellectual development is not straight forward; it is most likely mediated by a host of other environmental conditions including level of stimulation, nature of child care practices and the quality of interaction between mother (and other care givers) and infant in the family. It has been observed that the quality of mothering and mother-child interaction is related to the probability of malnutrition in case of the child (Vazir *et al.*, 1988). Thus, the effect of malnutrition, which happens to be a more visible aspect of poverty, has to be viewed in the total context of poverty and the environmental conditions associated with it. Further, nutrition is much more than the food intake and, as such, specific aspects of nutritional deficiency such as conditions of micro-nutrient deficiencies like anaemia and deficiencies of iodine/thiamine/niacin etc. must be related to cognitive and behavioural functions. Except for early and severe form of malnutrition, the earlier assumption about relative irreversibility of the negative effects of childhood malnutrition are not supported by the recent findings.

Apart from the nutrition related problems, relationship between poverty and mental health is an area of concern. The incidence of psychiatric disorders among the poor and the disadvantaged groups is much higher than the advantaged group. Instead of social class as a global variable, income and education, respectively, seem to be better predictors of psychopathology. Overall, mental health problems are much more frequent in the lower end of the population distributed over different levels of social class. Two broad theoretical positions have been suggested to account for this relationship — *social causation* and *social selection* views. The former point of view suggests that the differential experiences of growing up in different social classes are related to individual differences in coping styles, stress tolerance and access to supportive social relationship. Experiences in lower social class lead to low self esteem, intellectual rigidity, sense of fatalism and greater susceptibility to stress which are associated with mental health problems. The social selection view, on the other hand, proposes that, in any given population, the more incompetent tend to drift towards the lower class and, hence, they are more vulnerable to psychopathology. Indian studies are not very clear in their analysis of adequacy of these two positions.

Indian researchers have primarily focused on the distribution and incidence of various types of mental health problems among the poor and disadvantaged groups. Sharma, Michael, Reddy and Gehlot (1985) found that psychiatric morbidity among slum dwellers in Jaipur was higher for distant migrants than for those who migrated from nearby villages. Discussing the need for health services for the poor, Sridhar Sharma (1985) points to the inverse relationship between poverty and health status. Mishra, Sinha and Berry (1996) have shown that people experiencing culture change have increased acculturative stress and poor health status. In their study, Mishra *et al.* (1996) examined the health status of *Birhors*, a nomadic tribe and *Oraons*, a sedentary tribe, both from Chotanagpur plateau and found that the former group had greater physical, psychological and psycho-physiological problems than the latter. This is explained in terms of the transitional nature of the *Birhors* as opposed to the sedentary *Oraons* who adapted quite well to external influences. Further, stress was negatively related to differentiation, assimilation and coexistence modes of acculturation.

Conditions of poverty and disadvantage have been viewed as leading to emotional disturbance and neurotic traits of restlessness among chilren. A survey by Bhatia, Singhal, Nigam and Malik (1989) has shown that among the high SES children nail-biting was prevalent in a relatively younger age (2-5 years) whereas it was prevalent in a higher age (9-12 years) among the low SES children. Lapore, Palsane and Evans (1991) noted that, in case of the low SES urban individuals, chronic strains were associated with greater level of psychosomatic symptomatology and lower level of perceived social support. The effects of chronic stress were found to be attenuated by income and chronic strains rather than daily hassles were the major sources of stress. Various adjustment problems of SC and other disadvantaged children and adults have also been reported in a number of studies (Chaudhary & Minhas, 1993; Omprakash, 1993; Punithambal, 1990; Rangari, 1987; Ushashree, 1987). SES and adjustment problems show a negative relationship (Rathore, 1990). Although middle and high SES children do not differ, adjustment problems are prominent among the low SES children. However, it is not the belongingness to disadvantaged groups or SES *per se* but the environmental conditions associated with poverty and disadvantage which lead to mental health and adjustment problems. Specific environmental conditions like broken home status and parental deprivation have been related to adjustment problems. Disadvantaged children and young adolescents are exposed to unsupportive social climate and usually fail to adjust to the demands of an unfriendly environment, developing, in the process, unrealistic perceptions and inadequate coping strategies. While the dysfunctional health consequences of poverty and disadvantage have been amply documented, it is necessary to understand the processes through which such conditions affect the quality of mental health and to develop appropriate strategies. Poverty and disadvantage are broad labels to identify certain characteristic modes of experience to which certain groups of individuals are subjected. As a result of such experiences coupled with cultural transmission as well as macro level social processes, individuals growing up under conditions of poverty and disadvantage develop personality and motivational characteristics which make them vulnerable to various problems of performance and mental health. The next section examines these aspects of development of the poor and disadvantaged.

Socialization, Personality and Motivational Development

Poverty and disadvantage imply a set of ecological and socio-psychological conditions characterized by inadequate physical facilities and lack of proper stimulation in the home environment, poor or no schooling, and lack of social emotional support and role models. Current psychological research tends to relate these conditions with a host of negative personality dispositions. But the processes of socialization through which these characteristics come to be acquired under conditions of poverty and disadvantage are perhaps least understood. In an innovative study, Saraswathi and Dutta (1990) used micro level daily time schedule analysis of the life of children and adolescent girls growing up in rural poverty and urban slums and found some developmental constraints like limited scope for social mobility, non-competitive coping style, highly circumscribed life style with narrowly defined goals of socialization and poor know-how to outgrow the limitations of life in poverty. Some strengths of the poverty condition observed by Saraswathi and Dutta (1990) included existence of a family climate, a practical and realistic orientation with acceptance of destiny, availability of an informal support system and awareness of the need for positive social change. These aspects of life in poverty might help explain the resilience noted in case of poor people.

The Indian research on socialization, clearly, does not go far enough to further our understanding of the processes through which individuals in conditions of poverty and disadvantage develop certain characteristic modes of behaviour and patterns of personality. Cultural practices, ecological and environmental conditions and individual's social interactional experiences particularly during childhood are held to mediate personality development. Indian studies on personality characteristics of the poor and disadvantaged show some expected trends. Mohan and her colleagues (Mohan & Gill, 1988; Mohan & Verma, 1990) have shown that the deprived children exhibit high neuroticism and low extraversion compared to their non-deprived counterparts. Poverty and disadvantage have been related to social maladjustment, immature behaviour, autism, alienation, withdrawal and other antisocial and psychotic traits (Helode & Kapai, 1986; Kumar & Mehta, 1983). Prolonged deprivation of children in poverty and disadvantage seems to predispose them to delinquency-prone attitudinal orientation (Gaur, 1992; Mohan & Nalwa, 1992). Compared to their non-deprived counterparts, the deprived young adults have been found to be more external and chance oriented (Kumar & Tripathi, 1986; Ashok K. Singh, 1983). Deprivation has also been positively related to alienation as well as external control (A.N.V. Reddy, 1992). Gaur (1992) has shown a positive relationship between SES and Machiavellianism.

High SES individuals, compared to those in the lower SES, are more extrapunitive (Quraishi & Hussain, 1982) and show greater frustration under failure (Yadav, 1992). Poverty has been related to low adaptive behaviour in form of lack of self direction and responsibility, anxiety and maladjustment (Gunthey & Sinha, 1983). The low SES children are found to be less competitive and more cooperative (Pal, Verma & Vasudeva, 1989). Such cooperativeness tends to increase when the low SES children are involved in maximizing individual gain but not when they are involved in loss through maximization of difference in gain (Jayant & Karandikar, 1985). Srivastava and Lalnunmawii (1989) found that rich Mizo children studying in English medium schools engaged in cut throat competition more frequently than their government school counterparts from low SES. Children in destitute homes, deprived of parental and family care, show greater degree of maladjustment, low super ego strength, lack of acceptance of group moral standards, greater disregard for roles, unreflectiveness and lower levels of mental capacity, although, on the positive side, they show more enthusiasm, tough mindedness, self sufficiency and resourcefulness (Nagar, 1989).

Some studies have examined the relationship between caste and personality. Senger, Singh and Srivastava (1985) found the SC adolescents to be more ascendant, neurotic, and unmindful of others' feelings compared to their non-SC counterparts. They also have less desire for achievement and recognition and greater uncertainty. On Edward's Personal Preference Schedule (EPPS), the SC adolescents were found to have low need for achievement, intraception and aggression, and greater need for affiliation, succorance, abasement and nurturance. Similar patterns of personality traits were also obtained on High School Personality Questionnaire (HSPQ) and 16PF (Dubey, 1984), R. Singh (1992) has also reported similar findings in respect of the relationship between personality traits on EPPS and caste status. Social disadvantage has been shown to have negative impact on several personality variables such as decision, responsibillity, emotional stability, friendliness, heterosexuality and masculinity.

Poverty and disadvantage have generally been shown to affect individuals' self concept lowering their self esteem although the findings in this respect are not unequivocal. Ameerjan and Thimappa (1988) found no caste difference in self concept to which SES was positively related. S. Singh (1983) reported low self efficacy judgement among deprived children. A.N.V. Reddy (1992) has shown that prolonged deprivation and awareness of deprivation were related to alienation, locus of control and perceived self. G. Misra (1990a) has shown that socio-economic status moderated the effect of perceived competence on performance. Awasthi and Janabandhu (1988) found that self-ideal discrepancy was higher in the lower SES groups. Thus, conditions of poverty and disadvantage are generally found to be associated with negative self concept and under-estimation of personal efficacy which may account for lower levels of aspiration and low motivation characteristic of the disadvantaged population.

Social Class Differences in Value System

Motivation of the poor and the disadvantaged are also related to their value system and preferences. Indian studies show a clear trend of SES and caste related difference in values. Studies by Bhargava and Mittal (1991) and Mathur and Kalia (1984) have shown that, among the caste groups, Brahmans have greater preference for theoretical value whereas the Vaishyas and the SC groups show greater preference for social and political values, respectively. High SES adolescents have been found to be more theoretical than the middle and low SES ones (Ratnakumari, 1991).

In a recent work, A.K. Srivastava, Banerjee and Tripathi (1996) interviewed low and high economic status parents from urban, rural and metropolitan areas to find out their value preferences in respect of their children. Honesty, obedience and hard work were preferred values of the parents irrespective of their residential background. Urban, metropolitan and high economic status parents also showed preference for truthfulness as a desired value for their children whereas the rural parents preferred benevolence and humanity. Further, the rural and low economic status parents laid emphasis on economic values for children including their material contribution and contribution in extending the family tree. The high economic status, urban and metropolitan parents, emphasized psychological values in chidren's role such as in making life meaningful, bringing husband-wife closer. These Indian studies do show patterns of values differing across socio-economic strata. However, the genesis and transmission of such differences are not clearly understood. With reference to related aspect of time orientation the poor are found to be characterised by a lack of future orientation (Agarwal & K.K. Tripathi, 1980, 1984).

Motivational Consequences of Poverty and Disadvantage

Pareek (1970) has discussed poverty and motivation as having a figure-ground type of relationship. According to him poverty leads to low need for achievement, low extension need, high dependence and typical pattern of socialization leading to powerlessness. The dynamics of needs and powerlessness lead, in turn, to behaviours such as disproportionate risk taking, chance rather than control orientation, lack of interest in feedback, lack of activity and initiative. Later reviews by G. Misra (1982a) and D. Sinha and G. Misra (1982) also show that reinforcement history of persons in poverty as well as the cultural context jointly affect their motivational orientation. The Indian literature on poverty and motivation is generally focused on three aspects of the relationship: aspirations and task motivation of the poor, their achievement motivation and the attributional process. Recent studies clearly show linkages between poverty, motivation and behavioural patterns among the poor.

A positive relationship between SES and level of aspiration has been reported in a number of studies (e.g. Pal & Dixit, 1983; Pal & Tiwari, 1984). Singh and Misra (1985) reported low task persistence among the highly deprived class. The highly deprived group showed greater performance decrement under the experience of helplessness. Mal and Jain (1990) noted that the high deprived pupils had greater helplessness than low deprived ones and attributed uncontrollable outcome to internal, stable and global causes. The deprived individuals give up the task more than their low deprived counterparts under helplessness condition (Tiwari, 1994).

Deprivation has been shown in several studies to be negatively related to need achievement (n-Ach) (Misra, 1982a, Sinha & Misra, 1982; A. Tiwari, 1987). Similar findings have been reported in relation to SES (Hussain, 1983; Sudhir, 1989) and low caste status (S.K. Ojha, 1991). R. Singhal and G. Misra (1992) have reported that the low and high social class groups reported larger number of individualistic goals while family-related goals were dominant in the middle class.

Some recent studies on causal perception as mediators in behavioural outcomes of motivation have investigated the process of achievement attributions in the deprived groups. It has been reported (Jain & Mal, 1984) that low deprived groups as compared to high deprived ones considered effort and ability as major causes of success and bad luck as a major cause of failure. The advantaged students reported more variegated causal beliefs than the disadvantaged ones. Causal beliefs were generated more in failure than in success condition (Misra, 1985). Effort and ability emerged as major causes of success. G. Misra and S. Misra, (1986) found that socially advantaged students attributed failure to luck, perceived greater controllability, confidence in performance expectation and higher level of future expectation than the disadvantaged. S. Singh and G. Misra (1988) noted that high and low deprived individuals perceived ability as equally important under competence condition whereas under helplessness condition, the high deprived blamed ability more than their low deprived counterparts.

G. Misra and Jain (1988) have observed that deprived groups either attribute all outcomes to internal causes or assume greater responsibility for failure and externalize success. Thus, "the pattern of attribution seems to reflect the deep rooted feelings of lack of control over environment and the stance that outcomes are either predetermined or are independent of one's effort" (G. Misra, 1988, p. 77). R. Sharma and R.C. Tripathi (1988) found that the success of high caste students was attributed by teachers more to family, ability and effort whereas failure to chance and task. The failure of SC students was attributed more to their family, ability and effort. Finally, children's attributions were more influenced by teacher's expectation than student's caste.

It seems, people from deprived sections of our society develop a dysfunctional perspective on reality which has unwarranted consequences for planning, goal setting and task involvement. It should be pointed out that this motivational perspective being rooted in cognition is more flexible than the dispositional approaches. In fact, attributional retraining has been used as an intervention for motivational change.

Aggression is a very frequent response to frustration. The life conditions of the deprived and socially disadvantaged groups are characterized by difficulties and frequent disruptions in the process of goal attainment. This has prompted the researchers to examine reactions to frustration among deprived groups. Rao and Singh (1981) reported that extrapunitive reactions were more prevalent in the low SES children. Shukla, Misra and Singh (1994) found that female SC, ST and caste Hindu students show common pattern of reactions to frustration characterized by extrapunitive responses followed by intrapunitive and impunitive responses. However, the degree of felt relative deprivation was positively related to intrapunitive reactions in ST group and negatively in the SC group.

Coping with Poverty

How people from poverty conditions deal with their everyday problems has received some attention from researchers in India. Using an open-ended measure, Anoop

K.Singh and J. Pandey (1985) content analyzed the coping responses of the poor and observed that appraisal-focused coping was frequently adopted in dealing with economic and personal problems while collective coping was used in case of family and social problems.

Sinha and Misra (1989) investigated the problems of SC students who were first generation entrants to the university system. They found that a majority of such students joined university for instrumental reasons, based on a family decision rather than an individual one. During initial phase of stay in the university, physical and cultural proximity provided tha basis of their friendship and they felt greater degree of emotional disturbance. Difficulty in communication, lack of sufficient economic resources, limited friendship range, difficulty in attending lectures, difficult language and lack of illustration in lectures were some of their major problems. In general, they experienced greater stress and viewed university set-up negatively. Their self-esteem was low and they had low internal and more external control orientation. Their time perspective was predominantly past oriented and they viewed the future as influenced less by ability and more by situation. Their coping styles were characterized by lesser degree of affirmation and acceptance, greater degree of conformity, feelings of inadequacy, withdrawal, ignoring the situation and blaming. They relied more on significant others, God, and luck for success. In contrast, advantaged students emphasized effort, motivation, persistence and cleverness in dealing with success.

In general, the findings suggest that the motivational functioning of deprived groups is somewhat weak and fails to support positive behavioural changes necessary for pursuing useful goal. This demotivating state blocks any attempt toward social mobility and status enhancement.

Poverty and Social Behaviour

The relationship between poverty and pattern of social interaction at the level of collectivity has been a topic of interest in the disciplines of sociology and political science.

Violence, social tension and political movements are often linked with economic inequality, discrimination, administrative failures and corruption, Ahuja, (1988) and Srivastava, (1988) observed that uneven economic development of various parts and regions of the country, failure to carry the benefits of economic development to all sections of society, failure of many ambitious poverty amelioration programmes and administrative failures are some factors causing tension. Vagrecha and Gon (1985) found that outbursts of a mass protest movement in the beginning of 1974 in Gujarat were positively related to economic stress. They have argued that a community may experience stressful situation like economic stress and react in form of protest and violence. Social mobility in India is closely related to one's caste. Ram (1990) noted that social mobility of the SC groups in general is limited and not often successful. They do not recover social identity even if they are at the highest level of achievement. However, social mobility may result in positive acceptance by the reference group. There is also a chance of close association between social mobility and marginalization among the SCs.

Perceptual and Cognitive Functions

So far, this review has discussed the literature on the relationship of poverty and disadvantage with some of their direct and visible consequences such as malnutrition and mental health problems and consequences associated with the underlying dynamics of growing up under typical conditions. The latter include patterns of socialization, motivation and development of personality and values etc. which are assumed to mediate between poverty, *per se*, and its consequences. Poverty has to be understood both as a set of contextual conditions as well as certain processes which together give rise to typical performance of the poor and the disadvantaged. Of all different aspects of such performance, cognitive and intellectual functions have been held in high prioirty as these happen to be closely associated with upward socio-economic mobility of the poor.

Researchers have looked at the consequences of poverty and disadvantage in terms of cognitive processes including learning, memory, perceptual processes, language, intelligence and creativity. An underlying assumption in most of these studies has been that cognitive processes and performances are experientially shaped and, therefore, any kind of disorganization in the child's experiential world would interfere with her cognitive development.

Some major research programmes on disadvantage in India by R. Rath and his colleagues (R. Rath, 1972; R. Rath, A.S. Dash & U.N. Dash, 1979, Sinha, 1977; Sinha & Shukla, 1974; Tripathi, Misra, 1975, 1976; Amar K. Singh, 1976) have explored the consequences of social disadvantages suffered on account of several factors such as caste status, economic poverty, tribal status, residential background, experiential deprivation and quality of schooling. These programmes have sought to show the course of developmental changes in cognitive processes. In general the trends demonstrate adverse effects of deprivation and disadvantage and the gap between deprived and non-deprived has been found to increase with age (G. Misra, 1983).

Reviewing the research linking caste with cognitive processes, J.P. Das and Khurana (1988) pointed out that caste is an empty variable and that history of experience is more important since caste differences only represent environmental differences. Das and his associates have shown that the cultural complexity and sophistication associated with growing up in high caste Brahman families make children more competent than those from low caste Harijan families (J.P. Das & Singha, 1975). The confounding association of caste and deprivation is quite clear in many studies. It seems, caste related differences are due to inefficient use of cognitive strategies and not due to any deficit as such.

G. Misra (1982b) has reviewed the consequences of prolonged deprivation in respect of a variety of cognitive processes including pictorial depth perception, time perception, perceptual identification, psychological differentiation, categorization and verbal reasoning. The studies generally show that the low deprived groups were most competent followed by medium and high deprived groups. The deprivational effects were independent of the caste status. G. Misra (1982b) concluded that the experiential variation (impoverishment or enrichment) affects cognitive functioning rather than caste or any other distal variable which stands more for a social address.

Pushpa (1990) has shown that prolonged deprivation was negatively related to cognitive attainment of children. G. Misra and Tiwari (1986, 1990) observed that residential background, quality of schooling and aspects of home environment were consistently linked with cognitive development. R. Dash and A.S. Dash (1982) found that tribals scored lower than non-tribals on DAT, RPM, Bender Gestalt Test and Story Pictorial EFT and that residential background and quality of schooling interact with age in terms of provisions for inputs. Further, diverse home environment variables were consistently linked with cognitive development. In recent years, Indian researchers have paid greater attention to specific cognitive processes. Some major trends emerging from these studies are briefly discussed below.

As basic processes, learning and memory have received considerable attention. The findings generally show low level of performance on various measures of these processes. S.N. Shukla (1991) found that verbal learning of unrelated conceptual and phonetic materials was positively related to the caste status of children. Prolonged deprivation has been found to be a good predictor of learning ability (Quraishi & S. Das, 1991). However, there seems to be no consistent relationship between the preference for learning style and the SES of children (Chauhan & Singh, 1985).

Coding and organizational processes in memory like category clustering and extra-item transformation function at a lower level in the deprived children (P.S. Mishra, 1998) whose recognition and cued recall for episodic and semantic tasks has also been found to be poor (S. Srivastava, 1990). Recall of other types of material as well has been shown in other studies to be negatively influenced by prolonged deprivation (B.K. Tiwari, 1986; Zafar & K. Alam, 1986). Caste status and quality of schooling are found to affect positively the performance on various measures of STM and LTM (Dey, 1992; A. Mishra, 1992; G. Misra & A. Shukla, 1984). Experientially deprived children seem to have poor mnemonic competence, the deprivational effects increasing with age.

Examining the relationship between text processing and prolonged deprivation, T. Singh and C.B. Dwivedi (1993, 1994) found that high deprived children were slow processors, although their performance on short-term retention and error detecton tasks was similar to the less deprived ones. It was also noted that exposure helps the highly deprived process the text faster, whereas exposure adversely affects processing in the low deprived. Children with high degree of prolonged deprivation were found to perform poorly on problem solving and concept formation tasks and to be inattentive to the demands of the testing situation (S. Verma & Mohan, 1993).

Another aspect of research on poverty and deprivation deals with their effects on perceptual skills which are perhaps more directly affected by possible experiential deprivation. Various aspects of perceptual processes, including representational processes, pictorial perception, psychological differentiation etc., have constituted the focus in studies relating poverty and disadvantage to perception. G. Misra and associates (G. Misra, 1982c; G. Misra & A. Shukla, 1986; A. Shukla 1990; G. Misra & B.K. Tiwari, 1992) have shown that low deprived and older children displayed greater degree of representational competence. Perceptual identification of colour and shape was found to be the easiest while encoding was the most difficult task. Pattern reproduction in children was adversely influenced by experiential deprivation and the effect was greater at the younger age level (N.M. Tripathi, 1991). However, the disadvantaged children seem to show a kind of catch up growth. Broota and Pahwa (1984) found that, in tasks of matching objects, urban subjects evinced greater frequency of form preference than rural and institutionalized ones. M. Verma (1992) has shown that children from impoverished environments display centration, though the effect of deprivation was non-significant during early years. In classification tasks, disadvantaged ones took recourse to the taxonomic mode (S. Mishra, 1992).

Several studies have examined the relationship between poverty and psychological differentiation. The high caste and high SES children are found more differentiated in their performance on Embedded Figures Test (EFT) (Majeed & Ghosh, 1983; S. Sharma & Ahuja, 1990). Residential background has also been found to have significant effect showing greater field independence in urban than rural children (Tharakan, 1987). A.K. Srivastava (1989) reported that schooling has facilitative effect with greater differentiation in modern school children than those from traditional schools. Working within an ecological framework, G. Misra and B.K. Tiwari (1992) have observed that home environment and schooling had significant effects on psychological differentiation. In particular, intellectual stimulation, quality of physical environment, perception of school, health status of the child and sufficiency of income were important predictors of differentiation. D. Sinha and R.C. Mishra (1988) found that the Christian and superior school children show greater disembedding than non-Christian and ordinary school children.

Lower caste status, lack of education and urban contact were found to have a negative influence on the perception of symbols (D. Sinha & R.C. Mishra, 1982). The joint effect of these variables was pronounced and education tended to level off some of the differences. The effects of disadvantage were greater for unfamiliar symbols. R.C. Mishra (1987, 1988) also found that the effect of caste status was levelled off by education. However, the effect of urban contact did not improve performance of SC children. In addition, education and urban contact were positively related to comprehension of pictures involving perspective and sequential arrangement. G. Misra (1982b) reported that high deprived individuals have difficulty in the use of three dimensional cues in pictorial representation.

These studies tend to suggest that deprived children show relatively lower levels of performance on complex perceptual tasks demanding diverse skills and competencies. The effects of deprivation on performance on simpler or less complex tasks seem to be less pronounced.

Linguistic Skills of the Disadvantaged

The chapter by Mohanty (this volume) discusses the implications of *linguistic deficit hypothesis* in the context of the linguistic skills of the disadvantaged in India. As pointed out there, the linkages between social class and linguistic behaviour in the Indian context become more important on account of several factors including discontinuity between school and home languages, hegemony of English in academic and professional circles and association of English language with social prestige and upward mobility. Several studies from different linguistic regions i.e., Hindi (S. Shukla & A.K. Mohanty, 1986; Anjali & Sinha, this volume), Malayalam (Nair, 1980), Telugu (Reddy, 1987), Oriya (A.K. Mohanty & M. Mohanty, 1985) show a strong association between low social class and linguistic handicaps. However, as Annamalai (1982) has argued, the apparent linguistic deprivation in children of the lower classes fails to recognize the linguistic background of the child. Sahu and others (Sahu, 1989; Sahu & Devi, 1982; Sahu & Patnaik, 1987) have shown that the disadvantaged children were poor readers and comprehenders. However, the socially disadvantaged were found to be proficient in oral reading when the effect of IQ was partialled out. Deshpande (1985) has reported negative effect of experiential disadvantages on language development. However, the difference between advantaged and disadvantaged students was not significant in private schools. R.K. Mishra and B. Mishra (1992) noted that deprived young children have difficulty in comprehension of *Wh*-words. B. Mishra and L.B. Tripathi (1991) have found that, in communication in high deprivation homes, phonological corrections and suggestions were more frequent communicative intents, whereas low deprivation homes were marked by the use of labelling and requests for information.

The findings suggest a strong impact of the modes of social communicative processes and family interaction on the quality of language used by children. As a result, within social class differences may be greater than between social class differences. As A.K. Mohanty (1990, also this volume) has argued, poverty and deprivation need not be associated with the language of the otherwise deprived; language is a product of certain socio-cultural forces which combine to relegate some varieties of language use to a disadvantaged status. Thus, the disadvantage lies more in the differential treatment of languages than in the fact that some languages are poorer or deficient.

Intellective Functions and Creativity of the Disadvantaged

Using Jensen's theory, Jachuck and her associates (Jachuck, 1984; Jachcuck & Khandai, 1983) have shown negative effects of deprivational factors (e.g., SES, caste) and cumulative deficit on intellective measures. The differences have been explained in terms of environmental factors. In her later studies, Jachuck (1993) has reported significant positive effect of high SES and preschool experience on intelligence test performance.

Intelligence test scores have been shown to be adversely affected by parental deprivation (Pathak, Saxena & L.S. Mishra, 1983), low caste status (Basavanna & Rani, 1984), low SES and poverty (I. Das & Mona, 1990; Murthy & S.C. Panda, 1987). However, there are also some studies which do not show caste differences in intelligence (Rangari, 1987). Incidence of mental retardation has been found to be higher among lower class groups, (48 per cent) (Mata Prasad *et al.*, 1988). In a survey of mental retardation in rural children, Anima Sen (1992) reported that parental aspiration, SES, exposure to mass media, food, nutrition and health were at higher level in normal than retarded children. Mukherjee, *et al.* (1991) showed that performance on RPM was negatively related to physico-economic and cultural deprivation much more than to emotional deprivation component of prolonged deprivation.

Raina (1993) has discussed the complex relationship between deprivation and creativity. The Indian researchers have related creativity with a variety of background variables. High SES and low deprivation have been shown to be positively related to creativity on verbal measures (Ahmad, 1980; Dutt, 1988; C.Mishra, 1987). Low caste status (Chaudhary & Bindal, 1986) and residential disadvantage are found to be negatively related to creativity (Dhillon & Mehra, 1990). Curiosity has been found to be positively related to SES (Kauser, 1986).

The relationship between intelligence test scores and deprivational factors (e.g., low caste, low SES, prolonged deprivation, social disadvantage etc.) suggests greater risk of intellectual handicap among the deprived children (See chapter 9 by Singh of this volume). The existing studies provide very little information beyond a rough estimate of group level differences in performance on certain tests. The contemporary analysis of intelligence has moved away from traditional psychometric concerns to new approaches including analysis of component processes.

Some Indian studies have used various Piagetian tasks of cognitive development to compare the poor and the disadvantaged populations with their advantaged counterparts in the society. Generally, these studies show trends similar to those on intelligence and other cognitive skills. Jachuck and Behera (1988) observed that conservation was better in the children from enriched than from poor homes. U.N. Dash and J.P. Das (1984) found that low SES schooled and unschooled children did not differ in concrete operational skills. Bevli, *et al.*, (1990) have reported SES differences in the attainment of various logical operations. Bevli (1990) suggests that language and arithmetic achievement, school facilities and teacher's attitude are crucial for cognitive growth as assessed through Piagetian tasks.

These research efforts show negative role, to varying degrees, of poverty and disadvantage in shaping cognitive functioning of deprived groups on a range of tasks. The performance differences between deprived and non-deprived groups generally tend to widen with age. The cumulative deficit of the disadvantaged is a phenomenon of concern and draws attention to the role of contextual factors in amplifying the effects of deprivational factors. Interventions, therefore, can only be successful if adequate attention is paid to this aspect of deprivational experience.

Poverty, Disadvantage and Educational Achievement

Gangwar (1990) found that rural students with higher levels of school achievement had better study habits than their urban counterparts. SES has been found to be related to positive attitude towards school experience (Satyarthi, 1982). Basavanna and Rani (1984) have noted that social rather than economic impoverishment influences the skills necessary for academic achievement more negatively. Higher caste status has also been linked with better study habits (B.N. Panda, 1991). The disadvantaged students prefer dependent and non-participatory learning style while advantaged students prefer independent and participatory learning style (B.P. Verma & Sheikh, 1992).

Pande and R.C. Tripathi (1982) found that school climate was perceived to be more supportive by those who regularly attended school which, in turn, influenced performance. The role of caste was important for teacher expectancy which was greater for non-Scheduled Caste (NSC) than SC students. S. Singh and A.K. Sinha (1986) found that social deprivation rather than caste was a more potent predictor of intelligence, educational achievement and punctuality in the class.

Poor academic achievement has been found to be associated with low SES (Biswal, 1992; Ganguli, 1989; B.N. Panda, 1991), low social class (M. Mehta, 1992) and prolonged deprivation (V.P. Sharma, 1993). Mukherjee *et al.*, (1991) noted that achievement was more adversely affected by economic and cultural deprivations than by emotional deprivation. Gupta, Mukherjee and Chatterjee (1993) observed that in rural and urban areas different factors contributed to the prediction of academic achievement. Whereas intelligence, home environment and rearing experiences were important in urban children, intelligence, childhood experiences and travel were important in rural boys, and intelligence, housing condition and motivational experience in rural girls. Prolonged deprivation was associated with poor achievement. Amar K. Singh (1980, 1983) has shown negative effect of social disadvantage on school achievement. He argued that parental support and favourable familial conditions may partly compensate for these negative effects. Ushashree (1980) reported longitudinal findings showing negative relationship between social disadvantage and academic achievement even if the intelligence level was similar. Lack of motivation appeared to be more important in explaining the level of academic achievement.

It appears that poor school achievement of deprived pupils is a complex problem related to cognitive readiness, home environment and school climate. In general, poor intellectual, cognitive functioning and lower levels of academic achievement associated with poverty and disadvantage are expected problems given the cyclic relationship between these conditions and the conditions that are crucial in impeding cognitive growth. Poor or slow cognitive development, in turn, affects, general task performance as well as academic achievement and motivation which are associated with prospects of economic and social mobility. Thus, poverty is further perpetuated in a vicious cycle.

Explanations of Deprivation Effects

The gaps between psychological characteristics of the high deprived and low (or non) deprived groups have generally been accounted for on the basis of one of the two propositions i.e., *deficit* and *difference*. Based on the assumption that conditions of poverty and disadvantage present limited learning opportunities which restrict psychological development. Most of the findings documenting group level differences lend support to this view. In contrast, some researchers taking a "difference" view argue that the disadvantaged groups are not deficient. They merely show some differences in the nature of performance. It has been argued that the results supporting a 'deficit' positon are quite context specific and reflect limitations of data collection techniques.

A related issue is the distinction between competence and performance. It has been argued by some researchers that the measures used in the study of cognitive development of different groups reveal the nature of performance and do not essentially reveal differences in the level of competence. For example, as opposed to the linguistic deficit hypothesis, it is now held that advantaged and disadvantaged groups do not differ in linguistic competence. The observed differences are largely social in origin, situational or contextual (See chapter by Mohanty, this volume). They reflect the characteristics of the situation in which competence is expressed and assessed. Support for this position comes primarily from the analysis of motivational factors, linguistic performance, difference on Piagetian tasks and lack of difference during early stages of development.

The Indian studies showing lack of substantial difference on the measures of mental ability and learning, on one hand, and relatively consistent difference in achievement measures, on the other, implicate that the disadvantaged groups are perhaps different rather than deficient. G. Misra and L.B. Tripathi (1980) have argued that the types of ethos of deprived and non-deprived are such that a large area is common to both while some areas are different. The area common to both groups comes within the jurisdiction of deficiency hypothesis while areas exclusively falling in the reach of separate groups are amenable to the difference hypothesis.

Genetic factors provide another explanation of deprivational effects. It has been argued that deprived children perform poorly because they are genetically different. Moreover, the demonstrable environmental influences appear to account for much variance in intellective performance. Indian studies have hardly paid any attention to the possible role of genetic factors in cognitive development and linked it to disadvantaged or deprived status.

In Indian context caste appears to many researchers as a genetic variable, though distinct and separate genetic identities of various castes and subcastes can hardly be established in the contemporary Indian social structure. Caste differences represent variations along the socio-cultural, educational, economic and other experiences. Birth in a given caste does not seem to be linked with any specific level of competence. It is the experiential context linked to it which renders a person cognitively more or less competent. G. Misra and L.B. Tripathi (1980), for instance, found that high and low caste groups with similar experiential background demonstrated almost similar level of performance on cognitive and intellective tasks while those belonging to same caste with high degree of experiential deprivation scored significantly lower than their some caste low deprived counterparts. Caste in itself has unknown direct contribution as far as an individual's cognitive growth is concerned. Its correlation with cognitive performance reflects its association with experiential opportunities.

Specifying the functional relationship between deprivation and performance necessitates studies relating varying degrees of deprivation with performance. This is crucial in view of the observation that environmental deprivation is a threshold phenomenon. It operates adversely after a certain level (Jensen, 1977, 1984). Indian studies, due to extensive use of extreme group strategy, fail to offer any generalization in this context. Seeking to analyze this issue, G. Misra (1982b) compared performance of high, medium and low deprivation groups based on their scores on PDS. The low deprived people displayed a higher level of competence as compared to those from high deprived group. The performance of medium deprivation group yielded an interesting pattern which questions the frequently assumed linear relationship between deprivation and performance. On all the tasks, performance of medium deprivation group was better than higher deprived group and inferior to low deprived group. But, on most of the tasks, the performance differences between medium and low deprived groups were non-significant. The medium deprivation group was not markedly different suggesting that deprivation of moderate order does not lead to deleterious effects on performance. The non-monotonicity of relationship between performance and deprivation has also been noted by other researchers (Chatterjee, 1982). Yet another aspect of this issue relates to sensitivity to deprivational effects on the intellective level of the individual. J.P. Das (1973) has proposed a *modified threshold hypothesis* according to which, if we recognize a threshold for intellectual capacity, children above this threshold are hardly affected by the usual disadvantageous conditions whereas children below this threshold are affected strongly. It seems, ability and deprivation interact and jointly influence the level of performance.

The environmentalist position which situates the cause of poor level of performance of the deprived in child rearing practices is often considered ethnocentric as it projects the upper class/caste child rearing and competencies as standard. The cultural difference explanation also draws from the assertion that the tests are culturally biased. The use of western tests in non-western cultures is problematic in many respects (Misra, Puhan & Sahu, 1997). Use of culturally appropriate tests and measures is a minimum requirement in studies of individual and group differences. In India, not much attention has been paid to this problem. Further, the notion of culture has often been treated casually and as a global variable. The imperatives of culture involving the economic, political and other institutional arrangements of society which amplify certain cognitive skills has not been seriously examined. Little is known in respect of the phenomenal world of the deprived and disadvantaged groups. An adequate explanation must also attend to the context of cognitive skills, understanding the ecological resources and activities influencing these skills and the world view of the people who suffer from various forms of disadvantage and discrimination in a society with built-in inequalities.

Concluding Comments

The present review of studies on deprivation and disadvantage reveals that a variety of indicators of poverty are correlated with the status of physical development, cognitive competence, personality characteristics and motivation. In general, the development of individuals growing up in adverse circumstances lags behind those who come from relatively privileged backgrounds. The studies reviewed document that status variables like social class, caste, membership of tribal groups, social mobility and other macro level factors like economic inequality and lack of educational opportunity are correlated with attainment on diverse psychological measures dealing with cognitive, motivational and personality functions. However, most studies have paid scant attention to the processes through which the effects of poverty and deprivation are generated, moderated and transmitted.

It seems that the adverse effects of poverty and disadvantage are mediated by several intervening processes that operate at individual as well as group levels. This implies that the remedial efforts should attend to not only the problems in domains of individual competencies (e.g. cognitive, linguistics, motivational) but also to the family, school and neighbourhood. Unfortunately the dominant tendency of researchers has been to explain the lower level of achievement of the deprived ones on the basis of internal psychological characteristics rather than the contextual factors which constitute the phenomena of deprivation and poverty. That is why the researchers often fail to evolve meaningful and effective interventions for the poor and deprived. The researchers have often failed to realize that psychological processes are not independent of the social context in which they operate. They are formed in the social context and are always subject to modification. A processual view of psychological functions would provide a more realistic perspective and enable us to intervene for changing the quality of life of the deprived people more constructively.

8

Social Class and Language Development

ANJALI AND DURGANAND SINHA

A review of studies shows that social class and environment emerge as two major determinants of linguistic competence. Bernstein (1962) demonstrated that lower social class children use restricted code characterized by short, grammatically simple sentences. Bhargava (1974) obtained similar results that middle class children uttered longer sentences than their lower class counterparts. Studies aimed at studying the effects of sociocultural disadvantages on language development found that lower class children scored low on language tests (Muralidharan & Banerjee 1973; Sahu, 1979; Sahu & Sahu, 1981) However, on measures of cognitive competence, which consisted of tests of verbal reasoning and linguistic ability, they scored low (Jachuk & Mohanty, 1974; Panda & Das, 1970; Rath, Dash & Dash, 1979).

Researchers, who were critical of using mere SES as an index of deprivation emphasized that certain inadequacies and deficiencies of stimulations present in the home environment, impede the development (Misra & Tiwari, 1992; Muralidharan, 1970). Muralidharan and Banerjee (1975) and Singhal (1969) observed that social stimulation in the form of parental education and support are important variables in development of various linguistic skills.

There are certain shortcomings in both the approaches. Those who emphasize social class, do not clearly bring out the mechanism through which it exerts its influence on development. Environmentalists focus mainly on the characteristics of environment, not on its determinants. However, researches on both variables show that there is a close correspondance between them though not direct but mediated through certain intervening variables. In India, poverty, illiteracy and inequality in job opportunities are associated with class and caste. All these factors combine together to create a milieu of deprivation which restricts physical, psychological and linguistic experiences of child.

Secondly, while the nature of home environment has been investigated in general, less has been talked about specefic verbal environment in language studies, particularly in India. All kinds of communication by mother and other social agents create a verbal environment and provide linguistic inputs to the child from which the child picks up grammatical rules and semantics. Quality and quantity of these verbal inputs are, therefore, crucial. Studies have shown that structural properties of maternal linguistic inputs are correlated with children's language abilities (Holf-Ginsberg & Shatz, 1982) and nature of verbal interaction between mother and child varies in different social classes (Hess & Shipman, 1965). Shukla (1988) observed that instructional style of mothers affected language of their children. Against this backdrop an attempt was made to analyze the implications of social class differences in linguistic environment for language development.

An Empirical Analysis

Socialization, which is an aspect of home environment is an important intervening variable. Due to preference for male child (Srinivas, 1978) and discriminatory treatment meted out towards females (Tikoo, 1985) girls are also deprived in certain ways. All these factors constitute a general ecology of child. Stimulant or deficient nature of ecology influences the development of linguistic skills in certain ways. The objective of the present study, therefore, was to investigate the effects of social class on language development as mediated by linguistic environment of home. It was hypothesized that upper class children would score higher than lower class on language measures as well as on the measure of linguistic environment.

In order to achieve the above objectives a sample of 84 mothers and their children from extended families living in Allahabad city was asked to participate in the study. The sample was equally divided into six subgroups of 14 each following a 2 (Sex) X 3 (Social Class) factorial design. The mean age of children was 32 months and that of mothers, 27 years. Only those children who had at least one grandparent or surrogate grandparent living with them in the same house were included in the study. Since mere presence is not effective for the child, families where grandparents were suffering from prolonged illness and disabilities for over one year, were excluded.

The study involved several measures. A brief description of these measures is given below.

Social Class : A scale consisting of 19 items related to father's education and occupation, family income, residential accommodation, physical aspect of home environment, educational and rearing experiences, recreations and travel was used to measure the social class of family. Total of scores obtained on the scale was used for classification of social class.

Linguistic Environment Inventory : A semi-structured interview schedule, comprising of 7 categories, namely, (1) variety of speech spoken in the family; (2) stimulations through toys, games and reading materials; (3) linguistic interaction of child with other family members; (4) affect and warmth; (5) opportunities for learning linguistic skills in home; (6) visit to places where linguistic exposure is prevalent such as theatre, drama, puppet show etc. and (7) opportunities of meeting with visitors in family, was used to measure the linguistic environment of home. Responses were coded on 5-point scale. The high correlations between each category showed that the domain was more or less unidimensional. Therefore, a composite score was given for all the categories which was indicative of the nature of linguistic environment. An alpha coefficient for whole inventory showed the internal consistency of the measure (.93, p <.01). A significant correlation between linguistic environment score and social class score (r = .89, p <.01) established the concurrent validity of the inventory.

A battery of three tests was used to measure two aspects of language development, i.e. comprehension and production of speech.

Grammar Comprehension Test (GCT) : Hindi version of an adaptation of Bellugi-Klima's Grammatical Comprehension Test by White *et al.* (1973) was used. Back translation was employed to ensure accuracy of translation. The test was a performance test which included a set of toys, pictures, dolls and other play materials. Certain modifications were made to make it appropriate for Indian situation e.g. topi (cap) was used instead of 'Hat'. With the help of these toys the child executed certain instructions given by the researchers. Each correct response was scored as 1 and incorrect as 0. Total number of correct responses was taken as his/her index of grammar comprehension. The retest reliability coefficient was $r = .56$ ($p < .05$).

Word Meaning Test (WMT) : A test consisting of 26 stimulus words, ranging from more concrete objects (e.g. knife, bicycle, etc.) to less concrete objects (light, air, God etc.) was used to measure their vocabulary. The child was asked to talk about a particular object. Responses on these words were recorded verbatim. Content analysis of the responses revealed that they could be coded into one or all of the four categories, i.e. identification, relevant cues, function and structure of objects. They were scored in progressive manner. The reliability of scoring system was established. Three judges scored a sample of responses scored by the investigator (Mean $r = .91$, p <.01). Inter-coder reliability was also determined (Mean $r = .86$, $p < .01$). A split-half reliability coefficient of the test ($r = .91$, $p < .01$) showed high internal consistency.

Expressive Skill Test (EST) : Children were shown 9 carefully chosen, pictures which depicted boys, girls and women in different situations (e.g. home, playground). Their descriptions about pictures were recorded verbatim. Mean length of utterance (MLU) was calculated. A total MLU score on 9 pictures indicated the verbal expressive ability of child. An inter-coder reliability between two judges and investigator (r = .77, p <.01) indicated the reliability of coding system.

Linguistic Environment Inventory was administered first on the mother. During this period attempts were made to establish rapport with the child. When the investigator was assured that the child was prepared to respond, language tests were administered. Only one test was administered each day.

Results

Mean scores, obtained on all the measures by boys and girls of all social classes, were calculated. A 2 (sex) × 3 (Social Class) ANOVA, revealed that the main effect of sex was significant for linguistic environment [F (2,78) = 4.20, p <.05] (mean scores 218.45 and 205.91 for boys and girls, respectively), vocabulary [F (2,78) = 18.65, p < 01]; (means for boys and girls 74.38 and 89.16, respectively) and expression [F (2,78) = 8.08, p < .01] (mean for boys 2.60, girls 2.99) but not for grammar comprehension (mean score for boys and girls, 24.23 and 24.40, respectively). An internal comparison of means by Newman Keul's Test revealed that boys and girls differed significantly in production of speech. Girls scored higher than boys on WMT and EST. However, they received less linguistic stimulation in home in comparison to boys. In respect of the social class, the mean scores for the upper, middle and lower classes were 288.46, 198.46 and 149.60 for linguistic environment, 26.82, 23.14 and 23.00 for GCT, 97.14, 83.64 and 64.54 for WMT and 3.86, 2.95 and 1.58 for EST, respectively. Results showed main effect of social class on all the measures, i.e. linguistic environment [F (2,78) = 176.63, p <.01], vocabulary [F (2,78) = 30.15 p <.01], grammar comprehension [F (2,78) = 19.12, p <.01] and expression [F (2,78) = 16.26, p < .01]. The results showed that upper class children scored significantly higher than middle and lower class children on Linguistic Environment Inventory, GCT, WMT and EST. The F ratio for interaction effect of sex and social class was statistically significant only in case of expressive skill [F (2,78) = 3.25, p <.05] which indicated that socialization practices for boys and girls were different in upper and lower class but not in the middle class. To achieve precision in data, analysis of covariance was also employed. Though there was no change in mode of causal relationship, magnitude of F ratios changed.

Conclusion

The preceding findings suggest that socio-cultural disadvantages associated with social class do have a detrimental influence on language development. Lower social class children showed poor ability to comprehend grammatical rules and to explicate structural and functional qualities of stimulus word (e.g.; shape, colour and to express verbally). These findings are in line with the general conclusion drawn by others (Rath, 1972; Panda & Das, 1970; Mishra, 1990a) that social class belongingness affects significantly the development of linguistic skills. Sahu and Jena (1983) reported similar results. Their findings showed that disadvantaged children have lower performance in three linguistic abilities viz. receptive, associative and expressive, compared to their advantaged counterparts. Stating in more general terms, SES and family characteristics are the best predictors of cognitive development (Sigman, Newman, Jensen & Bwibo, 1989).

Despite scoring low on Linguistic Environment Inventory, girls showed greater proficiency in vocabulary and expression in comparison to boys confirming Menyuk's (1963) data. Possibility of biological factors in this regard cannot be ruled out.

Scores on Linguistic Environment Inventory indicated that the verbal environment in lower class families was less facilitating and less stimulating compared to middle and upper class families. This trend is supported by few other Indian studies (Shukla, 1988).

The analyses of findings in totality tend to suggest that social class determines the nature of verbal environment, stimulating or restrictive. Child's interactions and experiences with that particular environment, in turn, directly influence her language development. In broader terms, ecology, which consists of both social class and environment is a major determining factor. Therefore, results can be best understood in an ecological framework for Indian situations as proposed by Sinha (1977).

The 'upper layer' in Sinha's (1977) model relates to the linguistic environment of home. The three factors, namely, *physical space.* i.e. availability of toys, games, etc; *roles* and *linguistic interactions* of each social agent, affect and warmth expressed toward child, opportunity to meet visitors; and *activities* such as visiting other places; cultural activities, would constitute the 'upper' layer of ecology. Social class would constitute the 'outer' layer of ecology. Geographical and physical environment of home, nature and level of father's occupation, education and income would constitute the elements of this layer.

Due to poverty and consequently lack of physical facilities (e.g., games, reading, materials) children of lower social class have restricted opportunities to learn new concepts which retarded their comprehension and vocabulary skills. Studies have shown that availability of these things help children to organise information into meaningful concepts (Scanlon, 1977; White & Owens, 1989). In addition, majority of lower class women have to work to earn their living (Radha, 1984) and therefore, they have less time for verbal interaction such as story telling, sharing experiences etc. with their children. Miller and Moore (1989) observed that stories play major role in language socialization. Even in language delayed children, the shared context between mothers and their children was an important factor (Moseley, 1990).

Apart from poverty, illiteracy, on the part of parents, affects the quality of life in general (Entwistle, 1958) and verbal interaction, in particular. This observation is supported by Muralidharan and Banerjee (1975) who found parental education and home support as crucial factors in children's school readiness. Moreover, characteristics of father's occupation affect child rearing practices, values, and home environment (Miller & Swanson, 1958). It has significant, though, indirect impact on verbal climate of family. Thus the present study has shown that factors of both layers of ecology of poverty interact with each other to affect the nature and course of development of linguistic skills of children.

9

Are the Poor Less Intelligent? Or Much Ado About Nothing

ANUP KUMAR SINGH[1]

The first human necessity is education. For all that reason learning is fundamental to social life. Man is born knowing nothing but capable of learning everything. He is subject to what he learns.

—Luis A. Machado (1980)

Intelligence is a highly valued (and perhaps, highly misunderstood) psychological notion in modern society. Terms like intelligent, genius, and idiot are not only part of the psychological science, but are also very much part of everyday language. Research in this area has been marked by many debates. One such debate concerns itself with the relationship between poverty and intelligence (Block & Dwarking, 1976). Researchers report inconsistent findings about this relationship. They also disagree about the explanations of the poverty-intelligence relationship. Some psychologists argue that there is no difference between poor and nonpoor groups in intelligence while others contend that they exist and are caused by differences in their environments. Another group of researchers proposes that intelligence related differences are due to genetic factors. In this paper, literature on the relationship between poverty and intelligence and related issues is reviewed.

1. This paper was originally published in *The Indian Journal of Social Work*, Vol. XIX, No. 4 (October, 1988). Reprinted by permission.

Review of Literature

In the past few decades, several studies conducted in different countries have documented that conditions of poverty result in the decline of intelligence. Baker, Shutz, and Hinze (1961) found that socio-economic status (SES) was positively associated with intelligence quotient (IQ). In Britain, Douglas, Ross and Simpson (1968), using National British Survey data, noted that middle class children scored higher on intelligence tests than lower class children. In Turkey, Kagitcibasi (1979), who measured the intelligence of rural and urban children of different socio-economic backgrounds through Draw-A-Man Test, found that a low SES group scored lower in comparison to a middle SES group. Moreover, rural subjects of the most remote village had the lowest scores and urban middle class subjects had the highest.

Pinto (1980-81) compared logico-verbal abilities of 5, 9 and 13 years old children from urban and suburban districts of Rome, on intelligence, vocabulary, Byrne's Progressive Picture Composition, and two Piagetian tests. He found that social class did not affect nonverbal intelligence at three age levels but it affected verbal intelligence. Firkowska-Mankiewicz and Czarkowski (1981) examined intelligence of 11 year old children from Warsaw on the Raven Progressive Matrices (RPM) and the Wechsler Intelligence Scale for Children (WISC). They found that subjects of a high social class had higher IQ scores in comparison to children of a lower class. In Argentina, Sans (1982) compared IQ scores, using WISC, of two SES groups. The results showed that a high SES group outperformed a low SES group. In addition the difference was more salient in the case of verbal subtests.

In New Zealand, Silva, McGee, Thomas, and Williams (1982) studied five year old children of six socio-economic groups. They collected information on the children about parent's background, family and housing characteristics, child's experiences and activities. Stanford-Binet Intelligence Scale, Reynell Development Language Scale, and MacCarthy Scales of Children's Abilities, physical growth, and health problems. The results revealed that SES did not affect physical growth and health problems. But high SES children scored higher on intellectual ability tests than low SES children.

In Hungary, Eotovs (1983) studied nursery school children on the RPM. He observed that SES positively affected intelligence scores. In a longitudinal study conducted at Guatemala city, Bogin and MacVean (1983) examined children of different SES groups on the measures of physical and intellectual development. They found that high SES children scored higher on intelligence tests than middle class children, while middle class children scored higher than their lower class counterparts.

In another study conducted in Britain, Mascie-Taylor (1984) studied the relationship of intelligence with 29 biosocial variables. He found that children of higher social class had higher scores than lower class children. This effect remained even if parental, biological, familial, and contextual factors were controlled. Chalip and Stigler (1986) examined 1st and 5th graders of lower and higher SES in Taiwan on the RPM and on mathematics achievement. They noted that higher SES subjects outperformed their low SES counterparts in both tests.

The Indian studies have reported mixed findings. Tripathi and Misra (1975) have noted a linear relationship between deprivation and intelligence. Mohanty (1980) observed that socio-culturally advantaged children performed better than disadvantaged children on the RPM (Coloured form). Rangari and Palsane (1982) investigated the intelligence of scheduled caste (SC) and nonscheduled caste (NSC) male and female students of five SES levels. They found that SC and NSC students of first, second, and fifth SES levels did not differ in their intelligence. It follows that caste difference is more pronounced for the middle class subjects. In contrast, studying the effects of ecological background (better community vs. slum) and poverty levels on IQ scores, Husain and Jehan (1983) found that poverty did not influence intelligence scores. However, subjects of a economically rich community had higher IQ scores in comparison to slum children.

In another study, Singh and Sinha (1983) investigated the intelligence of Santal and non-Santal students on the Wechsler Adult Intelligence Scale. They found that non-Santal students had higher IQ scores than Santal students. Sinha (1980) compared tribal (Oraons) and non-tribal students on non-verbal intelligence. He found that tribal and non-tribal students did not differ on total intelligence scores and different subscales, i.e., Passalong Test, Block Design Test, and Cube Construction Test. In a study conducted in Orissa, Jachuck (1984) compared disadvantaged and advantaged children on Level I and Level II abilities. She did not find any effect of disadvantage on Level I ability. However, the advantaged group scored higher on Level II ability. She explained the findings in terms of environmental factors.

Basvana and Rani (1984) examined the impact of caste and economic deprivation on the Standard Progressive Matrices (SPM) for junior school boys. The subjects were equally divided in four groups based on caste and economic deprivation. The results revealed that lower caste subjects scored lower on verbal and numerical ability tests as compared to high caste subjects. In a meta-analysis White (1982) explored the relationship between SES and academic achievement. He defined academic achievement in terms of the achievement test, class ranks, grades, and intelligence scores. He found that academic achievement was weakly related with SES.

In summary, the findings reveal that the relationship between poverty and intelligence is inconclusive. The magnitude of correlations varies in different studies. Also the effect of poverty is more evident on verbal tests than on non-verbal tests.

Critique of Intelligence and Intelligence Tests

Intelligence and intelligence testing have been criticised widely. The two major criticisms are : the lack of validity, and the bias against the disadvantaged community. First, the lack of validity is concerned with two issues. Is there anything like intelligence? If yes, do the IQ tests measure intelligence? Second, if IQ tests measure intelligence, are they fair to different groups?

Many social scientists argue that intelligence is a redundant concept. It says nothing. If somebody does not know some words, is unable to solve some abstract problems or manipulate objects, then he is not cognitively inferior. Barring a few cases when cognitive functioning is disrupted, basic cognitive processes are the same in all human beings. The idea that success in solving abstract problems rapidly reflects high intelligence is an elitist idea to maintain *status quo* in the society.

Ginsberg (1972) is very critical of IQ tests. He argues that they do not measure the intellect. He contends that there are four major myths regarding intelligence tests. These are : (a) Intelligence tests measure intelligence which is unitary mental ability, (b) the difference in IQ scores reflects fundamental difference in intellect, (c) IQ tests measure competence, and (d) they can measure innate intellectual abilities. On the other hand, IQ tests (a) measure multiple abilities, (b) reflect motivational and subcultural differences, (c) measure performance, and (d) indicate experiences.

Another group of theorists argues that even if IQ tests measure a bit of intellectual ability, its validity is doubtful. The criteria against which the intelligence tests are standardized are unsatisfactory. In most cases, school grade and chronological age have been used to validate intelligence tests. The school grades are not so much related to intelligence as they are related to work habits, home environment, and desire to do better. Regarding chronological age, the higher scores with increasing age reveal greater practice and familiarity. The validity of IQ tests is also plagued by circularity. The elements of intelligence tests are derived from the school related materials and they are, in turn, validated against school performance. The evidence of validity is inferred by high correlations of items with the total scores, which is misleading. Richardson and Bryner (1984) suggest that items which relate closely to the total scores are selected *a priori*, and then they will closely correlate with the total score *a posteriori*. But this does not happen in reality. Therefore, validity becomes a methodological artifact.

The use of intelligence tests turns against the poor because tests are valid and relevant only for the middle class. Montagu (1975) points out that intelligence tests are arbitrarily standardized on the middle class and, therefore they discriminate against the lower classes. The content of IQ tests is unfamiliar, strange, and irrelevant to low SES children. The intelligence tests are such that the majority of the poor will score lower on them. As IQ tests do not reflect the intellect of individuals, its use for testing results in dangerous social consequences. It rejects the intellect of individuals rather than selecting it. Davis (1960) has pointed out that, "Half of the ability of this country (the United States) goes down the drain because of the failure of intelligence tests to measure the real mental ability of children from the lower socio-economic groups and because of the failure of the schools to recognize and to train this ability." In the same fashion, Codd (1985) questions the use of the Test of Scholastic Abilities (TOSCA). TOSCAs are used to distribute population on the basis of mental ability. It is bound to show that some people are intellectually superior than others, which is unethical.

In summary, intelligence testing has been criticized on many grounds. Some social scientists have contended that intelligence is a myth. It is a way to justify inequalities in society. Moreover, intelligence tests are inadequately validated. The IQ tests favour middle class individuals. Lastly, the social consequences of intelligence testing are threatening to the poor.

Nature-nurture Controversy and Intelligence Research

The nature-nurture controversy has important implications for the poverty-intelligence relationship (Schiff & Lewontin, 1986). The nature thesis proposes that intelligence differences across different social classes and racial groups are due to genetic factors; therefore, there is bleak hope of boosting intelligence. On the other hand, the nurture thesis holds that the poor have less intelligence due to impoverished environment; thus, intelligence can be boosted by enriching environment. In the following section, we shall critically examine the genetic perspective with special reference to the poverty-intelligence issue.

The Genetic Bases of Intelligence and its Critique

The roots of genetic theory of intelligence can be found in the philosophical work of Herbert Spencer, the bio-physiological approach of Francis Galton and the psychological studies of Cyril Burt. Jensen is a modern proponent of this perspective. Jensen (1981) states that there is a general factor of intelligence which is abstract, universal, and unaffected by socio-cultural factors. Some intelligence tests, particularly non-verbal ones, can measure the general factor. The intelligence is determined by polygenetic inheritance. According to him, although factors like associative mating, dominance and inbreeding, epistasis and genotype-environment interaction contaminate the effect of heredity on intelligence, they have little actual effect. Jensen (1969) proposes that there are two intellectual abilities : Level I and Level II. Level I refers to associative types of learning, while Level II engages complex intellectual processes. The former involves registration, storage, and recall while the latter refers to transfer, generalization, abstraction, conceptualization, reasoning, and problem solving. Both abilities are inheritable. He advances the hypothesis that the intelligence of the Blacks is inferior to their White counterparts in the United States. In addition, there are social class differences in intelligence which are also inheritable.

Critics of the genetic theory of intelligence have questioned this position on several theoretical, conceptual, methodological, and statistical grounds. For example, Kamin (1974) has re-examined the original genetic research on intelligence conducted by Cyril Burt in England. He notes a variety of methodological and statistical flaws. He concludes that there is no substantial evidence to show that intelligence is inheritable. We shall critically focus here on some of the issues which question the validity of the genetic theory.

Role of situational factors : Situational factors, such as testee's motivation, prior testing experience, test anxiety, test administrator's language, race, and social class, substantially affect test scores. The test items have little significance for poor children. Therefore, they are not motivated to perform well on the test. There is evidence to suggest that the difference between a lower and a higher SES group disappears when the test situation is made less threatening to the former. In a recent study, Miller and Eller (1985) have examined the effects of money and praise rewards on the level of intelligence of middle school black-white and lower-middle class subjects. They found that lower class Afro-Americans showed an increase in intelligence scores when motivated by the condition of monetary reward, while middle class Whites scored higher in the praise condition. The sequencing of money first and praise second was conducive to higher IQ scores in lower and middle class White females and middle class males. Overall, the findings showed that motivation of the testees significantly contributes to increase in the intelligence scores.

Conception of environment : The genetic theorists conceptualize environment narrowly and heredity broadly. Sometimes, they equate SES and home with environment. Thus, heredity is everything except social class and home conditions. The genetic theorists bypass the cultural, historical, and inter-generational aspects of environment. The rich and poor have different histories of experiences. The cultural dimension of environment helps one to understand that different cultural groups value different elements of intelligence, and they may score low on those elements of intelligence which are not valued in a given culture. Lastly, the intergenerational aspect refers to the phenomenon that social conditions of the parents set limits for the intellectual achievement of a child. There exists social inheritance besides genetic inheritance.

Culture, environment and intelligence : Cross-cultural

psychologists point out that the intelligence tests, conceptualized and developed in the Western cultures, cannot be used in other cultures. The people of one culture should be judged intelligent on the elements that they consider to constitute intelligence and not on what Westerners think. Berry (1976) observes that people of a culture develop specific abilities to adapt to their environment, and if they are successful in their environment, they are intelligent. Cultural groups differ in their meaning systems, and they value different aspects of cognitive skills. They are exposed to differences in technologies, social systems, the physical world, and way of living. Accordingly, they emphasize different facets of cognitive processes. The scores thus, show qualitative differences rather than quantitative deficits.

Different interpretation of H^2 : The genetic theorists argue that heritability quotient, H^2, reflects the contribution of heredity for the trait in question. H^2 is the main statistical tool to show the importance of heredity. But it is a weak statistical tool. Fisher (1951) called it an "unfortunate shortcut". It does not reveal the relative contribution of nature as the genetic theorists claim. H^2 is also a methodological artifact because it is higher when environment is homogeneous and lower when the environment is heterogeneous. The genetic studies often select a homogeneous environment and, in turn, obtain higher H^2.

Another issue concerns the different H^2 for different elements of intelligence and socially desirable and socially neutral attributes. The socially desirable and culturally specific attributes reveal more heritabilities. Gottesman (1966) found higher heritability for dominance (.49) and sociability (.49) than for flexibility (.15) and self-control (.27). He also observed differential H^2s for verbal (.52) and non-verbal (.25) tests of intelligence. Bronfenbrenner (1975) noted that H^2 is the lowest for the lower class and the highest for the middle and upper classes. Thus, H^2 reveals something more than heredity. He suggests that H^2 is, "an index of the capacity of a given environment to evoke and nurture the development of that ability or trait"

(Bronfenbrenner, 1975, p. 140).

Relative contribution of environment and heredity : The genetic theorists propose that heredity contributes to 70 to 80 per cent of variance in intelligence. It is impossible to fix figures for the relative contributions of heredity and environment, for they are correlated. Although heredity is determined at birth, it unfolds itself only through a complex transaction with environmental factors. As we have discussed earlier, H^2 is not just a measure of inheritance, it also represents environmental facilitation to develop potential abilities.

Besides the criticisms of the genetic theory outlined earlier, several other arguments are advanced against this position. Some theorists propose that heritability does not mean that intelligence is not malleable. They propose that in a better environment, phenotype may change drastically. Other theorists contend that it is necessary to distinguish between broad and narrow heritabilities. They contend that broad heritability, which is often used in genetic studies, reveals little about the contribution of heredity. Finally, many social scientists criticize the pessimistic tone and the racism of the genetic theory.

To summarize, the genetic theory of intelligence has been questioned on several grounds. Firstly, genetic theorists ignore the situational factors. Secondly, the environment is very narrowly conceptualized in genetic studies. Thirdly, heritability reflects much more than the relative contribution of genetic factors. It represents the capacity of a given environment to stimulate and nurture the trait. Lastly, it is impossible to arrive at exact figures for the relative contributions of environment and heredity.

Conclusions

How does poverty affect intelligence? We began by this question and examined numerous studies conducted in India and abroad. On the basis of a close perusal of literature, we conclude that the findings in this area are inconclusive, ambiguous, and non-supportive. Further, the concept of intelligence is polemical. Different theorists define intelligence in different ways. Some researchers define intelligence in terms of how they measure it. Thus, intelligence is what intelligence tests measure. Evans and Waites (1981) have pointed out that, "operational definitions of intelligence are unsatisfactory because scientific measurement must be embedded within scientific theories" (p. 118). On the contrary, measurement leads to conceptual development in intelligence research.

Cross-cultural research has documented that the concept of intelligence varies from culture to culture and from one subculture to another. The non-western cultures emphasize more social elements in defining intelligence. Because values and conceptions of intelligence vary qualitatively across cultures and subcultures, differences in IQ scores show qualitative differences and not quantitative deficits. There is no culture fair test because, to be culture fair, the test requires that people of different cultures should score equally on it. However, no test has ever shown this quality.

One should distinguish between statistical and meaningful differences in order to understand the intelligence gap between poor and non-poor persons. A statistical difference is not necessarily a meaningful difference. Sometimes, interpreting statistical difference as meaningful difference may be a great fallacy. A closer scrutiny of lower and middle class children shows that they exhibit equal verbal reasoning, and problem solving skills in their respective environments. The problem, arises when the lower class children are tested on middle class norms. If poor children have a middle class environment, they will show similar skills. Thus, even if intelligence is determined by genetic factors, there are chances of great improvement. A difference of 10 to 15 points on an intelligence test does not show a fundamental difference in competence. It is more important to maximize potential and put it into performance for better results than to statistically demonstrate surface differences. Our contention is that all human beings have incredible capacities, and we need to understand them, maximize them and use them.

10

Achievement Cognitions in Deprived Groups : An Attributional Analysis*

GIRISHWAR MISRA AND UDAY JAIN

Attribution theory assumes that the search for causes is one of the basic cognitive functions (Kelley, 1971). This causal search has been used by Weiner (1979) to explain achievement behaviour in a variety of situations. It is assumed that human beings try to locate causes of behaviours and their outcomes. These attempts yield innumerable causes. However, these causes, as Weiner (1986) has stated, involve at least three dimensions, namely, *locus of causality, controllability* and *stability*. The empirical evidence suggests linkages between these causal dimensions and important properties of behaviour (Hewstone, 1983). They have been found to be systematically related to affective reactions to outcomes and expectations about future outcomes. For instance it has been noted that internal (ability) attributions are related to expectations and persistence. Since attributions involve cognitions they prove to be relatively more flexible and manipulable than needs or personality dispositions. An analysis of attributions in the disadvantaged and deprived groups, therefore, is more pertinent to unravel the situations in which possibilities of change are greater as compared to other trait based personality approaches to motivation. Within this general framework this paper

* Revised version of a paper published earlier in *Indian Journal of Current Psychological Research, 1988, 3,* 45-54.

attempts to examine the patterns of attribution in relation to disadvantage and deprivation.

Deprivation and Attribution

The Case of Experimentally Manipulated Outcomes

Jain and Mal (1984) investigated the pattern of performance attribution as related to deprivation in an experimental situation. The low and high deprived high school students from the age range of 15 to 17 years (M = 16.2) were randomly assigned to the conditions of success and failure. Their level of deprivation was assessed with the help of Prolonged Deprivation Scale (PDS) of Misra and Tripathi (1978). The experimental task involved anagram solution. The subjects were asked to attribute their performance to effort, ability, luck and task difficulty on separate 5-points rating scales.

The results yielded a significant main effect of deprivation for ability but not for task difficulty and luck. The main effect of outcome was significant for all the causes. In addition, the deprivation × outcome interaction was significant for ability, effort, and luck. The low deprived subjects attributed their success more to internal than to external factors and failure to external factors. Such results are similar to the pattern found in Western cultural studies. The HD students, however, provided internal attributions for both success and failure outcomes. This seems to suggest that deprivational experiences shape attributions which emphasize helplessness and low self esteem.

Performance in School Examination

It is held that education is closely linked with career building and social mobility. However, the disadvantaged students face difficulty in integrating themselves with the prevailing system and lag behind their advantaged counterparts. This leads to poor performance and greater drop out rate which appear to reflect motivational differences. G. Misra and S. Misra (1986), therefore, explored the deprivational effects on attribution in the context of school examination. The sample consisted of 80 students (40 males and 40 females) of first year senior or higher secondary grade equally drawn from low and high deprived groups based on a short form of PDS. The success or failure in school examination was determined with the help of a measure of perceived success and examination marks.

The results showed significant interaction of outcome and social disadvantage, for luck, (p <.05) and preparation at home (effort), (p < .01) The advantaged pupils attributed success less to luck (M=1.85) than disadvantaged ones (M= 2.65). On the other hand, advantaged students attributed more to luck for failure (M=2.60) than their disadvantaged counterparts (M=2.20). In case of effort advantaged pupils attributed success more to preparation at home (M=3.90) than failure (M=3.35). The disadvantaged students rated it higher under failure (M=3.85) than success (M=3.05) condition. The result also yielded a significant 3-way gender × outcomes × deprivation interaction (p <.05) for attribution to luck. It was observed that under success condition disadvantaged as well as advantaged females attributed more to luck than their male counterparts. In case of failure, advantaged females scored higher than males while disadvantaged males and females displayed almost identical pattern.

Thus it is clear that the disadvantaged students' attributions are characterized by unstable and external causes which are demotivating for task involvement and decrease expectations.

Generality of Attributions

The question whether attributions are situation specific or share cross situational generality is an important one in attribution research for theoretical as well as applied reasons. To this end, Misra (1985) assessed attributions for outcome episodes using open ended items. The participants were allowed to generate causes for outcomes spontaneously in three contexts i.e., academic, interpersonal and competitive. A content analysis of the causes revealed that in the academic context the rural disadvantaged group yielded significantly larger number of causes for failure than success. In the inter-personal and competitive contexts urban advantaged group yielded significantly larger number of causes for failure than success. In general relatively larger number of causes were generated for failure than success.

The dimensional analysis indicated that in academic context success was largely attributed to internal causes, with greater emphasis on effort. This was followed by attributions to other internal factors and environmental resources. This pattern was shared by all the groups except the rural advantaged and disadvantaged groups who showed less ability attribution than their urban advantaged counterparts. Attributions for failure were diverse, though the category of environmental resources, was considered as the most salient cause for failure. Also, the rural group indicated significant others' and lack of effort as important causes for failure. These results indicate that causal search is more pronounced under failure condition and disadvantaged participants gave relatively fewer number of causes than their advantaged counterparts.

Self-esteem and Attribution

It has been documented that the disadvantaged students are often characterised by low degree of self-esteem; and attributions to external and unstable causes are related to variation in the strength of self-esteem. With this line of thinking, Jain (1986) examined achievement attributions of low and high deprived tenth graders varying in the degree of self-esteem as measured with the help of Beckman and Mellev's (1977) scale.

The analysis yielded significant joint effect of deprivation and self-esteem (p <.05) for task attribution. The low deprived (LD) with high self-esteem subjects considered task as less a cause of success (M=1.90) than their high deprived (HD) counterparts (M=2.35). The two groups with moderate self-esteem did not differ significantly (M=2.70 and 2.90 for LD and HD groups, respectively). In contrast to the LD group with high self-esteem the LD group with low self-esteem attributed more to task difficulty (M=2.40) than their high self-esteem counterparts (M=2.00).

The deprivation × self-esteem × target context, interaction reached significance level for two causes i.e., luck, (p < .01) and task difficulty, (p <.01). At high self-esteem level the difference in luck attribution between the high and low deprived groups was greater for personal than other's success. At the moderate self-esteem level the differences were lesser for personal than other's success while at low self-esteem level similar differences emerged for luck attribution for success. The HD subjects with high self-esteem attributed luck more as a cause for personal success (M=3.60) than their LD counterparts (M=3.10). the reverse was true for the participants with moderate self-esteem level as other's success was attributed more to luck by LD (M=4.0) than by HD (M=2.90) group.

In case of task difficulty (M=2.20) the LD subjects attributed lesser to task difficulty for personal success than for other's self success (M=2.60) at high esteem level whereas HD group did not differ. At moderate self-esteem level the HD subjects attributed to task difficulty more (M=3.30) than the LD group (M=2.50) for personal success; but for other's success the HD group attributed task difficulty lesser (M=2.50) than LD group (M=2.90). At low self-esteem level the attributional pattern was just the reverse of the one found at high self-esteem level, i.e, the LD group attributed more to task difficulty (M=2.60) for other's success as compared to HD group (M=2.00).

The main effect of deprivation was significant for luck (p <.01) and effort attributions, (p < .01). The LD subjects attributed luck to a greater extent than the HD subjects (M=3.10). The HD subjects attributed to effort more (M=3.83) than LD subjects (M=3.18). The main effect of self-esteem was significant for effort, F (2.54)=9.22, p < .01 and task difficulty, F (2,54)=40.77, p < .01. Effort as a cause for failure was rated higher by low self-esteem subjects (M=3.90) and least by the high self-esteem subjects (M=2.95).

The deprivation × self-esteem interaction was significant for ability, (p < .01) and effort, (p <.05). It was found that at the high self-esteem level HD subjects gave higher rating for ability (*M*=4.20) than the LD subjects (*M*=2.50). At moderate and low levels of self-esteem, however, lesser differences were noted between the LD and HD groups. The HD subjects consistently attributed effort less as a cause for failure than LD subjects across the three levels of self-esteem (*M*=2.60, 3.15, 3.80 for HD, and 3.30, 4.20, 4.00 for LD groups).

The interaction of deprivation and target context also reached the significance level for ability, ($p < .01$ and luck, $p < .05$). For personal failure HD group attributed to ability more (*M*=3.90) than the LD group (*M*=2.77) while the reverse was true for ability attribution to other's failure. In case of luck the mean difference was greater between the two groups for personal failure : LD group attributed more (*M*=4.43) than HD group (*M*=3.16) and the same was true for other's failure but the difference was lesser than personal attribution.

The above results indicate that in success condition there was no significant difference in attributions made across the two deprivation levels. The level of self-esteem, however, influenced attribution for luck and task. Target context affected effort attribution which was stronger in case of self than other's success.

Class Perspective and Achievement Attribution

Deprivation is a pervasive phenomenon in India where about 40 per cent of the total population lives below poverty line. Obviously poverty is very closely related to the distribution of resources. With this line of thinking Sinha, Jain and Pandey (1980) examined attribution of causality to poverty. They found that high income subjects perceived significantly less poor's lack of ability to earn money and wrong habits as the cause of poverty in comparison of low income subjects. In contrast, the low income subjects attributed significantly more to fate, government, and dominant people than high income subjects. The interaction of income and ownership was significant for self as a cause of poverty. It was largely due to the fact that the low income non-owner participants attributed more to self. A significant interaction for fate indicated that high income owners and non-owners did not differ significantly in their attribution. However, low income subjects attributed more to fate than high income subjects and attribution to fate was maximum in the low income non-owner group. Finally, a 3-way interaction was found for attribution to government. It was noted that owner internal subjects attributed to government as greater cause of poverty than their counterpart externals. However, non-owner internals and externals did not differ.

In general, the results showed that low income adults viewed themselves as the cause of poverty more than what the high income people perceive them. The poor people blame themselves more for their own poverty. Also, it is the low income non-owners who blame themselves more than any other group.

In a subsequent study Pandey, Sinha, Prakash and Tripathi (1982) observed that political ideology influences the attribution of poverty. It was found that the neutrals and right activists attributed significantly more to self, i.e, habits and ability of the poor, and to fate of the poor as causes of poverty than did the left activists. The left activists, however, attributed significantly more to governmental policies and economic dominance of a few in the society as the causes of poverty than the neutrals and right activists. The differences between the neutrals and right activists were not significant.

In another study Jain (1987) examined the way class stereotypes influence achievement attribution. In the light of earlier studies it was expected that owing to differential expectations from persons belonging to high and low social class groups would attribute performance differently. The participants (N=180) were high school students and came from middle class families with family income around Rs. 1000 per month. They witnessed the performance of a stimulus person and were informed about the outcome by the experimenter and finally attributed for the performance of stimulus person.

It was observed that as age progresses from 9 to 13

and 17 years the mean expectation increases for high status stimulus person (*M*=34.37, 39.35, 47.62 respectively), (p <.05). On the contrary, the expectation decreases for low stimulus person with age (*M*=33.13, 32.0, 29.01, respectively for 9 years, 13 years and 17 years).

The main effect of status of stimulus person was not significant for any of the causes as well as expectancy of outcome. However, status × outcome interaction was significant for luck (p <.01), effort (p <.01), and ability (p <.01). Success of high status person (*M*=3.8) and failure of low status person (*M*=3.5) were attributed more to ability. Success of low status person (*M*=3.6) and failure of high status person (*M*=3.5) were attributed more to luck. Finally, the success of low status person and failure of high status person were attributed more to effort (*M*=3.7, and 3.6 respectively).

The main effect of outcome was significant for task difficulty, (p <.01) and expectancy, (p <.01). Attribution to task difficulty and higher expectancy characterized success than failure. Interactions of age with status of stimulus person and outcome did not reach significance levels. However, the interaction of age × outcome × status of stimulus person was significant for ability, (p <.01) and effort (p <.01). Attributions of ability for the success of high status person increased with age whereas, mean rating for the success of low status person was almost similar across all the age groups. In the failure condition the ability attribution increased with age for low status person and remained similar for high status person. In case of effort attribution for success of high status person mean ratings were lower (*M*=2.6, 2.7 and 2.9) than for low status person (*M*=3.2, 3.4 and 4.0). In failure condition lack of effort was ascribed more for high status person (*M*=3.2, 3.3 and 3.9) than the low status person (*M*=2.3, 2.4 and 2.8). The subjects expressed stereotypical beliefs about persons of high and low economic status. These stereotypes develop with age and influence attributions for achievement outcomes.

The study exemplifies the linkage betwen stereotypes and attribution. The use of ability, effort and luck attributions was jointly influenced by the economic status of the stimulus person and outcome. Since the stereotypical beliefs emerged in the present study were in favour of higher expectation in the case of high economic status person, failure was attributed to lack of effort (unstable cause) and bad luck (external cause). On the other hand, in consonance with the stereotypical beliefs failure of low status person was considered more due to lack of ability (a stable internal cause) than to lack of effort or bad luck.

The success of low economic status person was attributed more to high effort and good luck than to high ability which was considered a cause of success for the high status person. Thus class stereotypes seem to bias attributions which might provide social feedback and facilitate the development of a specific perspective.

Changing the Attributions

In recent years the application of attributional model in dealing with achievement performance has considerably increased. They are rooted in the fact that attributions are directly linked with effective consequences and future expectancies (Weiner, 1986). Against this background Singh and G. Misra (1988) examined the effects of competence and helplessness manipulations on achievement attributions by high and low deprived students hailing from scheduled caste (SC) and high caste groups (N=64). These students were selected from middle school and pretested on PDS. The participants received the failure or success feedback on completion of a task and then rated their feeling of competence on ten, 7-point sementic differential type, scales. Finally, they also completed attributional questionnaire.

It was noted that the low deprived group attributed performance more to internal causes than their high deprived counterparts. The SC students attributed their performance more to luck than Non-SC students. A significant interaction of competence and deprivation for ability indicated that ability was perceived equally important by the two groups under competence condition but not under helplessness condition. Under helplessness condition HD group attributed more to ability than LD group. This pattern of attribution implies that the HD group may cease their effort even in situations where success is possible due to the feeling of helplessness. Thus, deprived pupils' attribution seems to be dysfunctional for their future performance which may be a potent cause for their poor academic performance. The results also revealed a significant competence × deprivation interaction for luck; where LD pupils perceived luck less important across competence and helplessness conditions.

The findings showed that disadvantaged students use stable and controllable causes to explain performance under helplessness condition. Therefore, one strategy to improve the achievement of socially deprived pupils may be to change their dysfunctional attributions through appropriate cognitive training.

Conclusion

The present findings indicate a reasonably consistent pattern of attribution. We have learned that the disadvantaged and deprived students and adults perceive achievement outcomes in one of the two ways : they either attribute all outcomes irrespective of their valence to internal factors or assume greater responsibility for failure and externalize success. This is contrary to the attributions made by the advantaged or privileged ones. As a matter of fact the attributions by the advantaged groups replicate the findings observed in western society namely, success is because of 'my characteristics' and failure is due to 'anything except me'. This pattern corresponds closely with the attributions made by the privileged participants for the deprived people. This congruence between actors and observers is remarkable.

The deprivational effect on attribution can be interpreted in many ways. First, it may be due to lack of discrimination of outcomes. The disadvantaged participants may not be able to distinguish between success and failure outcomes. Here distinction between outcomes involved not only differences or distinct identities of causes or outcomes but in terms of the entire cause-consequence scheme. What we mean to indicate is that saying "he is successful" is not saying "he is successful because of his brilliance" or "he is successful because he is tactful". These statements refer to the same outcome but implicate different meanings. The evidence reviewed in this paper indicates that the disadvantaged as well as advantaged participants distinguish between success and failure and use causes to explain success and failure, but they are perhaps using different schemes of `cause-outcome configuration.' It is not unlikely that the disadvantaged, because of their limited experiential background and repeated experiences of behavioural irrelevance or noncontingency, do not develop an adequate cause-outcome scheme. This proposition needs further enquiry.

Secondly, the deprived sections of society have assimilated the views held by the privileged people about themselves. It is argued that the poor people accept the views of significant others. The results of this study are consistent with this view to the extent that there is similarity between attributions by the deprived people and attributions made by the nondeprived people for deprived people. But this does not indicate assimilation hypothesis as a logical conclusion.

The third explanation is that attributions made by the disadvantaged groups are true and veridical. This view is very close to the first explanation and assumes that attributions are the acts of naive scientist (Heider, 1958). People hold theories of attribution. They use the informational input in attributing to causes. Such inputs available to the advantaged and disadvantaged people are different and seem to be consistent with their attributions.

Considering the present set of attributions on the part of disadvantaged groups veridical, is discouraging. Such attributions made by the deprived sections are dysfunctional and suggest a state of depression and helplessness. The only hope is that they are learned and acquired and are, therefore, susceptible to change. One of our studies has demonstrated that competence manipulation leads to changes in attributions and it is possible to convert external determination into self determination (G. Misra, 1988). It is felt that retrieving from the state of helplessness at the larger societal plane is also possible and we can look forward to a social order which ensures equity and equality of opportunities for all sections of society.

SECTION-III

REACHING OUT : STRATEGIES FOR INTERVENTION

11

Interventions for Alleviation of Poverty and Disadvantage : An Overview

GIRISHWAR MISRA AND UDAYA N. DASH

The past few decades have witnessed noticeable economic progress in many developing countries including India in the form of positive gains in income, consumption and life expectancy, decrease in child mortality, and increase in educational attainment. All over the world, however, more than one billion people are still living in conditions of poverty and disadvantage. Studies show that the problems of poverty, population, and environment are intertwined, and that the burden of poverty is spread unevenly across and within countries. The burden of poverty often falls heavily on certain groups like women, children, girls, and people from low caste and minority groups. The concern for reducing poverty has assumed a significant place on the national agenda. Poverty has been a major concern in a developing country like India for the last five decades. During 50s and 60s, growth was considered as the primary means of reducing poverty and improving quality of life (QOL). In the 70s, attention was shifted to the direct provision of help promoting growth in income. The success in poverty reduction was achieved by the following two strategies : (a) productive use of the poor's labour, and (b) providing basic social services. It involved politically sensitive trade off between the poor and the non-poor.

The present paper provides an integrative review of

the governmental and non-governmental efforts in anti-poverty programmes, and examines various aspects of psychological interventions in dealing with the cognitive, motivational and affective characteristics of the poor and the disadvantaged so as to maximize the efficacy of the poverty alleviation programmes.

The World Development Report, 1990 indicated that progress in Asia depends critically on developments in China and India. If economic reforms falter in China or if India is unable to maintain its momentum, the prospects for reducing poverty will be far less bright. Alternate projections based on slower growth and policies less favourable to the poor show an additional 150 million poor, mainly in India.

A variety of governmental and non-governmental interventions was taken up during the Five Year Plans to introduce measures to help people outgrow the poverty trap. In addition, psychological interventions have also been tried out at different levels. The focus of the governmental interventions has been on macro level policy changes, while psychological interventions have been tried out at a micro level to address issues with individual or a small group as the unit of analysis. The analyses of intervention show the emphasis on the mechanisms of reaching out to children and adults in poverty settings, the nature of inputs needed (e.g., education, early stimulation, nutrition, empowerment), organizational efforts, and strengths and weaknesses of the people.

Governmental Interventions for Poverty Alleviation

The commitment to poverty eradication has a politico-historical background. It was an issue during India's freedom struggle and was the concern of the Indian political and social movements before independence. It was reflected in the Gandhian spirit of working for the uplift of the downtrodden — the poorest of the poor, or the spirit of what Gandhiji termed as *antyodaya*. Thus, it was natural that economic and social justice constituted a significant goal for the nation after independence. There was clear consensus in the political circles on poverty alleviation as an instrument for the establishment of democratic values in the country. After gaining independence, the Indian Government opted for a socialist pattern of society, and the problem of poverty assumed greater significance. In the documents of Five Year Plans, poverty was treated as a central problem and a variety of programmes were undertaken to reduce it.

Planned Interventions at the National Level

Beginning with Dadabhai Nauroji who analyzed poverty in India in 1876, the political leadership in India considered poverty as a key issue. The National Planning Committee constituted in 1938 under the chairmanship of Pandit Nehru considered elimination of poverty as an important goal. Immediately after Independence in 1947, the Economic Programme Committee of the Congress party recommended measures for a quick and progressive rise in the standard of living. Article 38 of the Constitution stipulated a social order in which justice—social, economic, and political—will inform all the institutions of public life. Article 39 proposed the right to adequate means of livelihood, and Articles 41, 46, and 47 stipulated that the State must create provisions for care and assistance to the poor people. Thus, elimination of poverty received due attention while framing the Constitution of free India.

The Planning Commission was constituted in March 1950 to assess the national resources for formulating plans for their effective utilization. The First Five Year Plan (FYP) (1951-56) aimed at raising the living standards and providing the people more opportunities for a richer and more varied life. Community Development and National Extension Services were introduced to transform the village life. The second FYP (1956-61) opted for a socialistic pattern of society and for attaining the goals of raising the living standards by enlarging the opportunities through rapid industrialization. The third FYP (1961-66) considered combating poverty as the most important problem, and envisaged programmes for rural workers especially in densely populated areas during periods of less employment in the slack agricultural seasons. The fourth FYP (1969-74) was committed to raise the standard of living of the people, especially the less privileged sections of the society. The plan document stated that while increased production is of utmost importance, it is equally important to remove or reduce and prevent concentration of wealth and economic power. In the fifth FYP (1974-79) elimination of poverty received the highest priority. It aimed at raising the consumption levels of the lowest 30 per cent of the population and held that the existence of poverty was incompatible with the vision of an egalitarian and just society. The sixth FYP (1980-85) recognized that accelerating growth process was not the solution. In addition to stimulating growth in backward areas, improving the poverty eradication programmes, and bringing in institutional reforms were also emphasized. It was expected that the population below poverty line in 1984-85 would be reduced to less than 10 per cent by the end of 1994-95. The seventh FYP (1985-90) was conceived to assist the country in establishing an economy and polity which is modern, efficient, progressive, humane, and is based on equity and justice. Anti-poverty programmes were launched on a massive scale, and special attention was paid to the problems faced by the socially disadvantaged groups like the SC and the ST, and women and children. The eighth FYP (1992-97) differed radically from the earlier plans in that it held planning to be essential for macroeconomic care of the poor and the downtrodden who were mostly outside the market system, and had little resource endowment. It emphasized structural reforms, liberalization, market orientation and globalization. The ninth FYP (1997-2002) asserts that a sustained and long lasting solution to the problem of poverty depends on the creation of adequate employment opportunities through a broad based programme of development and economic growth. Empowering the SC, ST, backward class people, minorities, and women is receiving major attention. The promise for poverty reduction, employment generation and providing basic minimum services in a time bound manner are the key features of this plan.

It is evident that the objective of elimination of poverty has figured in our national plans from the very beginning. The anti-poverty programmes and policies can be broadly grouped into three major types viz., *land reform, asset provision, and income and consumption support.* During the initial years of independence, structural changes in terms of land reform were introduced by the Indian Government. A major project called the Community Development Programme was launched to enhance the quality of social and economic life of the masses living in the villages. However, owing to lack of relevant technological and institutional reforms, it could not achieve its goals to a large extent. The effort for poverty elimination was undertaken in three phases. In the first phase which continued till the end of 1960s, there was emphasis on redistribution of land and improving the plight of the poor tenants, on eliminating intermediaries, on tenancy reforms, on imposing ceilings on large holdings, and redistributing the surplus land among the poor specially the agricultural labourers and marginal farmers. The *Bhoodan* movement of Binoba Bhave was a non-governmental initiative of this kind. The implementation of these reforms took time and the well-to-do villagers could consolidate their position. As a consequence, redistributive land reforms could not help much. The other important programmes included Composite Programme for Women and Pre-school Children, the Small Farmers Development Agency (SFDA), Training Rural Youth for Self Employment (TRYSEM), the Integrated Rural Development Programme (IRDP), the National Rural Employment Programme (NREP), the Development of Women and Children in Rural Areas (DWCRA), the Rural Landless Employment Guarantee Programme (RLEGP), Jawahar Rozgar Yojna, and Indira Rozgar Yojna. Out of these, the impact of IRDP has been the largest.

Detailed micro-level analyses show that the participation of the poorest lot in most of these programmes has been very limited. Many beneficiaries happen to be those who are above the poverty line. Also, a large proportion of the funds do not reach the poor owing to the role played by intermediaries and corruption in the delivery system. There is, therefore, a large variation in the level of effectiveness of these programmes in different states. In an analysis of NREP, Achiever-Gent (1992) found better performance in the state of West Bengal. It had two main objectives: (a) to provide work to the unemployed labourers residing in rural areas, and (b) to construct durable assets that will improve the infrastructure in those areas. The enhanced role of public participation facilitated the planning of the projects more appropriate to the demands of the local conditions. The findings did not provide support in favour of the elite domination hypothesis. Recent revival and improvement of the Panchayat Raj has given political parties a prominent role in shaping the process of development by providing local authorities with information about the local circumstances and also monitoring the performance of the Panchayat members.

Because of the failure of the expected "Trickle Down" effects of economic growth, the anti-poverty programmes were redesigned in a targeted form. In the absence of a decentralized micro level planning, these programmes remained fragmentary and isolated, and could not yield the expected outcomes. It is sad that the institutional framework often goes against the implementation of these programmes (Copestake, 1992). The new technology generally could not reach the poor people. There was no stable and sustainable shift in their earning capacity, security, and self-respect. Also, the cost effectiveness of such programmes in respect of asset transfer was questionable. In order to ensure the benefits of the programmes, the planners need to address themselves to the existing bureaucratic hurdles in implementing methods for achieving more effective mobilization of the existing or already committed resources (Giriappa, 1992).

The problem of integrating poverty alleviation programmes (PAP) with development strategies poses a difficult challenge. Hanumanth Rao (1992) has noted that in the mid 60s, increasing production became the goal, and attention was paid to the developed regions and the prosperous farmers. The concern was not as much with the small farmers or with extending technologies and practices for increasing the chances of employment in poverty-stricken areas. The PAPs follow a top-down structure and are heavily dependent on the functioning of bureaucracy. They are largely ill suited to the local resource endowments, and there is reluctance to involve the NGOs. The involvement of the intermediaries increases the chance of leakage and lead to greater degree of inefficiency. The integration of PAPs with the overall developmental programmes in the rural sector is a tough challenge. It may be mentioned that stimulating household small scale rural industries, and accelerating the pace of social development in rural areas would certainly be of great help. Designing appropriate institutional mechanisms for planning the activities under the PAPs within the framework of area development planning and their effective implementation present the major challenge.

In an appraisal of public sector interventions made for poverty alleviation, Vyas and Bhargava (1995) have noted that if the strategies for poverty alleviation are adequately planned and implemented, even without spectacular economic growth or a drastic reorganization of the institutions and structures, the poverty ratio could be reduced. They observed that the states achieving greater success in poverty alleviation have also made sizeable investments in the PAPs. If the poor have access to assets including skills and capabilities, the chances are greater that poverty alleviation will take place, even at slower rate of economic growth. The low deprived farmers held more positive attitude towards innovative agricultural practices, and expressed desire and intention to seek information about them through mass media (Agarwal & Mishra, 1993). The success of governmental plans was attributed to 'good luck' by the high deprived farmers and to 'effort' by the low deprived farmers.

Tripathi, Bhusan, and Pradhan (1990) found that IRDP in Orissa had a positive impact on the income level of the households. While examining the impact of bank lending programme for the self employed poor in Bombay, Everett and Savara (1984) found that women's organizations constituted a pressure group to keep the government honest in its effort to reach the self employed. Sachidananda (1983) observed that poor perception of rural social reality, lack of effective implementation strategy, lack of information about the programme, and corruption were crucial determinants of the failure of the developmental programmes. Though the general guidelines for the IRDP have been designed at the national level, the implementation of the programme for achieving optimal success has been far from being uniform across the country. In a study of the tribal people of Bastar, Singh (1995) found that positive attitude and expectation of gain significantly influenced the involvement of farmers in community development programmes. Some reformative attempts by the Bhartiya Sanskar Nigam Samiti, a Jain organization (Shyamlal, 1992) in the western part of Rajasthan also have not yielded very encouraging results.

The scheme of Integrated Child Development Services (ICDS) was introduced in 1975 as a major programme to combat the effects of poverty on human development at national level. It is perhaps one of the world's largest and most unique outreach programmes for early childhood care and development. It aims at promoting holistic development of children between 0 to 6 years through strengthening the capacity of caregivers and communities and improved access to the basic services at the community level. The ICDS reaches out to 3.8 million expectant and nursing mothers and 21.6 million children. Using *Anyanwadi*, ICDS attempts to take care of nutritional needs of children and early child care and preschool education. The ICDS is now operating in 180 focal high poverty districts. Evaluations show that children attending *Anganwadies* display higher level of cognitive development and health status than those who do not attend (Mistry, Kaul, & Dhar, 1986; Sood, 1992). Chadha and Sen (1993) did not observe any clear cut differences between the two groups of children. A national level evaluation of the ICDS by the National Institute of Public Cooperation and Child Development

(NIPCCD, 1992) has revealed that nutrition, health, and preschool education components of the scheme had positive impact on children. In a study conducted in South India, Vazir and Kashinath (1995) reported that the ICDS programme seemed to benefit younger beneficiaries (36-47 months) more than the older beneficiaries (48-72 months). The educational content of the programme was more suitable for younger children, though children from all age groups displayed higher level of motor and mental development.

In recent years, many non-governmental organizations (NGOs) from within as well as outside the country have shown interest in interventions for the psychological development and economic uplift of the people living in conditions of poverty and disadvantage. Though the attempts have largely been region specific, some of them have been effective in bringing policy changes at the governmental level. They address to a wide range of issues related to social and economic development. So far the impact of the NGO activities were felt at a larger scale in the southern part of the country, but now they are spreading to other areas as well.

The issue of poverty alleviation is related to the entire process of planning, the institutional structure, the class character of those who are in power, and the structural changes that have taken place in the economy (Minocha, 1990). The Indian planning has been overly concerned with high rate of growth and market economy with very little emphasis on institutional changes necessary for effectively dealing with the issue of poverty. The imposition of the culture of the capitalistic societies is hardly commensurate with the socialistic ideals. The relative dominance of the private sector in our mixed economy has contributed to an increase in the level of poverty in the Indian society.

Psychological Interventions for the Uplift of the Poor

Extreme and pervasive poverty, inadequate infrastructural facilities, weak industrial activities, and retarded state of human development tend to create a 'poverty syndrome', which is likely to affect the whole range of interpersonal behaviour and relationships (Sinha, 1998).

Psychological interventions are rooted in the assumption that human development is critically shaped by the experiential base received by a person. The interventions generally aimed at strengthening and equipping individuals from disadvantaged and deprived backgrounds with skills and competencies necessary for effective functioning in the society. Rath (1982) has suggested complementary programmes to enrich the cognitive background of the disadvantaged children for increasing their academic motivation, to effect changes in the living conditions of the people, and to build a positive self image among the slum dwellers. Sinha (1985, 1990) has pointed out that the detrimental effects of poverty are accentuated by the unfavourable proximal environment of the child. Thus, interventions should address not only to the cognitive-attentional drawbacks but also to the conditions prevailing in the family and school settings. Focusing on the school settings, Sandeep and Pushpa (1981) propose to coordinate efforts for developing curriculum, teacher training, modification of school organization and innovations in teaching methods for the disadvantaged pupils. In an interesting theoretical analysis, Dalal (1991) has proposed an educational resourcefulness model which emphasizes that *self efficacy, sense of personal control* and *planfulness* have to be capitalized to derive benefits from the opportunities to learn. He has also outlined such a programme for the school setting.

Misra (1990) has argued that the provision of resources alone cannot ensure social uplift, unless the people learn to accept and properly utilize it. Interventions, therefore, should be planned to create in them a sense of empowerment to effect changes in their environment. Researchers should identify components in the environment at the individual and community levels, which create and maintain poverty and deprivation. Programmes for cognitive enrichment, attitudinal change and motivational training can yield substantial results, only if necessary environmental support is available. As argued by Prillettensky (1989), psychology is expected to perform the dual role of *consentization* and *annunciation*. Consentization refers to the process whereby people attain an illuminating awareness of not only the critical environmental conditions that shape life but also of their own capacity to transform the reality. Annunciation is viewed as the act of announcing a just social arrangement in which the well-being of the people is facilitated. Recently Mehta (1994) has argued for empowerment of the poor so that they may assert collectively to influence and change the socio-economic conditions for realising various social goals. Referring to several successful experiments in India, he has recommended for adopting a participatory approach to development in economic, political, and educational fields. Education, meaningful work, participation in civic and other activities contribute to efficacy, enhanced self respect and stimulate a process of relearning to assert. Pareek (1994) points out that since the expectancy of reward from hardwork through initiative has been low for centuries in a feudal society, the individual has lost the capacity to take initiative for change.

Cognitive performance and classroom behaviour have also been considered as important goals of psychological intervention. Dash and Rath (1985) observed positive impact of cognitive stimulation on performance of the non-schooled disadvantaged children. Mishra (1990a) has shown that pictorial experience and training facilitated the perceptual task performance of 5-6 year-old children, and more so for the deprived than the privileged ones. Koul (1986) also reports the efficacy of the mastery learning strategies for enhancing motivation. While studying classroom behaviour and scholastic achievement, Lidhoo and Khan (1990) demonstrated that counselling of bright underachievers from rural background led to self acceptance, self understanding, and enhanced academic performance. Since the deprived and poor children lack parental competence and support relevant to the context of schooling, Singh (1983) argues that schools need to function as a substitute for parents and families. He has even advocated for the creation of 'ashram type' schools for rescuing the socially disadvantaged from the impact of adverse home conditions. Reddy (1991) found that SC and non-SC students differed only in scholastic achievement, which the former were able to compensate through guided tutoring and training of skills.

Studies on infants from poverty background are rare. Anandalakshmy (1990) observed that an intervention programme is most likely to succeed, if it includes the involvement and interest of the mother and is conducted in an environment familiar and stress-free for the infant. Thus, one should aim at educating mothers on the value of stimulating play activities and providing them with skills that would enable them to offer a stimulating environment for their infants. Working with the problems of children in urban slums of Kolaba, Mumbai, Desai (1989) has also argued for a holistic approach to the education of the disadvantaged child based on an analysis of the contextual realities of the child (e.g., child's family and the community). Since the emergence of cognitive-perceptual skills in the advantaged and disadvantaged groups is similar, Sinha (1982b) has argued that interventions should start at an early stage, and attention be paid to the family atmosphere. The evidence from the tribal children of Madhya Pradesh (Murlidharan & Kaur, 1987) suggests that educational intervention produced positive gains in language and cognitive development. A 3-6 year follow-up study by Kaur, Linda, Razorio, & Maheswari, (1992) showed that the intervention through Anganwadi could not lead to significant changes; rather high drop out rate, stagnation, and poor academic performance were common.

Over the years, the extent of relative poverty in India has increased, thus indicating that the promise for achieving a "socialist pattern of society" did not yield a good return. A regime of controls was instituted to check concentration of economic power, and a number of steps was taken to create an egalitarian society. These measures included land reforms, ceiling of urban property, direct and indirect taxation, industrial licensing, provision of MRTP act etc. The ineffectiveness of these measures has been documented by several researchers. The

Governmental policies were influenced by an issue based conception of poverty, ignoring the complex sociopolitical issues that need to be addressed before poverty elimination programmes can be launched in an effective manner. As a consequence, the policy formulations have catered to the interests of the vested groups, and the relative inequalities have become cumulative. With a view to deal with tnese issues, a process of liberalization of the economy was initiated in the eighties, but that was again fragmentary.

The recent process of economic reforms started since June, 1991 leading to privatization and globalization. The steps involved in India's structural adjustment programme (e.g., deregulation of economy, liberalization of the service sector, increase in private investment) may have benefited a small section in the society, but they have detrimental effects on the deprived groups. It is unfortunate that despite an increase in expenditure on rural development and social services during the Eighth Plan period (1992-97), the role of government in directly addressing the issue of poverty alleviation are countered by the large scale macro-level changes. The so called 'safety net' is inadequate in preventing the declining living standards of the poor. The high rate of inflation coupled with a lack of an efficient public distribution system has brought about considerable shrinkage in the purchasing power of the poor. The market economy has diverted the resources to the production of luxury goods and has encouraged consumerism. However, as Tendulkar (1998) has noted, the economic policy reforms can at best be only indirectly responsible for the observed movement in the poverty indicators in the post-reform period. He argues that the rural poverty situation in 1993-94 could possibly have been improved with better management of the government interventions in the food economy.

Poverty Alleviation Programmes and the Development of Poor

The poverty alleviation programmes have been evaluated

by some researchers in respect of their effectiveness as perceived by the beneficiaries. An analysis of attribution for success and failure by the IRDP beneficiaries and non-beneficiaries (Tiwari & Mishra, 1988) revealed that the salient causes of individual outcome were 'environmental resource' and 'effort'. While the privileged beneficiaries considered lack of ability as a cause for failure, the poor non-beneficiaries used 'ability' more than 'effort'. In another study (Tiwari, 1990a, b), the beneficiaries who perceived themselves more poor exhibited low level of achievement motivation than those who viewed themselves less poor. Those showing middle level of productivity gave more internal attributions, while low productive farmers used greater external attributions. The beneficiaries attributed more to controllable and internal causes (Tripathi, 1993). However, the effect of mass media was significant. It was suggested that the educational programmes should be more flexible, need based, contextually oriented, and culturally relevant, and that the formal schooling need to be supplemented by adult education and non-formal education.

In a study in Orissa, Jachuck and Chatterjee (1989) reported the significant effect of preschool education on cognitive abilities of children. But the high-SES non-preschool children compensated for their lack of preschool experience. Dash and Rath (1985) observed that cognitive stimulation was more important in the non-schooled disadvantaged. They found that intensive cognitive training in sequential and shape discrimination improved the performance of both schooled and non-schooled groups, though the non-schooled demonstrated more improvement than the schooled. Rath (1992) investigated the relative efficacy of verbal self instructional training, and operant manipulation of response and reward in the remediation of impulsive tempo in the disadvantaged children in Orissa. Data from children of low-SES tribal families of marginal farming and daily labourers showed that both kinds of training were effective in modifying the impulsive tempo of children. Singh (1983) reported that high self efficacy treatment (i.e., competence enhancement strategy) improved the intellectual performance of the disadvantaged children. Verma and Verma (1994) noted significant gains in the problem solving performance of deprived children using techniques like brainstorming, generation of alternatives, and hypothetical problem solving for a period of 16 weeks. Khattri and Gupta (1981) have reported that 14-16 year old children in the disadvantaged group did show reduction in the use of abusive language due to intervention, and this effect generalized beyond experimental conditions.

The psychological interventions have dealt with micro-level issues at the individual level. But they have pointed out the cognitive, motivational and affective characteristics of the poor and the disadvantaged, which must be taken into cognizance in macro-level policy planning. The South Asian workshop of the International Society for the Study of Behavioural Development held in Chandigarh in 1995 deliberated on the culturally relevant intervention strategies for the psychosocial development of children and youth in poverty. The participants advocated for the integration of knowledge from field studies and research for effective policy planning, and for promotion of a participatory approach to all aspects of intervention strategies with an emphasis on decentralization and flexibility at all levels of planning and implementation .

Community Based Initiatives

In recent years, a number of NGOs have undertaken community based initiatives to help the poor people, particularly children. Many of such interventions emphasize community participation and providing alternative educational and vocational training opportunities. (See Dalal, this volume). In order to get a feel of such efforts, we may consider the activities of some such NGOs. *Cini Asha*, an NGO in Calcutta, runs an integrated programme to improve the QOL of the urban poor. It addresses several concerns of the poor including health, education and income generation. The *Mobile Creche* tries to create a 'home away from home' for children of construction workers and migrant families in India. It is set up by contractors in partnership with the Mobile Creches. The day care attention allows mothers to work with less anxiety about their children's needs. *NANBAN* is a centre for street and working children in Madurai, which extends support to child's efforts for integration with the mainstream. *Butterflies* is an organization in Delhi which deals with children — largely runaways, victims of poverty, and abused, and destitutes.

Attention has also been paid to the problem of illiteracy and lack of related skills. Education is an essential component of any intervention for poverty and should be closely related to the social realities of the target groups. *Alripu* is a Delhi based NGO involved in education adopting a nonpedagogic approach which allows learners to progress at a pace with the music they set to build learner's confidence in the learning process. *Eklavya* of Bhopal works through the formal school system and attempts to bring about a change through schools run by the government. It offers an alternative kind of formal schooling, teaching material and evaluation strategies. *Gyan-Prabodhini* has been working with youth in poverty settings in Maharashtra. It extends opportunities for all-round development including leadership qualities, motivation and vocational training.

BOSCO in Cochin integrates street children with society. It provides shelter to those who have no house and provide them with opportunities for spiritual, intellectual, social and physical development. The *Vatsalya-Foundation* of Bombay aims at mainstreaming and rehabilitation of street children. *PRACHITI*, at Pune trains youth from slum for social work.

Swadhyaya has emerged as an important social movement under the leadership of Pandurang Shastri Athwale. Located largely in Maharashtra and Gujarat, this movement has mobilized the poor people for community participation, spiritual awakening, and involvement in productive activity. It is an unique social experiment which is transforming the life of the poor people in a significant manner.

Concluding Observations

Alleviation of poverty has been a persistent concern of the social and economic policies of the Indian government. This has led to adoption of macro level strategies as a part of National Five Year Plans. They have involved a variety of programmes including land reform, asset provision and income generation and extending consumption support. The implementation and outcomes of these strategies have not yielded consistent results across all the regions of India on account of bureaucratic hurdles and corruption. A shift in favour of targeted programmes has partly improved the situation. It is also felt that integrating poverty alleviation programmes with developmental programmes will be more effective. The economic reforms in 1990s have diverted the resources needed for the anti-poverty programmes towards promotion of market economy and consumerism. The structural adjustment programme has adversely influenced the poor, by decreasing public expenditure on social services and anti-poverty programmes. The poor do not have the necessary capital to respond to the changes in the market. It is, therefore, important that state must intervene through public distribution, anti-poverty programmes and reservation of jobs for the economically and socially disadvantaged.

The detailed analyses of behavioural consequences of programmes like IRDP and ICDS and psychological interventions at individual and institutional levels indicate promising results. The diverse programmes run by NGOs' have employed many innovative strategies to enrich the lives of people particularly women and children living under difficult circumstances. These programmes are need based and sensitive to the local conditions. The success of these programmes indicates that efforts for poverty alleviation can be fruitful if we address the setting as the context in which people operate as well as empower people. The future of poverty alleviation programmes will, therefore, depend on the extent to which the concerns of policy and people are constructively responded to, within the context of societal functioning.

12

Cognitive-Behavioural Training with Disadvantaged Children

SUDHAKAR RATH

The existing Indian literature reveals that disadvantaged and socio-economically deprived children, particularly scheduled caste (SC) and scheduled tribe (ST) perform poorly on various academic, problem-solving and ability measures. In addition, they also suffer from linguistic, social, cognitive and motivational problems both at home and primary school settings (for a review see Misra & Tripathi, 1980; Sinha, Misra & Tripathi, 1982; and chapters in this volume). Some studies such as that of Mishra (1991) and Reddy (1991) reported that irrespective of caste, tribe, and social status, there did not exist much difference in the innate abilities of children. Inspite of comparable intelligence, in general, the SC and ST children are found to be inferior in various problem-solving and academic situations. The poorer performance of the SC and ST children has been attributed to the dynamics of motivational deficiency and the lack of spontaneous and deliberate effort. It is proposed that sub-optimal mobilisation of effort may be due to the low (or sub-optimal) level of arousal, inappropriate causal attributional style (i.e., tendency to attribute failure to internal ability and success to external factors such as luck; see the chapter by Misra and Jain, this volume), and cognitive distortions. The family and socio-cultural milieu in which these children are brought up does not motivate them for higher aspirations or goals in academic and professional spheres. Due to illiteracy and poverty, the parental aspirations of these children are generally very low. These children lack appreciation of the value of education, and modern careers and perhaps do not realise the importance and significance of competition and success in academic and problem-solving situations. In spite of comparable intellectual and cognitive potentiality during early primary grades, the success rate of tribal and SC children in high school upwards is very low, and majority of them drop out after primary grades and join the work force (for supplementing family income). These children also suffer from several emotional and behavioural problems including attention deficit disorders and face tremendous difficulties in classroom adjustments. The present chapter seeks to show that Cognitive Behavioural Training (CBT) can be an effective method for augmenting cognitive and academic performance of disadvantaged children. The nature of CBT intervention and studies demonstrating its efficacy with disadvantaged Indian children have been discussed in the following sections.

The Historical Roots (Integration of Cognitive and Behaviour Therapy Traditions)

In the 1980s and 1990s, cognitive psychology made its pervasive impact on behaviour therapy with children and the consequence was the proliferation of research and growth of various cognitive-behavioural intervention models for effective management of childhood cognitive, behavioural and academic disorders. The happy marriage between cognitive and behaviour therapeutic models generally occurred in five distinctive ways. First, modelling effects were explained through cognitive information processing explanations. While traditional modelling is viewed as an application of principles of learning and hence identified historically with behaviour therapy, Bandura's (1977) explanation of modelling effects had become more and more cognitive in nature as he emphasized the role of symbolic cognitive processes (i.e. attention, retention, and some other mediational processes) in behaviour change which formed a major spring board for the development of CBT. Second, the developmental literature on language and cognition helped the formulation of self-instructional training (Meichenbaum, 1977) through which, children could be trained to produce internally generated verbal self-statements and talk to themselves in a self-guiding fashion so as to produce changes in thought and behaviour patterns. Third, the emergence of clinical problem solving followed a cognitive-behavioural procedure. Spivack, Platt and Shure (1976) documented the efficacy of problem solving/thinking strategies such as alternative thinking, means-end-thinking and consequence thinking for behavioural and cognitive changes in children. Problem solving like modelling had been historically associated with learning literature but it was most frequently explained through an information processing model in cognitive psychology (Mahoney, 1974, pp. 199-212). Since problem-solving emerges from the cognitive psychology literature and focuses on internal thought processes as mechanisms of change, clinical problem-solving has been usually classified as a cognitive-behavioural procedure. Fourth, extensive work on self-control clinical interventions contributed to the growth of CBT. While initially self-control procedures used to be conceptualised according to an operant model emphasizing the role of external factors, gradually the role of internal factors came to be recognized as important ingredient of self-control such as self-monitoring, self-evaluation, self-reinforcement etc. Bandura developed the concept of reciprocal determinism which maintains that the individual (one's cognitive process) and the environment reciprocally affect each other. Reciprocal determinism is the major component of CBT. Self-control is conceptualised as more cognitive in nature and most cognitive-behavioural intervention studies in children are actually conducted under the rubric of self-control (Kanfer & Karoly, 1982). Finally, cognitive therapy, which independently developed in the adult clinical settings rather than in laboratory settings, viewed external maladaptive behaviours as caused by maladaptive cognitive processes and hence it involved modification of cognitive processes. Beck (1976) and Ellis and Grieger (1977) maintained that behavioural disturbances occur because individuals engage in maladaptive cognitions such as inappropriate, irrational and illogical self-statements which are reflections of their assumptions and beliefs about themselves and the world. In fact, Beck's cognitive therapy has been a major factor in the development of CBT.

Behavioural events do not occur in isolation. Rather, behaviours are inextricably a part of the sequence of multiple events. Cognitive structures such as beliefs, schema and attributional styles are more organized features of cognition that develop after multiple behavioural events. A cognitive-behavioural model is, therefore, concerned with cognitive activities that surround behavioural events and seek to determine how anticipatory, concurrent, and post-hoc cognitions contribute to adaptive and maladaptive patterns of behaviours (Kendall, 1985; Kendall & Panichelli, 1995).

Common Features of CBT

Although the label of CBT intervention has been applied to a number of somewhat loosely related methods and procedures, the approach does have some common and distinctive key procedural attributes. CBT implies that children act in some ways as their own therapists or trainers and can be taught to employ self-mediated cognitive strategies (through self-guidance, self-verbalisation, self-instruction, self-monitoring, self-recording, self-reinforcement etc.) that exemplify a general strategy for controlling behaviour under various circumstances. For instance, the child may be trained to delay impulsive responding by scanning each object in the stimulus array on a match-to-sample task, to improve academic performance by slowly thinking through the cognitive responses requisite for correct performance on an arithmetic problem, or to decrease aggression by examining alternative patterns of responding during a frustrating situation.

Verbalisation (both overt and covert) is a typical component of training. Self-verbalisations that refer to appropriate forms of behaviour are presented to the child who is taught to actively rehearse such statements for use in problem-situations. CBT often involves the identification of a series of problem-solving steps (i.e., strategy) through which children proceed in order to solve a problem. In certain cases, the steps are abstracted to a very general level so that they may be construed as a plan of attack for virtually any task. In other cases, the steps are designed to be used with a particular type of problem or task. Further, modelling which has been used as a primary means of instruction involves exposing a child to a live or symbolic model who exemplifies the controlling strategy (cognitive modelling). Identification of cognitive absences and teaching the cognitive skills constitute an essential ingredient of CBT. Hence, therapy procedures essentially maintain an emphasis on the teaching of thinking processes and highlight the importance of an integrated behavioural system of contingencies to facilitate learning and maintenance of behaviour change (Kendall, 1985).

A Typical CBT Model

A typical CBT Model that has been successfully applied in case of children is patterned after the work of Meichenbaum and Genest (1980) and Kendall (1985, 1991) known as Verbal Self-instructional Training. Typical Verbal Self-Instructions (VSI) that are taught to children are designed to break down the process of problem-solving into several discrete steps. Each self-instruction represents one step of solving a problem. The content of the self-instructions modelled by the trainer/therapist and rehearsed by the child includes five types of statements. These statements proceed from the generation of a problem definition to stating the problem approach focussing on attention, and self-rewarding of correct responses. Coping statements are built in for use after an incorrect answer so as to facilitate the inhibition of a disturbing outburst. The coping statements generally avoid overly negative self-statements such as "that was dumb" or "I am dumb" and do encourage comparatively neutral statements about the error such as "I made a mistake, I will try again". In the sequence of self-instructions, the therapist and the child take turns completing tasks, each using the self-instructions. One of the goals of therapy is for the child to internalise the self-statements so that he or she is able to use them to think slowly through potential solutions to problems outside therapy. The use of self-instructions both by the therapist and child fades from overt (loud) through a whispering phase, and finally to covert (silent) speech. In order to help the child learn the self statements, a cue card is often employed. For example, a cue card might state "stop, look, listen and think" before responding. It can also be a list of the different self-statements that must be remembered. The therapist and the child work together in making the cue card and the child can put the self-instructions in her or his own words as long as the meaning of the self-statements is maintained.

Promises of CBT

The CBT programme seems to hold several inherent merits. Since CBT fosters self-control in thought patterns and behaviours that children learn through verbal mediation, the children become less dependent upon sources of outside environmental control. Since the locus of control is implanted within the child, it is expected that the treatment effects should be maintained and generalized to other problem situations and provide a source of natural nurturance. Self-instruction training has also the potency to enhance general coping skills in a wide variety of contexts. The CBT has been found to be a form of "cognitive prosthesis" which could be employed to help overcome inadequate performance by fostering a kind of thinking which children could not or would not, otherwise, be capable of. Verbalisations help the children in evaluating feedback by providing verbal mediators to distinguish relevant from irrelevant dimensions of the problems. The CBT promotes an interactive relationship between behaviour change and cognitive change in such a way that change in one domain facilitates change in the other. For example, behaviour change may induce a number of cognitive changes including increased feelings of competency, self-control and self-efficacy. It is a very flexible treatment method which can be tailored to different training tasks and to different verbal styles as per the needs of the individual child, because the content and sequence of the treatment procedure are independent of the tasks used in the treatment (Kendall, 1985, 1993).

Research Evaluation

The efficacy of CBT intervention has been empirically demonstrated in a variety of childhood disorders and problems. A major problem in schools is the high incidence of hyperactivity, impulsivity, and aggression among children. Studies have employed self-instructional training in order to evaluate the efficacy of the CBT programme on impulsive and low-self controlled preschoolers and primary grade children, particularly coming from low middle class and socio-economically disadvantaged groups. In general, the results of these studies indicated that the treatment groups significantly improved on a variety of outcome measures compared to the control groups of children (Arnold & Forhand, 1978; Kendall & Finch, 1979; Kendall & Wilcox, 1980; Kendall & Braswell, 1993).

A few researchers utilised the CBT intervention strategy to combat hyperactivity and aggressive behaviour in school children. Self-instructional training using problem-solving skills has decreased children's aggression as rated by parents and teachers (Kazdin, *et al.*, 1987). In a subsequent study Kazdin, *et al.* (1989) also reported positive results of CBT with antisocial children. Lochman, White and Wayland (1991) showed that when children were taught to self-monitor and observe situations in which they or others were angry, and to recognize how they react to anger and so on, their frequency and magnitude of anger depleted as a result of self-talk. Burte and Burte (1994) demonstrated that mediation alone cannot modify or correct attention deficit hyperactivity disorder (ADHD) and argued for cognitive therapy focussing on parent training counselling in addition to self-instructional training with children. Lochman and Lenhart (1993) emphasized the role of CBT for anger-coping-intervention for aggressive children. Davis and Boster (1993) demonstrated the efficacy of CBT intervention in management of aggressive and resistant youth. Research shows that aggressive children suffer from both cognitive distortions and cognitive deficiencies (Kendall & MacDonald, 1993) and hence CBT interventions have been shown to be a promising treatment programme for aggressive children (Kazdin, 1987).

The CBT intervention with over anxious children reduced children's anxiety level as evidenced in parent reports, independent clinician ratings and child self-reports. Kendall (1994) documented the efficacy of CBT intervention (16 to 20 individual CBT sessions) with diagnosed cases of anxiety disorder in youth. In terms of clinical significance, many treated individuals were found to be without diagnosis (at post-test and follow up) and to be within normal limits on several measures. Stark, Rouse and Livingston (1991) used CBT intervention which included behavioural training in social skills, activity scheduling, relaxation and assignments to be completed at home. Since depressive children lack motivation, self-evaluation, rewards provided an incentive for them to work to change. Cognitive modelling and problem solving provided an opportunity to generate alternative solutions and overcome sense of hopelessness. Cognitive restructuring was used to modify children's distorted thinking, assumptions and perceptions.

Manning (1990) reported the positive impact of cognitive self-instruction programme upon a fourth grade student exhibiting poor self-management skills (i.e., inability to focus attention, follow through and finish academic assignments). Loera and Meichenbaum (1993) demonstrated that the use of scaffolded instruction and self-instructional training helped deaf students to develop meta-cognitive and self-regulatory skills needed to become self-directive and more capable of managing problems in school and at work. Vahn (1988) used cognitive and behavioural training paradigm to develop social skills, cognitive restructuring, coping skills and anxiety management. Agran, Fodor and Moore (1986) investigated the effects of self-instructional training package on the job task sequencing. Findings indicated that training increased job task sequencing. Target behaviours were maintained upto 3 months and supported the use of CBT in vocational training. CBT programmes have also been found to be useful in improving targeted classroom behaviour (Corno, 1987), enhancing arithmetic skill (Leon & Pepe, 1983), promoting a child's tolerance for resisting temptation (Mahoney & Nezworski, 1985) and decreasing disruptive and non-productive classroom behaviour (Dulcan, 1986). Mahn and Greenwood (1990) showed that CBT intervention has the potential for enhancing application of academic skills through increased skill in problem definition, strategy selection and the development of planned behaviour in first graders. Studies have shown that CBT can improve children's performance in spelling accuracy (Kapadia & Fantuzzo, 1988), hand writing (Kosiewicz *et al.*, 1982), mathematics performance (Wood, Rosenberg & Carran, 1993), and reading skills (Chan, 1991).

CBT with Disadvantaged Children in Indian Context

Since CBT is a multifaceted intervention programme, it is assumed that the programme would be of immense value to the disadvantaged children in remediation of their cognitive distortions and deficiencies and varieties of problem behaviours as well as in improving general motivation, problem-solving behaviour and academic achievement. CBT uses modelling techniques to demonstrate problem-solving — identifying the problem, generating solutions and evaluating the behavioural and emotional outcomes etc. Problem-solving is taught in CBT to reduce cognitive deficiency; goal setting allows children to take personal responsibility for changes in behaviour and contingency based rewards provide reinforcements for the desired behaviours. Cognitive restructuring in CBT is used to modify children's distorted thinking, assumptions and perceptions. In general, CBT intervention does not simply promote one unified way of thinking rather, it provides children with a wide scope and opportunity to broaden their perspectives and to modify their detrimental cognitive, behavioural and affective style.

Rath (1992) examined the efficacy of verbal self-instructional training and operant manipulations of response cost and reward on disadvantaged tribal children. The independent and combined effects of self-instruction and operant behaviour modification procedures were examined on a number of problem-solving and teacher perception measures. The children were randomly assigned to different treatment and control groups. The results revealed that while operant manipulations of response-cost and reward had significant treatment effects on cognitive problem-solving measures similar to those used in the training sessions, the VSI technique was found to foster a general self-control which successfully inhibited impulsive thoughts, actions and hasty problem-solving behaviour and produced significant generalisation or transfer effects to novel task settings and situations. The combined strategy proved to be the most effective intervention. The approach combining verbal self-instruction and operant treatment served to strengthen reflective responding, enhanced motivation, increased self-control and better problem-solving and facilitated transfer and generalisation effects in the disadvantaged tribal Santal children. Rath (1995) further examined the CBT intervention with disadvantaged tribal and non-tribal low achieving school children. The results revealed that while the disadvantaged non-tribal children were very much benefited by the CBT intervention programme on several cognitive problem-solving measures as well as mathematics and language achievement measures, their tribal counterparts did not benefit much from the treatment programme. Further, the treatment effects were maintained for a period of four months, and evidenced clear generalisation effects to a variety of task situations and settings in case of non-tribal disadvantaged children. The author argued that these tribal children came from low quality "mediated learning" homes (Feurestein, 1980) with poor involvement in learning the strategies by themselves. They did not possess minimum required cognitive and meta-cognitive skills to cope with the treatment demands of the cognitive self-instruction regimen which required self-guidance, self-help, self-monitoring metacognitive strategy to plan, organize, direct, reinforce and evaluate one's own independent learning strategies without therapists' help as the training progresses. Hence, there is a need to develop CBT programmes that include parent training at home as collaborators or co-clients with their own children.

Rath (1998) also examined the differential efficacy, maintenance and generalisation effects of verbal self instructional training on reading disabled children. Type of sub-culture (Tribal vs. Non-tribal) was crossed with type of cognitive stage (concrete vs. formal operation) to produce four training groups with 15 subjects per cell. The subjects were trained for 10 weeks and retested for post-test and follow-up data. While VSI training was beneficial to non-tribals and children of formal operational stage, it failed in case of tribals and children of concrete operational stage. VSI effects were maintained over four months time and evidenced clear generalisation effects. The significance of child variable or subject variable was clearly demonstrated in their study and hence, VSI training cannot be recommended indiscriminately for all children without examining the individual differences among them.

Unresolved Issues and Concerns of CBT Intervention

Attempts have been made to review and evaluate the efficacy of CBT method. Conclusions have ranged from generally favourable (e.g., Kendall & Braswell, 1993; Kazdin, 1982; Powell & Oei 1991) to skeptical (e.g., Craighead, Meyers & Craighead, 1985; Ledwidge, 1979) to findings of serious, methodological and conceptual problems (i.e., Mahoney & Nezworski, 1985; Dush, Hirt & Schroeder 1989). The question of measurement of treatment outcomes in general continues to receive active attention. What is the objective method of evaluating the exact mediational role of self instruction? How can one assess the amount of self instruction used during the covert stage of training? Is it necessary and practical to use overt self instruction for some classes of responses, especially in a classroom situation ? More work is needed to evaluate the relationship between performance on cognitive measures and performance in naturalistic settings. There is a need to show that change on measures of cognitive skills is reflected in changes in measures of ordinary non-test performance in naturalistic situations. The heavy emphasis on laboratory task, self report and teacher report measures be supplemented with more direct measures of actual performance in day-to-day life.

The CBT programme consists of multifaceted intervention techniques including modelling, role playing, imagery, contingency management, overt and covert verbalisations, rehearsal, prompt feedback etc. each of which might produce significant therapeutic effects in its own right. Research efforts be made to determine the relative efficacy of different components included in the CBT.

The other important concern relates to the need to demonstrate durable, generalizable and important changes due to CBT intervention. Clearly, interventions yielding only situation and domain specific effects, which fade rapidly when the treatment is discontinued, are of limited value or consequence.

When researchers have tried to assess the impact of intervention using a wide range of measures, performance improvements have been limited to few psychometric and perceptual motor tasks. Generalisation to academic performance or achievements is rare and generalisation from cognitive task performance to social-adaptive behaviour trends not to be found (Kendall & Morns, 1991; Whalen, Henker & Hinshaw, 1985). The use of direct behavioural observation measures in the home environment and other social environment appear to be essential for an adequate evaluation of the utility of CBT with children.

Moreover many CBT intervention studies are plagued by the absence of adequate data on long term child behaviour change. Only minority of studies present follow-up data, and those that do generally restrict such reports to post-treatment periods of at most 1-2 months. Long term follow-up data are required to establish its durable effects. However, against this scenario of hopelessness, some studies have reported generalisation from training session to teacher rated classroom behaviour but not to parent rated home behaviour (i.e., Kendall & Braswell, 1982). Rath (1992, 1996) reported generalisation effects across different tasks (i.e., reading achievement) as well as across different settings (i.e., teacher ratings of classroom behaviour). In order to foster generalisation it is suggested that parents be involved as collaborators or as co-clients with their children. When significant family members (i.e., parents) are involved, they can provide positive feedback for a child's efforts to change, be encouraged to change their own perceptions of the child, and alter their expectations about the child's behaviour as well (Kendall & Panichelli, 1995). This has special relevance in CBT intervention with disadvantaged children.

The other major concern relates to the individual difference in children, otherwise known as "child variables or subject variables". Children are active moderators of treatment efficacy. Research findings are accumulating to suggest that the child's age, his/her maturity and adequacy of cognitive and language skill, attributional style, personality type, culture and sub-cultural affiliation may very well influence the outcome of CBT programme. Thus, both the nature of the CBT programme and the characteristics of the children should be considered and examined before tailoring or designing appropriate CBT for administration on children (Dush, *et al.*, 1989; Rath, 1995).

Another important concern relates to the procedures and content of the training itself which affect outcomes. Issues like nature, number and breadth of training tasks, the appropriate CBT procedures to be utilised, frequency and duration of training sessions are of vital concern in order to achieve positive results from CBT intervention. CBT programmes differ markedly on the above parameters and thus such parameters are important determinants of programme success.

In summary, although the potential merits of CBT hold a greater promise for remediation of varieties of childhood problems of the disadvantaged, there remains a wide gap between theoretical expectation and practical achievement in terms of actual research and training. The CBT intervention reveals failure of replication in some cases, a limited number of examples of the maintenance of training effects and inconsistent evidence in respect of training generalisation. Further research is needed in these directions to make CBT programme an effective training procedure to combat problems of disadvantaged children.

13

Intervention for Cognitive Development of Disadvantaged Children

R.C. MISHRA AND APARNA VAJPAYEE

During the last two decades, psychologists and educationists have shown a major concern with the study of the problems faced by children of scheduled castes (SC) and scheduled tribes (ST) considering them primarily as "disadvantaged". Research indicates that these children perform poorly on cognitive tasks, show learning difficulties as well as progressive achievement deficits in schools and finally stagnate and drop out.

Early studies (e.g., Das & Singha, 1975) demonstrated that deficiencies in the socio-cultural milieu of SCs were so deeply rooted that ensuring their homogeneity in terms of economic background was not enough to ensure their cognitive performance. Since then, efforts have been made towards more systematic and programmatic studies (Mishra, 1976; Misra & Tripathi, 1980; Sinha, 1977). While in some studies caste has been directly used as a variable, in others, the focus has been on the identification of deprivational variables associated with caste (e.g., Misra & Tripathi, 1980). It has been argued that the effect of caste on performance of various cognitive tasks can be evaluated only by analysing different kinds of deprivation.

The programmatic studies have tried to analyze the environment of children of different caste groups. Extending Bronfenbrenner's (1977) work, Sinha (1977, 1982b) has proposed an ecological model to comprehend the environment of the SC and non-SC children in Indian setting (see Sinha's contribution to this volume, for a discussion of his model).

In comparisons of the SC and non-SC children, Sinha (1982b) has presented a contrast between them at both the levels of ecology. His studies on the development of perceptual skills among SC, ST and non-SC children lend support to the ecological model. Later studies have widely used this model directly or indirectly as a guide for research on the relationship between socio-cultural variables and cognitive functioning.

Since caste and tribe constitute sociological variables, their usefulness for study in psychological research has often been questioned. Yet several studies related to the impact of caste on cognitive processes have been carried out. The literature clearly indicates the differences in cognitive performance of caste groups to be associated with the demands of cognitive processing (Das & Khurana, 1988).

With the assumption that a variety of differences (e.g., experiential, motivational, nutritional) may be associated with SC and non-SC groups, researchers have utilized a wide variety of psychological measures in comparison between the SC and non-SC children. A major conclusion of these studies is that the performance of SC children suffers particularly on tasks which require mediational processes. Explanation for poor performance of SC children has been given in terms of experiential deprivation suffered by them.

Intervention for Facilitating Cognitive Functioning

The findings mentioned above have generated considerable hope among psychologists, regarding the utility of their research for human welfare. Many of them have tried to develop intervention programmes for overcoming the performance difference of SC and non-SC children. Improvement in socio-economic conditions and educational status of the children of SC groups has been a major agenda of the Central and State governments. On the other hand, development of intervention programmes, such as of education and training, to ensure optimal performance of these children in test situations as well as in school settings has been a major agenda of discussion among social and educational scientists.

These deliberations have resulted into two kinds of propositions for changes in the context of SC groups. One, called structural change, focuses on changes in social, economic, occupational and educational structures of the SC groups (Singh, 1983). However, a number of difficulties associated with structural changes have led many psychologists to suggest that the solution of the problems of SC children needs to be searched out within their existing circumstances. They advocate the programmes of behavioural change which require the delivery of certain "arranged" kind of experiences and training. The suggestion appears to be useful in view of the fact that psychologists can have no direct influence on structural level changes. There is also evidence to suggest that attempts made in the direction of structural changes among groups lead to conflict and disharmony with other groups present in the social arena (Mishra & Sinha, 1991). These situations also favour the programmes of behavioural change.

Studies which emphasize behavioural changes are generally grouped as "intervention studies". They focus on the processes through which deleterious effects of socio-cultural deprivations or disadvantages on SC children's performance on psychological tests or in school settings could be overcome. Attempts are made to break the cycle of deprivation by enhancing children's experiences during the course of their development and thereby shift the direction of development from anticipated negative to positive outcomes (Sigel, 1990).

Children considered as socio-culturally deprived have often been characterized by low achievement motivation, low level of aspiration, low self-concept and poor orientation to learning. Experiential impoverishment (Misra & Tripathi, 1980), deficient environment (Mishra, 1976, 1982; Sinha, 1977, 1982a), poor socialization (Sinha, 1982b), cultural limitations (Mishra, 1996) and economic constraints (Zafar

& Alam, 1986) have been identified as factors influencing the performance of SC children on cognitive tests/tasks. Immediate application of intervention programme has been considered to be important to ameliorate the ill-effects of these factors. Studies involving intervention have usually shown significant gain in I.Q. scores suggesting that they have world-wide significance (Mayers & Hertenberg, 1987).

In India, Dash and Rath (1986) studied the effect of cognitive stimulation on disadvantaged and non-disadvantaged preschool children. Training on a number of cognitive tasks showed considerable improvement in the scores on other cognitive tests. The performance of both the schooled non-disadvantaged and the non-schooled disadvantaged children showed significant improvement with training, but the rate of improvement was greater in the case of non-schooled disadvantaged group. Children with formal preschool experiences perform better than those without such experiences (Jachuck & Chatterjee, 1989).

The programmes appear to be more effective where the parents are illiterate or less educated and where the home environment provides inadequate cognitive stimulation. Kagitcibasi, Sunar and Beckman (1989) have demonstrated greater impact of enrichment programme with the involvement of parents.

Mishra (1990a) reported that training increased the performance of both deprived and privileged groups, the performance of low caste children after training became more or less similar to that of the high caste children on some tasks, and the effect of training was stable in both the groups over a period of three months. Vashist (1990) developed a stimulation programme for the development of mentally retarded infants. Findings indicated that almost 90 percent of infants showed improvement in performance over three testing sessions, there was more improvement in areas of mental development, parents showed a sequential shift in the stage of acceptance, and almost 70 percent parents reached the stage of acceptance of infants' situation.

Kaul (1991) noted a significant difference between

children of high and low language stimulating homes. Nandurbarker (1991) tried out a stimulation programme which indicated progress of infants in motor as well as mental areas. He found development in all areas of mentally retarded children. A greater gain was observed in manipulative social skills. With parental understanding of child's mood and parental participation, infants showed improvement in social and language skills.

Padhy (1992) reported a stronger association between intervention and cognitive skills. Her study showed not only significant improvement in performance as a result of intervention, but also better integration over the testing sessions. The intervention effects were found to persist up to a period of six months after training. Baksi (1993) developed and implemented an infant stimulation programme for mothers through Anganwadi workers. Effective raising and better mental development of infants was noted with mother's stimulation. Beneficial effect of training has also been demonstrated by other kinds of organized programmes. Das (1993) noted that with increase in practice, the gap between high and low achievers' performance on all the tasks disappeared.

The studies reviewed above reveal that performance differences are largely reduced or levelled off if children of deprived background are given proper opportunity of schooling and exposure to training with appropriate perceptual-cognitive experiences. Such intervention programmes (Bharatraj, Bhawani & Vidyasagar, 1983; Das, 1993; Mishra, 1990a; Patnaik & Rath, 1982; Rath & Patnaik, 1979) have shown considerable improvement in perceptual, cognitive and intellectual performance of children. Short-term evaluation of their effects have particularly shown remarkable gains on the part of children. Mishra (1990a) found about 23 per cent increase in the score of deprived children on the SPEFT (Sinha, 1984b) after four weeks of exposure to pictures and training for task performance, using Kohs' Block Design Test and the IAEFT (Sinha, 1984). The persistence of findings has not been assessed systematically.

Studies examining the effect of training on deprived

children's performance still suffer from a number of weaknesses : (i) There is little comparative research in this area. In most of the studies the focus is on the gain of deprived children alone. (ii) In those studies in which deprived children have been compared with non-deprived, the subjects have not been matched for their socio-economic background. (iii) There has been less effort to monitor or evaluate the effect of different levels of training in terms of immediate and long-term gains. (iv) The maintenance effect has also not been assessed over different intervals of time (from short-term to long-term). (v) The effect of training, either short-term or long-term, has also not been assessed for children of different age levels. (vi) Lastly, the contribution of test sophistication, which may occur with experiential differences of groups, has also not been assessed.

Against this backdrop, the effect of three levels of training on immediate and long-term improvement in children's cognitive task was explored. It was hypothesized that the performance of high caste children on perceptual-cognitive tasks would be better than those of low caste children prior to training; training with perceptual and cognitive tasks would level off the performance differences of high and low caste children; children having longer duration of training would perform better on perceptual and cognitive tasks than those getting exposure to a shorter duration of training; and the positive effect of training would be maintained over a longer interval of time to the same extent in the high as well as low caste children.

The performance of 120 high and low caste children on some perceptual and cognitive tasks was compared at four different time points: (a) prior to training, (b) soon after training, (c) one month after training, and (d) six months after training. Thus, a before-after design was used in the study. The training schedule varied from (a) half an hour per week for two weeks to (b) half an hour per week for four weeks to (c) half an hour per week for eight weeks.

The sample comprised of 8-9 years old primary school

children drawn from some villages of Varanasi. The effect of training on this age group was studied because it is around this age that maximum differences between the performance of high and low caste or deprived and non-deprived children have been reported (Shukla, 1991; Tripathi, 1991).

Children of the two castes were matched on SES. Based on two levels of caste and three levels of training, six groups of children were studied. Some criterion and training tests/tasks were given to children. The criterion tests included : Story-Pictorial Embedded Figures Test (Sinha, 1984b), Picture Model Matching Task (Mishra & Sinha, 1991), Sequence Perception Test (Sinha, 1977), and Picture Interpretation Test (Sinha, 1977). Training tasks included Indo-African Embedded Figures Test (Sinha, 1984b), Block Designs Test (Kohs, 1923), Picture Comprehension Task (Mishra, 1976), and Object Perception and Classification Task (Vajpayee, 1995).

The analyses generally revealed that the performance of high caste children on various tasks was better than those of the low caste prior to training, but the difference in performance of the two groups was largely levelled off after training. Children having longer duration of training performed better than those having shorter duration of training. The positive effect of training was evident not only soon after training, but also up to a period of six months, showing a kind of "maintenance effect" of training. Such an effect was observed almost with all levels of training and for both the caste groups.

SOME KEY ISSUES IN INTERVENTION STUDIES

The findings of the study have brought out certain key issues pertaining to intervention studies. In the following section, these issues are discussed in some detail, along with their implications.

Caste as a Variable

Caste exists as a living social reality in India. Although

its roots lie far back in the history of Indian society, the concern with caste has perhaps never been as pervasive as during the last few decades. As we have noted earlier, there is a wide-spread belief that low caste status is associated with a lower level of development of psychological qualities and cognitive abilities which are essential for effective participation in the wider national life. The policy of reservation based on caste has basically echoed this spirit. Many new ramifications have been in evidence with the caste-based reservation policy during the last few years.

Researchers having interest in caste variable have identified a number of characteristics of individuals' life which tend to be associated with caste. For example, Ghurye (1961) had reported that endogamy, hierarchy, restrictions on community relations, restrictions on choice of occupation, civil and religious privileges, disadvantages and untouchability are the traditional features of caste in India. This conceptualization specifies certain differences among individuals of different castes evident in the structure of authority patterns, interpersonal relationships and existence of certain limitations on experiences of the wider cultural life. Psychological studies using caste as a variable have largely focused on these dimensions.

Psychological research associated with caste variable indicates two major trends. One is represented in studies in which caste has been directly used as a variable with the assumption that it is strongly associated with experiential differences of individuals, resulting at both physical and socio-cultural levels (Mishra, 1976; Rath, Dash & Dash, 1979; Sinha, 1977). This trend has been very wide-spread in research. Later studies (e.g., Misra & Tripathi, 1980; Mishra, 1990b) and reformulations (Misra, 1990) have indicated that experiential deprivation is a major factor producing differences in psychological performance of the SC and non-SC children not only in the test situation, but also in more practical situations.

Das and Khurana (1988) have questioned the legitimacy of caste as a psychological variable. They strongly feel that by its nature, caste is a sociological variable. They argue that in order to justify its existence as a psychological variable, we need to analyze the history of experiences in which we are really interested while comparing low *vs.* high caste performance. It is indicated that factors largely underlying the caste variable are environmental, such as physical factors associated with poverty, quality of education, parental expectation regarding the child's educational achievement, malnutrition, childhood diseases, etc. These may be differentially associated with high and low caste belongingness. Such variables have been frequently used in research on cognitive competence. The extent to which they can be reliably associated with a particular caste, they can justify the use of caste as a variable in studies of cognitive competence.

Research dealing with the relationship between caste and cognitive performance clearly suggests that cognitive deficiencies of the low caste groups have no genetic basis. Even if it is assumed that *Brahmans* and *Harijans* have retained their distinct genetic pool (Das & Singha, 1975), it is difficult to prove differences in their innate abilities (Das & Khurana, 1988). On the other hand, studies generally suggest little or no differences between the cognitive performance of children of high and low caste groups in the early years. The differences tend to become evident somewhere around the age of 8 or 9 years. Beyond that, we have two kinds of evidence. One suggests that differences between the two caste groups becomes greater, representing a phenomenon called "cumulative deficit" for the low class children (Whiteman & Deutsch, 1968), or "broomstick effect" for the SC children (Sinha, 1977). Another suggests that differences between cognitive performance of the two caste groups are levelled off around the age of 12 or 13 (Shukla, 1991; Tripathi, 1991). These formulations clearly refute the notion of genetic or inborn differences between low and high caste groups. On the other hand, we can think of certain biological factors (associated with pervasive malnutrition and childhood diseases) and experiential factors which are largely associated with the conditions of poverty and deprivation underlying the differences between the two groups.

Thus, in debates on the development of cognitive competence among low and high caste children, the balance seems to be tilted to the side of experiential factors. Physical factors (e.g., availability of toys, books and other cultural artifacts) stimulate the child to engage in certain activities which lead to the emergence of various cognitive structures. Piagetian theory considers children's experiences with objects and resultant activities to be of vital importance to cognitive development. Cultural artifacts, such as toys, pictures, etc. are regarded as "cultural amplifiers" (Berland, 1988; Cole, 1992) of cognitive development. The extent to which a culture can provide for such experiences, it can determine the level of development achieved by children in the cognitive domain.

The importance of human interaction in the acquisition and development of cognitive abilities has been greatly emphasized in the socio-cultural theory of cognitive development proposed by Vygotsky (1978) and extended by Cole (1990) and Rogoff (1990). This theory places great emphasis on culturally mediated practical activities and brings out the importance of children's interaction with adults in situations of guided participation. Rogoff (1990) argues that a kind of "apprenticeship" is required to master the cognitive skills. The importance of interactional factors has been empirically demonstrated in several studies of cognitive development with children of different socio-cultural groups (Mishra, 1996; Misra, 1990; Tripathi, 1991).

The difference in performance of high and low caste children can be interpreted in the context of these theoretical views and empirical evidence. The findings of present study demonstrate that the performance of low caste children was significantly lower than those of the high caste group almost on all the criterion measures prior to their exposure to the training programme. Since the children of both the groups were matched in terms of their SES, the differences in their performance cannot be attributed simply to experiences associated with economic factors. We feel that the experiential inputs which the low caste children received in their environment and the nature and quality of interactions that took place between these children and their parents, peers and other adult members of the community were largely responsible for their low level performance.

The Effect of Training

For a long time psychologists have been dealing with the effect of practice or training on individuals' later performance. Various theories of transfer basically deal with these effects. Experience and learning opportunities are important factors in the performance of cognitive tasks (e.g., Rogoff, 1990). The question may be asked about the mechanisms through which training brings about change in individuals' performance. Familiarity with test contents and operations (which often increase with training) have been hypothesized as one set of factors, called "non-test factors in test performance". Irvine (1983) indicates a positive evidence in support of their effect on test performance. The effects appear to be more pervasive on the performance of people of the Third World countries than those of the Western hemisphere. In the latter, factors like race, ethnicity and social class have been found to be more significant predictors of performance than training or education.

Irvine (1983) has also drawn attention to the problems associated with inferences drawn from the above-mentioned set of variables. It is easy to establish a direct linkage between training and test performance, because it requires a smaller leap. He calls it a "high level inference" variable. On the other hand, it is difficult to establish a direct linkage between caste, class, ethnicity and test performance. It requires a larger leap in terms of postulating mediating mechanisms. Hence, they are referred to as "low level inference" variables (Irvine, 1983).

The present findings suggest that the mechanisms of caste influencing test performance are largely those related to experience and training. As long as children were not exposed to training, caste differences in performance were quite significant. The same differences were reduced to a nonsignificant level when the low caste children were given training with various cognitive tasks.

At this stage, we may ask, "What kind of effect does training produce within individuals which results in better performance?" There are two contrasting viewpoints on this issue. Some researchers indicate that training produces "superficial effects", which are confined only to the level of performance (Cole, 1990; Lave, 1977; Rogoff, 1981; Scribner & Cole, 1973). Such effects have been interpreted as resulting from "test sophistication" or "test acculturation" (Berry *et al.*, 1986; Mishra, Sinha & Berry, 1996). It is argued that as a result of participation in testing programmes, an individual develops the habit of test taking. Thus, one feels more easy and comfortable in test situations. These states tend to increase test performance of individuals without any evidence for real change in their cognitive competence or ability. The other viewpoint suggest that training produces certain "real effects". It is argued that training brings about changes in the cognitive structure of individuals so much so that a trained person operates on tests differently by using strategies, plans of actions, and reasoning which are different from those of a non-trained person.

While these viewpoints still prevail, research evidence seems to be more in favour of "test sophistication" than "real change" in cognitive structures (Berry *et al.*, 1986). Since most of the studies focusing on the effect of training or exposure have generally looked for short-term effects, it is really difficult to claim any "real change" in cognitive capacity of individuals. The findings of our study with regard to maintenance of training effect generally suggest improvement in performance with training which does not show any major loss over a period of six months. To suggest a real effect, a longitudinal study pursued over a relatively longer period of time would be required.

Issues Related to Intervention

During the last one decade, psychologists all over the world have shown concern with the development of Third World nations. While development of physical resources has represented a major element in these programmes, development of human resource has been considered most important for achieving the goal of national development. The Third World countries have this resource in "surplus", and its proper utilization can greatly contribute to their overall progress.

With this basic idea in mind, a number of intervention programmes have been developed to bring about changes in the life of people in several parts of the world. They have appeared to be effective means of changing individuals' present state of affairs into a desirable future state. While most of these programmes have been rooted in economic, educational and health spheres of life, psychological concerns have been strongly represented among them in more recent years.

An analysis of these programmes would suggest that they have been largely designed for weaker sections of the society. There have been numerous criticisms of the "policy of reservation" by those engaged in intervention research. It is argued that a reservation policy devoid of time-frame generates a tendency of "look to others", a feeling of dependency, and reduced vigour to compete with others at the individual level, and for generating a variety of conflicts at the societal and national levels under the slogan of "distributive justice" (Eldering & Vedder, 1993).

In the Indian setting, Integrated Child Development Scheme (ICDS) has represented one of the most important programmes focused on mother child-health and preparation of children for school education. On the other hand, the national government's 1992 Plan of Action on Early Childhood Care and Education focuses on a wider range of dimensions of development that induce the notion of comprehension repertoire extension and role change.

Other programmes,, such as Success For All (SFA) (Slavin & Madden, 1993), Turkish Early Enhancement Programme (TEEP) (Kagitcibasi, 1993) and Home Intervention for Pre-Primary Youngsters (HIPPY) (Eldering & Vedder, 1993) developed in other parts of the world have brought out a number of psychological dimensions which may influence cognitive development of children. These programmes assert that it is the functional isolation of children from others in the community that affects their cognitive development. Thus, as long as a programme can generate participation of a child into the activities of a larger community by some psychological support extended over a definite period of time, it can ensure an optimum development of children of the deprived communities. Poortinga (1993) has argued that the intervention programmes have provided us with certain universal principles. What we need to do is to attempt a "cultural tailoring" of these programmes according to the local needs of people.

The present study suggests that through participation even in a short duration training programme, the children of the lower caste group were elevated to the level of those of the high caste in terms of their performance on criterion tests. A training programme with a long-term goal in mind and carried out with a precise set of tasks is likely to bring about more fruitful outcome than what we have been able to demonstrate in this study.

A number of critical issues have been raised with regard to the evaluation of the impact of intervention programmes. While the nature of programme in itself is a major issue of discussion, particularly from the point of view of its content (independent variable), defining and measuring the effects of intervention (dependent variable) has been an issue of equal importance. With regard to the first issue, there is some evidence to suggest that even programmes that have not been well implemented (Slavenburg, 1993), and programmes in which people have not directly participated (Dubey, Mishra & Pandey, 1987) have also resulted in positive effects. Such a situation does not permit the researcher to draw a causal inference about the effects of intervention on the basis of the programme. With regard to the second issue (i.e., the effect), we note that one can focus on short-term effect, or long-term effect, or both. While theoretically, there would be no need to examine the long-term effect if the condition for short-term effect has not been fulfilled, empirical studies provide us with a different picture. Despite showing failure at the short-term level, some intervention programmes have shown positive effects in the long-term. One way to reconcile such anomaly is to state the effects in personal terms (i.e., test scores, school success), or in social terms (e.g., reduced inequality in test performance or competence of two different groups). It has been shown that short-term effects are more evident at the individual level, whereas long-term effects are generally found at the societal level (Eldering & Liseman, 1993).

Policy Implications

Researchers interested in evaluation of intervention programmes have pointed out that policy makers generally seem to be interested in evaluation with a short-term agenda (Husen, 1990; Sinha & Mishra, 1993). There is hardly any funding for a long-term programme of evaluation. There is also greater interest in positive effects of the programme than in negative effects. In fact, reporting negative consequences of any intervention programme creates embarrassment not only to the designer of the programmes, but also to its evaluator. Review of evaluation studies suggests that no programme is complete in its totality (Eldering, 1991; Farren, 1990). Hence, it is difficult to use any one of them in policy. There is still need to develop, evaluate and review the prototypical programmes to make them effective for the communities. This cycle must be repeated until a successful programme is obtained, which can fulfil the expectations of both the designer of the programme and the people for whom it was designed. This involves a lot of time, money and commitment on the part of researcher. However, in view of their predicted effectiveness, one has to bear with these constraints. Evidence suggests that to invent a useful vaccine in medical sciences, more than 20 years have been spent. Our problems (e.g., educational equality) are more complex than those addressed in medical sciences. Therefore, psychologists have to abandon their hasty attitude to search out effective solutions to their problems.

The findings of our study have certain policy implications. The demonstrated enhancement in children's cognitive performance as a result of training suggests that such training programmes may be used as valuable tools for teaching children certain strategies which can contribute to their cognitive growth. The findings also suggest that a longer duration of training is more effective than a shorter duration in bringing about both immediate and long-term changes in performance. In planning and implementing an intervention programme it is necessary to monitor the programme over an extended period of time. This is usually more fruitful in generating stable changes in performance and contributing to the development of cognitive competence of disadvantaged children.

14

Poverty, Development and Disability : Some Lessons from a Community Based Intervention Programme

AJIT K. DALAL

Many sample surveys conducted in recent years to map physical disability in India have shown two characteristic patterns. One, physical disability is much more prevalent in lower socio-economic class than in middle and upper middle class. For example, the prevalence of childhood blindness in the population below poverty line is four times more than in the population above poverty line (Sen, 1988). Second, as revealed in National Sample Survey (1982), more than 50% of the India's population with disabilities is below the age of 18 years. The same pattern was observed after a decade in the second survey (NSS, 1991). Disability is thus a childhood problem in India. In contrast, the prevalence of disability is found to be higher in the older age group in developed countries (e.g., 46% in 65 plus age group in Canada, The Daily Activity Survey in Canada, 1992).

The unfortunate part is that 80 to 85% of the childhood disability is preventable through proper hygiene, nutrition, immunization, education, timely detection and treatment, These are the poor children in rural sector who suffer most because of the lack of health care facilities, sanitary conditions, malnutrition of mother and infant, Vitamin A and iodine deficiency, superstitions, etc. The families which are living at subsistence level very often have no resources to provide necessary health care to their children.

It can, thus, be argued that socio-economic development and disability are closely tied with each other. The success of preventive and rehabilitative measures is largely contingent on the success of community development programmes. The emerging view in this field is that the community based rehabilitation (CBR) programmes need to be conceived as a kind of community development programme in the field of disability. Realizing that disability is largely a disease of poverty, improving the quality of life of people with disability should improve the quality of life of a large disadvantaged section of the community. WHO Report (1991) suggested that 10% of the population suffers from some kind of disability. Taking a conservative estimate that 5% of them are youth and children and that an average Indian family has about 7 members, about 35% of the Indian population is directly or indirectly affected by some kind of disability. Any community based developmental programme targetting at people with disability is going to affect the lives of a very large section of the population.

Consistent with this rationale and philosophy, the Sirathu Project which we are documenting here has primarily focused on improving quality of life of people with disability and their families through community's own efforts. The Sirathu CBR Programme has three distinct features :

(1) The programme was initiated in a planned manner by the local community with its own resources. The programme aimed at greater participation of the people with disability and their families, particularly from the lower socio-economic status.

(2) The main thrust of the programme was to mobilize the resources of the existing socio-religious institutions, developmental schemes, service organizations. The community's primary role is seen as a pressure group to activate the existing programmes and provisions.

(3) To develop a low cost rehabilitation programme which can be self-sustaining on a long-term basis.

It may be appropriate to mention here that some of us from the Psychology Department of Allahabad University are associated with this programme as initiators. In this capacity it was an opportunity for us to work with local people in forming a local NGO (called '*Sambhavana*') and participate in their various activities. The major emphasis has been on psycho-social, educational and vocational rehabilitation. For us it is a social experiment on a limited scale. A preliminary report of the project activities was published earlier (Dalal & Pandey, 1995). Here we are reporting the stages through which this programme has gone since its inception to the present.

THE SIRATHU PROJECT

Project Area

The project area consists of five villages of the Sirathu tahsil, which are located 70 km. from Allahabad city. Around a thousand families live in these villages. This is one of the most backward regions of the Allahabad District. Barring a few high caste families, most of the inhabitants belong to lower castes, are illiterate and work as agricultural labourers. There is only one PHC for about 80 villages. These villages have no telecommunication facilities and are inaccessible in the rainy season. There are few developmental activities mostly undertaken by the government agencies.

Two features of this region are worth noting. These features, in essence, are common to most of the north Indian villages. One is a high degree of caste consciousness. The village community is divided into high, backward and scheduled (low) castes which do not trust each other and compete for the scarce resources. The centuries old dominance of high caste (brahmins and thakurs) is being challenged by the other castes. The issue is much politicized and this emerging caste consciousness is being exploited by the local leaders to build their power base. Two is the prevailing ethos is of dependency on external agencies for rehabilitation. The culture of dependency has build up in the last 40-45 years which is sustained by the practice of 'welfare' camps. In these camps, aids and appliances are freely distributed by government and non-government agencies. Self-reliance is least appealing in this set-up and any initiative to mobilize local resources is viewed with scepticism.

Entry Stage

The overriding consideration in selecting Sirathu to initiate a CBR programme was our personal contacts with some local people who showed keen interest in this endeavour. To explore the possibility of starting a programme we met local people and held meetings. People from all strata, caste and religious groups, including persons with disability, local panchayat members and government officials attended these meetings. There was a good deal of participation in deliberations by social, spiritual and political leaders of the region. Many suggestions were put forward to tap local resources. The response was overwhelming.

At some stage a small group of 6-7 members was formed to develop programme activities and to share responsibilities. These were the people who showed activism, which included one woman and two people with a disability. The block *pramukh* who was an elected representative of 115 villages of Sirathu *tahsil* was chosen to head this group. Incidentally he was an ex-convict but a political heavyweight in the region.

This posed a moral dilemma for many of us associated with the programme. Any community mobilization for CBR with the active support of the block *pramukh* was going to strengthen his power base. It was unpalatable to many that the success of CBR project with him at the helm of the affairs should improve his social image. On the other hand, the vast manpower and material resources at his disposal were important for the success of Sirathu Project. Anyway, his animosity was sure to seal the fate of our initiative. Though we wished him to be a nominal head, he intended to play an active role. This was not a unique situation, as often seen in eastern Uttar Pradesh and Bihar where as many as 60% block *pramukhs* have criminal cases pending against them in courts.

Because of these meetings and the air of expectations they carried accross, the programme generated much interest and enthusiasm in the community. Many people offered their voluntary services. The meetings were well attended. People had the impression that the CBR Project had a large funding. One reason for high expectations was the visit of our three guests from Canada. It created an impression that the present programme is part of a larger International project and a large sum would be available for our local programme.

The rumours about large funding, in effect, became a major menace. It did not matter how hard we tried to clarify that no such money was forthcoming and that we have to rely on our own resources. There was a good deal of suspicion and confusion. When it dawned upon the people that this CBR project had virtually no funding and that they have to venture out to generate funds, many became fence-sitters. The attendance in the meetings started thinning out. We were left with a small group of people. This determined small group of people was the main strength of the programme. Incidentally, the block *pramukh* realizing that our project no longer attracts large crowd lost interest and distanced himself from its activities.

Disability Survey : There were no records in these villages of the people with disability and their families. To fill this gap, an initial survey was conducted with the help of local volunteers. The purpose of this survey was to identify persons (including children) with disability, nature and causes of physical impairment, their special needs, abilities and expectations from the programme. The survey revealed that in these villages there were around 300 families with at least one member with physical disability. The most common causes of disability were post-polio residual paralysis, tuberculosis, blindness due to vitamin A deficiency, malnutrition and mal-union of fractures. More than 80 per cent of the people with disability belonged to the low SES group. A detailed record of 160 persons with disability was prepared.

Mobilization Stage

To salvage the programme, and to sustain interest of the community, the local group decided to initiate the activities which would render immediate benefits without big investment. The Government had many schemes, such as travel concession, scholarships, disability pension, and bank loan for self-employment. We discovered that these facilities were not accessible to the deserving persons due to bureaucratic hassles, corruption and callousness. A disability certificate was needed to avail any of the Government facilities. Only the Chief Medical Officer of the district, or Heads of the departments of the medical college in Allahabad city were authorized to issue disability certificates. For poor villagers it was nearly impossible to procure these certificates. Only 5-6 people in these villages had this certificate.

As our first major activity, three Certificate Camps were organized and we managed to bring the concerned medical officials to the village centre. This measure helped in availing disability certificates to more than 120 people.

This activity brought immediate benefits. For example, persons with disability not only got 75% concession in rail and bus travel, but their accompanying relative or friends were also entitled to the same concession. Many got small loans from banks to start their own business which benefited both people with disability and their families. The success of this venture may not have brought substantial material change in the life conditions of the people but did make people realize benefits of collective action. In many subsequent meetings, government officials, bank managers, medical doctors, and others were invited where community memebers had a dialogue about the implementation of various government schemes. This gave people hope and confidence that community initiated intervention can succeed and make things happen.

Breaking Mental Barriers

Prejudices and negative attitudes are the major barriers in social integration and rehabilitation process. Such prejudices are functional as they explain suffering and justify inaction. People are often seen shaking their heads and questioning 'how can people with disability do anything?'

To bring a shift in thinking and attitudes focus-group meetings were held. The professed objective of such discussions was to identify what people with disability *can do very well* for self-employment if a loan is provided to them for self-employment. The whole exercise was to shift community's mental set from disabilities to abilities, to sensitize them of the special abilities which persons with disability have. Everyone, including the persons concerned and their families were encouraged to join in the discussion. Few selected persons with disability were provided small loans by one other NGO and the local people provided them necessary support for setting up small business.

The goal of this activity was also to create some success models and to inspire others to follow suit. It was our hope that these models would set examples of what people can achieve who were earlier thought incapable of doing anything. This plan was, however, not very successful as we could not muster sufficient financial resources for self-employment scheme. It did open up a public debate about what people with disability can do, rather than what they cannot; a shift in thinking from negative-cynical to positive-constructive direction.

New Initiatives

With all this groundwork and expanding support base, a local NGO named *Sambhavana* (literally, meaning 'possibility') was formally constituted. A local office bearer of *Sambhavana* offered his own house for office space and building for two specific activities of this NGO: an integrated school and a vocational training centre. These two activities were later supported by the Rajiv Gandhi Foundation.

(1) *Opening of an Integrated School* : It was realized for a long time that children with major disabilities had no access to any education in that region. With its own meagre resources, an integrated school was started on 15 August, 1994 with one teacher and 25 children, 15 of whom had some physical disability. The children were imparted basic reading and writing skills and arithmetic. For most of the children with disability this was their first experience of formal schooling. Free transport was arranged for the severely handicapped children. The school did provide a forum for community members to come together, particularly the parents of these school children, to discuss and plan various activities of *Sambhavana*.

In April 1995, the school complex was renovated, essential furniture was procured and one more teacher was appointed. The school though could not get specially trained teachers and teaching aids for the severely disabled. The enrolment went up to 55 children, half of whom had a disability.

(2) *Vocational Training Centre* : Another major milestone was the beginning of a vocational training centre for the school children and their families. Rajiv Gandhi Foundation provided the needed money for this Centre. After long deliberations and market survey the group decided to start two kinds of skill training : incense making and bakery. There was a good local market for these products.

The bakery was rather more successful. Its products started selling and the Centre began churning profit. With the possibility that *Sambhavana* may become self-reliant, greater attention and efforts were divested to run the bakery. The school attendance improved, the families of these children were getting involved in our activities. This income-generating training programme caught the imagination of the village community and their participation was increasing. There were all indications that our CBR programme was becoming a success story.

The Crisis

This success was short-lived. In fact, the very success created new problems. It attracted the attention of those who saw in joining *Sambhavana* an opportunity to expand their power base and share its success. These were influential local people and many were more interested in commercial success of vocational training centre. There were frictions, conflicts and confrontations to influence decision making and programme activities. The priorities were also changing. We observed with dismay during one of our visits that the integrated school was shifted from the main hall to a side room and the bakery was taking over the whole premises. Even training people with disability in bakery business was of secondary importance in running the bakery.

And then a tragedy struck. A key person from our local CBR group and the secretary of *Sambhavana* met a serious road accident and was confined to bed. His absence exacerbated the crisis in the CBR group to the extent that the bakery could no longer operate. The atmosphere was getting vitiated and more energy was going in managing different interest groups than the programme activities. At one stage we had to take this painful decision of suspending all CBR activities. The prevailing opinion was to initiate a debate on how to make Sirathu project community based in real sense and to save it from being taken over by those who have vested interest. Lack of trained CBR worker was our one glaring shortcoming. We decided to send local volunteers for CBR worker's training and try to revive the programme on their return. The International Centre for the Advancement of Community Based Rehabilitation, Queen's University, Canada supported the training of CBR workers. We requested the Rajiv Gandhi Foundation to hold their financial support till the programme again stands on its own. At present we are exploring various possibilities of reviving Sirathu Project. We are inviting suggestions and opinion at all forums. We hope to revive the programme on return of our CBR workers from their six months' training.

A Retrospect

Looking back, despite many constraints and compulsions the Sirathu CBR Project did achieve modest success. It did succeed in creating an environment of hope and expectations that the things can change for better. Our meetings and discussions did arouse the interest of village people in disability issues. The encouraging part was that in all these deliberations and activities people with disability actively participated. The programme had ripple effect in changing many misconceptions and prejudices about 'what people with disability can do'. This change was evident from an increased enrolment of children having physical impairment in different schools of the region. An unintended consequence of this project was about 150 per cent increase in immunization in four years. We cannot however take all the credit for this increase.

The Sirathu Project has thrown up many issues for the protagonists of CBR approach. It is presumptuous that village communities are cohesive and motivated. In reality they are often faction-ridden, with different interest groups operating at cross-purposes. There are undercurrents of suspicion, mistrust and personal rivalries. The success of CBR lay in bringing together diverse groups to work for a common cause. The task is formidable. In reality, CBR programmes are highly vulnerable to local influences. Experience shows that rehabilitation programmes succeed where the local leadership is strong and stand on moral grounds.

Secondly, a major challenge for a CBR programme is to bring attitudinal changes. In a culture where suffering is accepted as *karma*, where people below subsistence level have learnt to be helpless, any talk of CBR is a far cry. We have to engage in a serious thinking about how CBR can work in a community which is oppressed and exploited for centuries. The work for rehabilitation in this milieu cannot be divorced from the larger concerns of socio-economic development. Thirdly, in resource starved underdeveloped villages only a low cost CBR programme is viable. The dictum is self-sustenance rather than self-reliance. It is in this respect that any CBR initiative must aim at tapping vast governmental resources. India is among few countries in the world which has an impressive range of legal and administrative measures to meet health, education, employment and economic needs of people with disability. It is a tragic fact that these welfare schemes remain out of reach of most of the deserving people. Success of the community efforts are to be measured in terms of revival of these defunct schemes. For this, the community has to be prepared to work as a pressure group to claim the benefits for their members with disability and their families.

The concept and practice of CBR has come a long way in India. With the initial euphoria subsiding, we now have a better appreciation of problems and prospects of CBR in action. The vast experience we have accumulated over these years should help us in meeting the challenges unique to Indian social reality. It is crucial for the success of CBR in India that we acknowledge the ground realities and learn from success, as well as, from failure stories.

Lastly, our experience has shown that health and rehabilitation could be very effective entry points for community development work. These are of concern to all sections of the community, irrespective of caste, class, religion, or region. At the same time, these are non-threatening issues in terms of upsetting the social and power hierarchy in the villages. It is relatively easier to ensure community participation for various health and rehabilitation programmes. The tangible success of these programmes can break the cycle of helplessness-poverty, and can potentially become vehicle for other community development programmes.

15

Self-Reliant Development of Disadvantaged Rural People and the Role of Development Professionals

DAMODAR SUAR

The basic philosophy of rural development (RD) is encompassed with the truth of an old saying : "Give a man a fish and feed him for a day, teach him to fish, and feed him for a life-time." The ultimate tests of RD, following the withdrawal of programme implementing agencies, are the rural people's self-reliance, their sustained initiative to improve the quality of life, and to maintain or multiply the given infrastructure and assets. But, many implemented plans and programmes have fallen short of expectations. The percentage of people remaining below the poverty line has declined following the implementation of poverty alleviation programmes. However, this downward slide does not depict the whole picture. As population grows, the absolute number of people remaining below the poverty line increases sharply.

PLANS AND PROGRAMMES

In governmental efforts for RD, during the first five year plan, emphasis was on community development, in the second, cooperative farming and in the third plan, Panchayati Raj model was adopted. In the fourth, the fifth, the sixth and the seventh plans, emphasis was put on area development, minimum needs programme, anti-poverty, wage and self-employment, respectively. When RD had not picked up (Jain, Krishnamurthy, & Tripathy, 1985, pp. 50-105), emphasis was shifted during the eighth plan to renovate Panchayati Raj Institutions for decentralisation of power and local self governance. IMF, World Bank, ODA, UNICEF and other international agencies pumped financial and other resources during the plan periods to further accelerate RD. The NGOs implemented various programmes at the micro level related to adult education, women development, health, agriculture and technology transfer. Also, industries joined as partners. All these plans and programmes can be broadly put under three categories (Figure 15.1).

When the area development programmes — Waste Land Development Programme (WLDP), Drought Prone Area Programme (DPAP), Command Area Development Programme (CADP), etc. — were executed, the emphasis was given on infrastructure development.

The assumptions were that once the area would develop in infrastructure facilities, growth impulses generated in the area would radiate to its hinter land. Thereby, the area and its nearby area would develop economically. In addition, there was another set of target-group programmes — through Tribal Sub-plan (TSP), Small Farmer Development Agency (SFDA), Income Generation Activities for Women (IGAW), etc. — meant for the landless labourers, marginal and small farmers, scheduled castes (SCs), scheduled tribes (STs), and women. Sometime in 1970, the area specific and target-group programmes were clubbed together. The beneficiaries were from rural area and belonged to disadvantaged groups. Such programmes were Integrated Rural Development Programme (IRDP), National Rural Employment Programme (NREP), Training of Rural Youth for Self Employment (TRYSEM), Rural Landless Employment Guarantee Programme (RLEGP), and Jawahar Rojgar Yojana (JRY). In all these programmes, the basic assumption was that by creating the scope for economic activities, people would respond, derive benefits and develop economically.

It was felt that no other investment would yield higher return than the investment in human resources of which

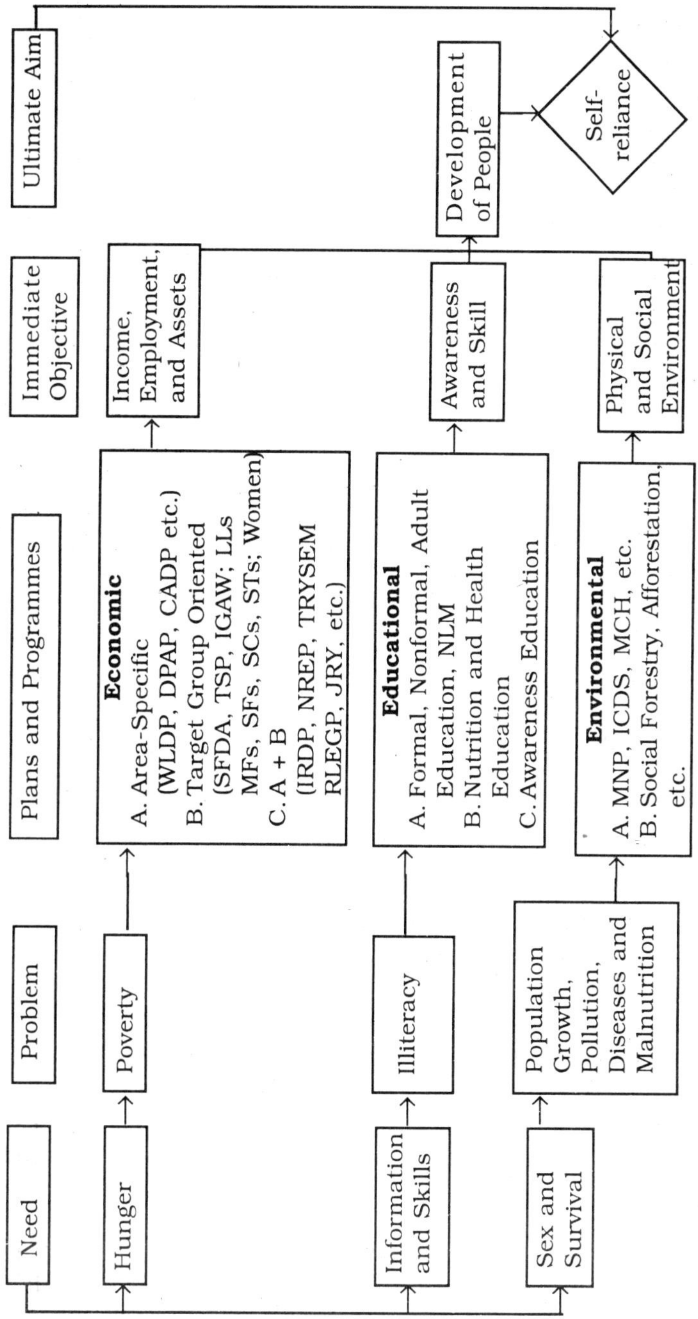

FIGURE 15.1 : *Plans and Programmes for Rural Development*

the most important component was education. Accordingly, formal, nonformal, adult, health awareness and nutrition education programmes, and National Literacy Mission (NLM) were launched. These programmes aimed at the development of awareness and skills to absorb new information and new orientation.

The betterment of weaker women and children, and the development of physical environment were looked into. Accordingly, Minimum Needs Programme (MNP), Integrated Child Development Scheme (ICDS), Maternal and Child Health Programme (MCH), Development of Women and Children in Rural Area (DWCRA), Social Forestry, Afforestation Programme, etc. were introduced to fight against population growth, malnutrition, diseases and pollution.

Many reputed firms like TELCO, TISCO, SAIL, Arvind Mills, CIL, Cadbury India, and others had joined as partners in community development. Their developmental efforts concentrated primarily on assets distribution and infrastructure development to boost up their long-term marketing strategy and to foster a good relationship with the surrounding communities.

In all these programmes, the disadvantaged rural people (DRP) were the poor, illiterates, SCs, STs, women, children, educated unemployeds, physically handicapped, landless labourers, marginal and small farmers. Given the whole gamut of programme inputs, it was anticipated that there would be socio-economic development of the DRP. This would improve the quality of life and would be reflected in their self-reliance.

The following discussion focuses on DRP with reference to the poor, SCs and STs only. The characteristics of DRP will be discussed. Then an attempt will be made to understand how these characteristics are transformed through RD programmes.

CHARACTERISTICS OF DRP

The DRP have different characteristics (Figure 15.2). These have been put under three categories broadly—behavioural, social and economic. These characteristics are also present among others but more prevalent among the DRP—a difference in degree but not in kind. Several other chapters in this volume, contain exhaustive discussion of the research evidence in support of such characterisation. Here, an attempt has been made to put together the recognised characteristics without citing any specific literature as supportive evidences.

Behavioural Characteristics

Dependence Proneness : Dependence proneness is built up in our authoritarian home background to seek the support, suggestion and protection from superiors. This is further reinforced in hierarchical and unequal power-distributed social structure. A gap between the development authorities and the poor helps to promote '*mai-bap*' image. Poor people, therefore, seek the suggestion and support from *mukhiyas*, political leaders and other influential persons for taking up prospective ventures like IRDPs.

Fatalistic Attitude : The DRP attribute the outcomes of their activities to fate, chance and God. If the DRP make themselves responsible for the adverse consequences which they face frequently, the stability of their selves is likely to disintegrate. However, unconditional surrendering to fate, chance and God fosters maintenance of *status quo* and stalls dynamism and initiative.

Low Self-Esteem : Prejudices and atrocities against DRP and their humiliation bring about low self-esteem. Poor people in Gujarat disliked taking debts because what followed from them included abuses, insults, helplessness and touching the feet of the lenders and swallowing insults and abuses (Hirway, 1986, pp. 142-147). When Beck (1994, p. 140) asked poor people in three villages in West Bengal, which do you value more, food or self-respect?" 49 out of 58 said they valued self-respect more. Despite their regular

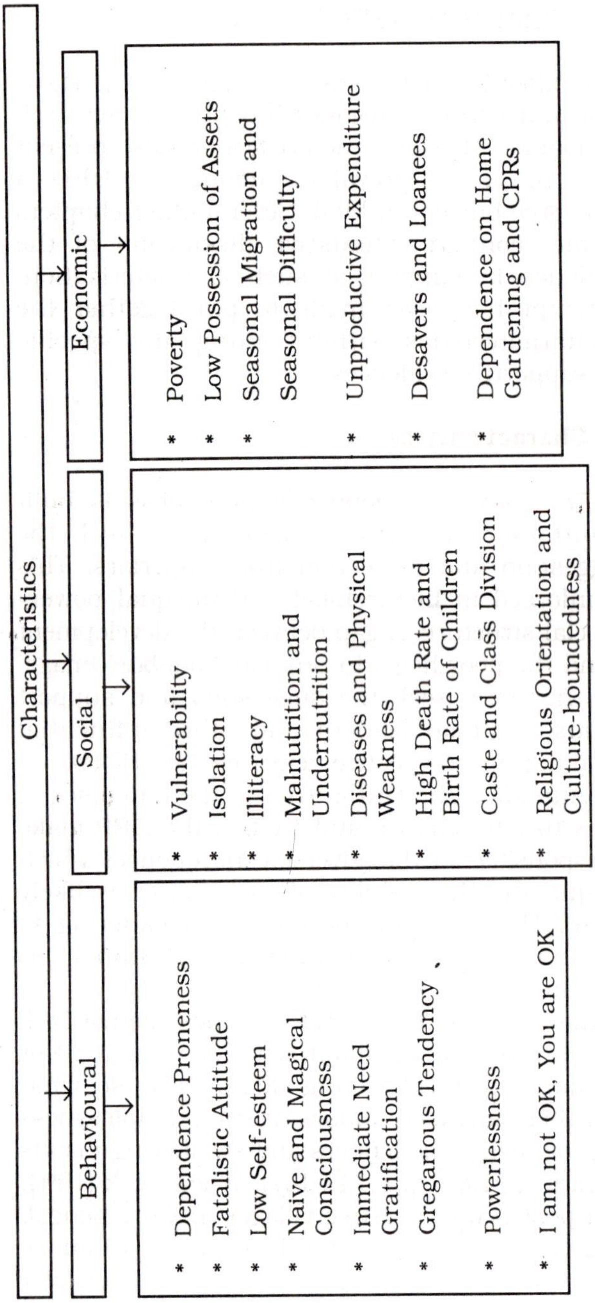

FIGURE 15.2 : *Characteristics of Disadvantaged People*

hunger, the poorest people felt it was more important to be treated with respect than gratify immediate need. Respects to them are long due.

Naive and Magical Consciousness : The DRP explain the complex social happenings by external and magical attribution rather than realistic ones. Ask a person, why are you poor? He replies, "God has made me poor and I have taken birth to serve the rich." This is a naive and magical understanding of the causes of poverty rather than a critical understanding. Two reasons explain such behaviour : (a) banking system of education, and (b) culture of silence. Fatalistic explanations for poverty are generated and propagated by the authorities, dominant elites and influential persons in rural area. The DRP have learned to accept the blame for their status without any contradiction and protest. This passive orientation hinders development and realization of local wisdom.

Immediate Need Gratification : The DRP consume their earnings and financial assistance immediately in meeting their compulsive survival needs, in observing festivals, marketing and in drinking. The Kondhs in Phulbani district of Orissa are craftsmen. Cutting the wood from forest, they sell it in nearby markets to satisfy their immediate survival needs. Perhaps, organising them, providing training to prepare finished products and creating marketing avenues will go a long way in their development.

Gregarious Tendency : The DRP like to take up different activities of cash-crop cultivation, afforestation and many more in group. One can observe this tendency in village markets, marriages, festivals, and in hunting occasions among tribals. The collective orientation in rural India, at least according to some researchers, may impede economic development, unless this is properly directed.

Powerlessness : The DRP are economically dispossessed, socially oppressed and politically voiceless. Also, their day-to-day struggle against survival lives them with no time and energy to organise and bargain.

The learned helplessness syndrome is so deep rooted that despite political empowerment, they get manipulated by the powerful.

I-am-not-OK, You-are-OK Orientation : The DRP are made to feel by the officials and significant others in the interaction that they are not OK. This introjective position leads them to withdraw and experience anxiety.

The above mentioned attributes (except, perhaps, collectivism and gregariousness) of DRP are dysfunctional to development. A deeper reflection reveals that the social structure and its power play are responsible for the development of dysfunctional characteristics. Along with gregariousness, they possess positive attributes of simplicity, honesty, diligence, resilience, spirituality, and affection for their development.

Social Characteristics

Vulnerability : Vulnerability means exposure and defenselessness. It has two sides : the external side of exposure to shocks, stress and risk, and the internal side of defenselessness, meaning a lack of means to cope without damaging loss (Chambers, 1995). The DRP are frequently hit by many kinds of crisis, such as, the death of a cow, goat, buffalo or bullock; diseases of crop, animals, or human beings; natural calamities like famine, flood or storm; and economic hardships such as mortgage of land, crop or other assets, dowry and other burdens. They do not have the means to cope with the shock and stress and to compensate for the losses.

Isolation : Isolation refers to remaining in peripheral and cut off status. Rural people live in dispersed and isolated area. Thereby, they are isolated in communication leading to lack of information, and limited access to social services, markets and banks. The degree of such isolation hits the DRP much more than other more advantaged sections of population.

Illiteracy : Illiteracy is more prevalent among the DRP than the others. Even if they know how to read and write, they do not know how to calculate accurately. Thereby, they are easily cheated by traders, creditors, middlemen and outsiders. Despite the massive educational programmes, their skills and knowledge are not augmented to meet the demands of production system and to help them harness the local resources effectively.

Malnutrition and Undernutrition : The DRP do not get the right combination of food. Also, they consume less than the required calories of food per day.

Poor Health Condition : Because of high female illiteracy, malnutrition, lack of awareness about preventive and curative health practices, non-availability of hospitals and dispensaries in nearby areas, exposure to toxic substances in natural resource-exploited area, child labour, and many such adverse conditions, DRP suffer from poor health conditions.

High Death Rate and Birth Rate of Children : The death rate of children is high because of malnutrition, mothers' hard-work, lack of health services, delivery of the child under unhygienic conditions, lack of health awareness and superstitions (non-offering of breast milk to the newborn for three days). With every successive death, the desire of the mother increases to give birth to more children, with the anticipation that few will survive. Also, poverty among women (measured in surrogate terms of female illiteracy, living in *kuchha* house, non-availability of drinking water, toilet, and health facilities) contributes primarily to high fertility and high infant mortality (Mukherji, 1997).

Caste and Class Division : The DRP are divided on the basis of caste and community status, and on political affiliations.

Economic Characteristics

Poverty : Despite the massive anti-poverty programmes, the number of poor people have never gone below 30% in rural area. The major sources of income of DRP are from agriculture, agricultural labour and common property resources. Their agriculture is complex, diverse and risk-prone. Barring a few, all are landless labourers, marginal and small farmers. With the lack of proper irrigation facilities, agriculture becomes a gamble against monsoon. That restricts cropping intensity. Along with these, non-availability of employment opportunities, obstruction in the use of forests and other local resources stretch the poverty bracket.

Low Possession of Assets : The DRP have little ownership of land and capital assets. Despite the abundant availability of labourers among them, many remain underemployed or disguised employed. Consequently, they borrow money from patrons, landlords, credit societies and rural banks mortgaging land, crop and other assets. Often, without repayment capacity, they lose their survival assets and retain only their own physical labour as the source of livelihood.

Unproductive Expenditure : The DRP spend a sizable portion of their meagre earnings on drinking, smoking and other such habits, and on dowry, birth ceremonies, funerals, and festive occasions. Out of each 100 rupees, they spend 10 to 13 rupees on such unproductive items (Suar & Chand, 1992, p. 15).

Desavers and Loanees : The DRP spend easily when they have money, a syndrome related to a psychological trait of seeking immediate gratification and lack of futuristic economic orientation. As such, they borrow money, sell assets, and remain hungry, as a result. This tends to make them desavers and loanees.

Dependence on Home Gardening and Common Property Resources : The DRP earn a sizable chunk of the household income selling leafy and other vegetables from home gardens. They get a vast range of fish, animals, fodders, building materials, wild foods, fuel, fertiliser, medicine, vegetables and many more from lakes, ponds, rivers, the sea, forests, hills, wasteland and roadsides. Common property resources (CPRs) account for between 19 and 29 per cent of the household's income (Beck, 1994, p. 133). CPRs provide income and employment when other activities are not available.

DEVELOPMENTAL INPUTS, CHARACTERISTICS OF DRP AND DEVELOPMENT

Here two conceptual arguments are developed. First, it was assumed that given the anti-poverty programmes, income, employment and assets would increase. Given the educational programmes, awareness and skills would go up. Given the environmental packages, population growth, malnutrition, diseases and pollution would decrease. The programmes are implemented in accordance with the causal (socio-economic) variables neglecting the process variables for the self-reliance of DRP. The implemented programmes have tried to counterbalance the social and economic backwardness of the DRP, as discussed earlier. The process variables or the throughput intervene between the developmental inputs and expected outputs (see Fig. 15.3). They comprise of thinking and reasoning (head traits, feeling (heart traits), and doing (hand traits : action and skills). These traits are called *Gyana*, *Bhakti*, and *Karma*, respectively in *Bhagavat Gita*. The change in thinking, reasoning and feeling will activate to develop skills and to initiate action.

The evaluation of programmes and projects has brought to our realisation that the success or failure of a programme relates to the mindsets and attitudes of beneficiaries. These process variables (or throughput) are taken for granted to change with the implemented programmes. The thinking, reasoning and feeling in various combinations constitute the functional and dysfunctional behavioural dimensions of the DRP discussed earlier. Unfortunately, programmes have not facilitated appreciable change in the dysfunctional behavioural dimensions. That is why, the input and expected output approach, ignoring the throughput, has not made a dent in bringing about self-reliance.

Second, there are two realities. Ours, which is powerful and theirs, which is weak. Our prevailing knowledge, statistical data on few variables, their logical analyses and conclusions ascertain that we know what the DRP experience and want. Accordingly, standardised, simplified and quantified packages are designed and delivered without learning about their need priorities, skills, local resources, and without their participation. The DRP experience their own realities which are diverse, complex, unquantified and holistic. They have their own definitions of need priorities,

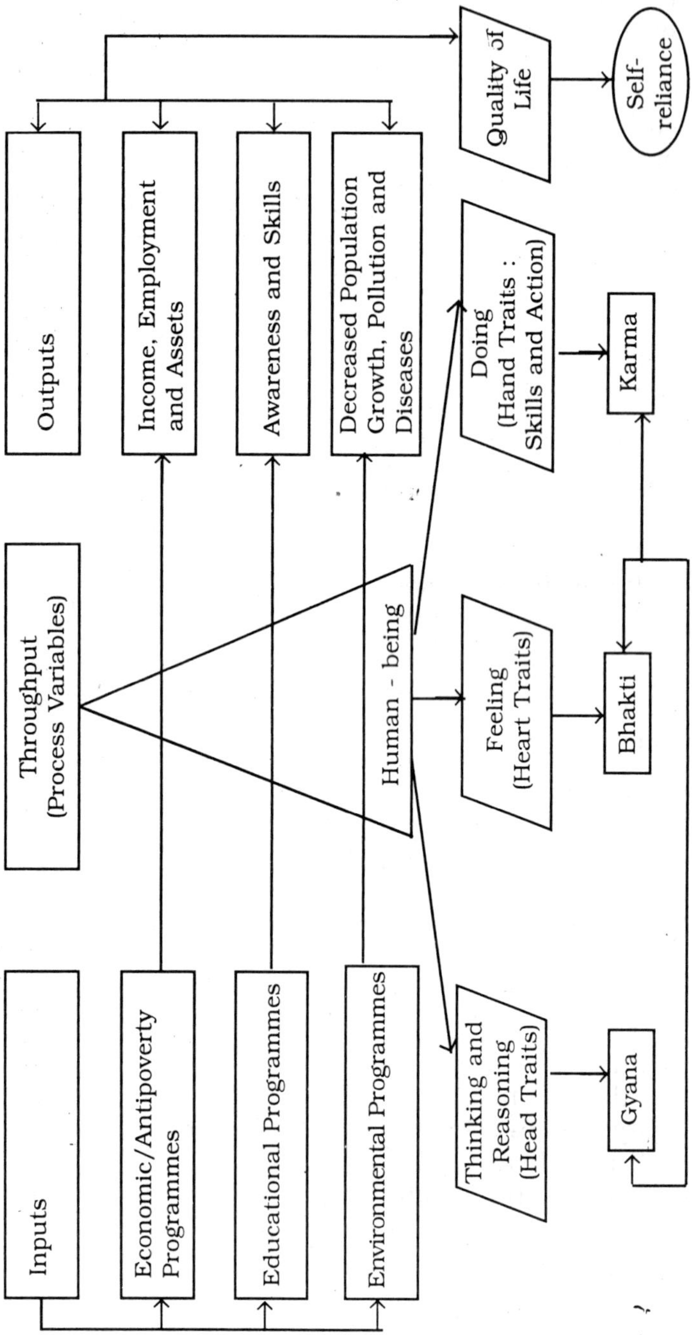

FIGURE 15.3 : *Inputs and Outputs Approach Ignoring the Throughput*

poverty and wellbeing in their own surroundings. The solution is one of balance between the two realities and in search for overlaps where their realities and aspirations can give rise to practical concepts which we can use to help empower them. The strategies which flow from the two conceptual arguments, need a further look.

MICRO-PLANNING, PARTICIPATORY RURAL APPRAISAL, CHANGE IN BEHAVIOURAL CHARACTERISTICS, AND DEVELOPMENT OF DRP

The people, their livelihood, skills, needs, natural resources and constraints differ from village to village. Hence, each village or the DRP therein constitute the unit for micro-planning (MP). With the implementation of Panchayati Raj Act, some directions are given for MP in governmental programmes (Suar & Prasad, 1995). NGOs use MP extensively. MP ensures democratic decentralisation with the involvement of villagers or DRP right from need identification to planning, execution, monitoring and evaluation of the project. In the process, villagers or DRP in collaboration with the development professional (DP), identify their most pressing needs; natural, social and economic resources. They discover different means and ways to develop themselves. The aim is to encourage self-help and self-reliance at the community or village level and to nourish the wisdom of the community or villagers for solving their own problems and improving their own life conditions (Figure15.4).

Rapport Establishment and Creating a Desire for Change

The first step in MP is the establishment of rapport and the creation of a desire for change. Before entering the village, the DP needs to collect the information from secondary sources about infrastructure, caste composition, agriculture, health, climate, income, occupation, employment, crop productivity, etc. to have some knowledge about the village. Staying in the village, the DP visits people, seeks to establish rapport through casual

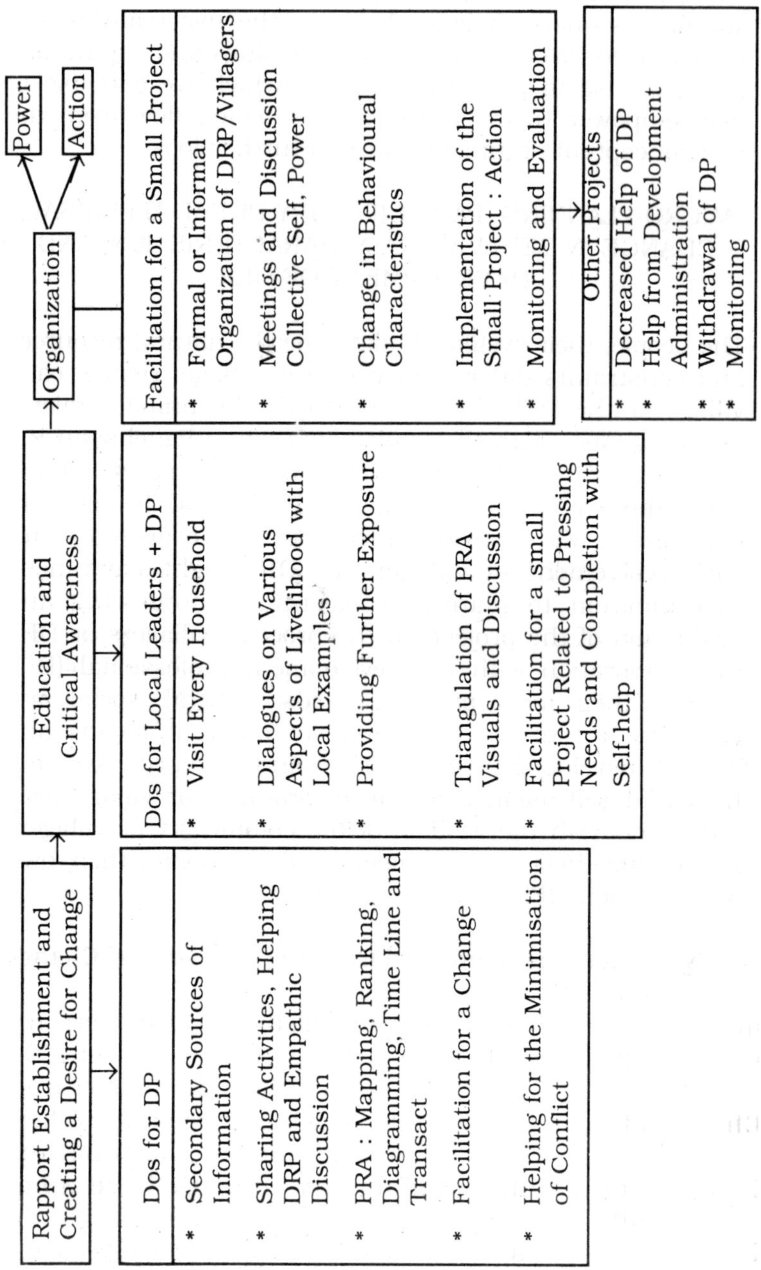

FIGURE 15.4 : *Micro-planning, Participatory Rural Appraisal, Change in Behavioural Characteristics and Development*

conversation, goes to village market; shares food, entertainments and festivals with villagers or DRP, participates in crop cutting, attends village meetings, takes the sick to the hospital with villagers and engages in many more rapport seeking activities to win the trust of the villagers or DRP. Also, the DP takes part in informal and empathic discussion with opinion leaders, elites, key informants and others. The discussion on resources, livelihoods, crops, festivals, role of women and other aspects, attracts others and helps the villagers or DRP to understand that they have problems. This is followed by participatory rural appraisal (PRA) to procure quick data and visuals through mapping, ranking, diagramming, time line and transact. Through PRA exercises, villagers or DRP analyse their conditions, express their own values, definitions of wellbeing and priorities, or in short, present their realities (second conceptual argument). This attracts the young, old, and women to participate and discuss with others on different aspects of the village. Triangulation takes place. All these bring the understanding among the villagers or DRP that they have local resources, skills and opportunities about which they had not thought earlier. With the facilitation of the DP, villagers or DRP understand that something can be done for a good change. They also feel that exploitation is existing and there are some people who are blocking their development. At this stage, the villagers or DRP experience helplessness to do something for their development. Also, there may be conflict of interest among different groups in the village. Then the DP can meet the conflicting groups with the local leaders, try to convince them, resolve the conflicts and encourage the DRP for their solidarity. A quick check list is given below to guide the DP to gauge whether the ground work is sufficient to proceed further.

Check List

1. Has he/she established the rapport with the villagers or DRP?
2. Have the villagers or DRP trusted him/her?

3. Do the villagers or DRP know about themselves, their resources, needs and constraints?
4. Are the villagers or DRP backed by genuine and honest leaders from their community or village?
5. Do the women know the different aspects of the village as the male members?
6. Are the conflicts among groups minimised?
7. Are the villagers or DRP sensing for a change?

Education and Critical Awareness

If the answers are in affirmative, next step is to educate and make aware critically the villagers or DRP. This is a transformational education which enables the people to analyse their problems in the context of resources critically, and develop solutions for them. With the local leaders, DP meets the families one-by-one, initiates dialogues,with local examples to improve their skills in agriculture, in preparation and use of bio-fertiliser, and in use of common property resources; how to use a bank, open an account, and to take a loan; about minimum wages, small irrigation scheme, home management, vegetable cultivation, legal aspects and many more. Dialogue does not impose, manipulate, domesticate and sloganise, rather it contains the truth, love and empathy for those who are going to suffer the consequences of their decisions. This can be furthered by communication strategies such as community reading of newspapers showing films related to group activity, irrigation and village development organising street dramas and skits on local issues; and inviting schools teachers, leaders from other villages, and government officials to talk on development. This will be automatically followed by discussion and reflection among villagers or DRP to understand the development issues critically. The idea behind this education and conscientization is that knowledge begets power.

The earlier PRA visuals would be further triangulated here. Dialogues, arguments, and revisions of PRA maps, models, diagrams and others will continue with increased awareness and knowledge. A participatory learning of villagers or DRP will take place simultaneously through discussion, revision of PRA visuals and decision. The villagers or DRP will settle down for a specific project to take up and plan accordingly. It is wise for the DP and local leaders to facilitate a small project. This may be related to the digging of a small pond, construction of a *kuchha* house for the school, of a check dam, a small saving scheme for women, etc. It is to be seen that the project is related to their needs and can be completed with the contribution of their money, materials and time. Otherwise, the project, which cannot be completed with self-help, will only breed frustration and the plan of that 'big white elephant' will remain as a show-piece. If necessary, training can be provided for building the capacity of the villagers or DRP to undertake the project.

Organisation

Following this, villagers or DRP will look for their solidarity to implement the project. The DP and local leaders can help organising them through the registration of a youth club, mahila mandal, a cooperative, and the formation of a *Gram Sabha*, women self-help group, etc. Indeed, organisation of villagers or DRP relies on honest and committed leadership, common goals, transparency, power-sharing, trust, cooperation and synergy among members. Meeting will be held and a concrete action plan will be prepared for the implementation of the project. Both cost-benefit analysis, budgeting, and contribution of the villagers or DRP for the project will be taken care of at this stage. Responsibilities will be delegated—who will do what, where, when and how. Records and accounts will be kept and leaders will emerge for different activities of the project. There should be something to do for everybody for getting involved in the project. It is their identified problem and must be planned and executed in their own way to solve it. Through conscientization, capacity building, organisation, collective discussion and decision, fear will be dispelled and every one will experience freedom and authority. A collective self will emerge. The dysfunctional behavioural characteristics of the villagers or DRP will change (first conceptual argument).

When the small project is going on, meeting will be held to evaluate its monitoring, successes and failures. Completing the small project, they will feel confident of themselves. Further meeting will be organised to discuss the benefits the project incurred. Doing so, the villagers or DRP will look to the future with vigour and optimism for bigger issues/projects to be tackled—watershed construction, marketing of local handicrafts and vegetables, mushroom cultivation, etc. At this stage, villagers or DRP can fight against corruption, exploitation, and injustice and make those open to public.

Again, they will formulate another project with decreased assistance of DP and may impress upon block, district or state administration to back them up. When villagers or DRP have crossed the take-up stage in implementing their identified plans and projects in their own ways getting organised, DP may withdraw himself/herself from the village. But, he/she should monitor their activities for some time to see that his/her efforts are bearing fruits.

This is a pragmatic approach based on our experience. The DP is just a facilitator. The development of the villagers or DRP depends on DP's commitment, altruism, empathy, and above all his/her desire to learn from the villagers or DRP—their society, needs, perception, priorities and personalities. This qualifies the psychologists to be DPs. Unfortunately, they are rare among DPs and where they are found, they tend to be in the areas other than their specialised fields.

SECTION-IV

CONCLUSION

16

Poverty and Disadvantage : Issues in Retrospect

GIRISHWAR MISRA AND AJIT K. MOHANTY

The preceding chapters in this book have sought to provide a general overview of the state of our knowledge and understanding of the psychological aspects of poverty and disadvantage. One can now stand back from the available knowledge and make an assessment. One can ask, for example, how distinctly psychological is the contemporary psychology of poverty and disadvantage? The chapters in this book have taken a consistent stand that understanding of poverty and disadvantage is much better promoted by a multidisciplinary framework and psychological approaches alone are bound to be too narrow given the essential socio-economic nature of the phenomena. Thus, psychological analyses of poverty and disadvantage can, at best, seek to supplement and enrich a more holistic approach. Over the years, the other dominant disciplines in the study of poverty like economics and sociology have come to realize the limitations of any narrow intra-disciplinary framework. Economists have tended to move away from purely economic criteria in study of poverty realizing that economic growth alone does not provide a complete picture of development out of poverty. Similarly, sociological views of poverty have also increasingly sought to incorporate other disciplinary perspectives. In fact, various disciplines seem to have unwittingly come closer in their view of poverty as a complex and multidimensional phenomenon.

The chapters in this book dealing with conceptualization of poverty have clearly shown that psychological views of poverty within an ecological framework or of poverty as a perceived phenomenon have come quite close to the views, in other disciplines, of absolute and relative poverty and of poverty as a social contextual process. Thus, on the whole, poverty has come to be viewed more as phenomenological than purely economic. In this sense, psychological aspects of poverty have been very much accepted as significant. Psychologists have generally viewed poverty within a "deprivation" paradigm. Organisms act upon and react to stimuli within their environment, creating learned associations on which to build the competencies. When there is a lack of relevant stimuli in the environment, the organism is impaired and cannot function as other members in the environment. There is also a lack of adequate feedback to facilitate learning. Thus we have deprivation, a state that often occurs in poverty and interferes by creating impairments to the cognitive, perceptual, and social functioning of an individual. Such impairments certainly deny the individual equality of opportunities and limit individual's choices. Reflecting a similar orientation in economics, the work of Amartya Sen (Dreze & Sen, 1996; Sen, 1982, 1985) has conceptualised poverty as 'capability deprivation' and focused on constraints in person's choices or freedom in functioning as important parameters of poverty.

> " 'Capability' refers to the alternative combinations of functionings from which a person can choose. Thus, the notion of capability is essentially one of freedom — the range of options a person has in deciding what kind of life to lead. Poverty of a life, in this view, lies not merely in the impoverished state in which the person actually lives, but also in the lack of real opportunity — given by social constraints as well as personal circumstances — to choose other types of living. Even the relevance of low incomes, meagre possessions, and other

> aspects of what are standardly seen as economic poverty relates ultimately to their role in curtailing capabilities (that is, their role in severely restricting the choices people have to lead valuable and valued lives). Poverty is, thus, ultimately a matter of 'capability deprivation', and note has to be taken of that basic connection not just at the conceptual level, but also in economic investigations and in social or political analyses." (Dreze & Sen, 1996, pp. 10-11)

Psychological dimensions of poverty are quite evident in such analyses and dealing with poverty is no longer to be viewed simply in terms of generating economic growth; expansion of human capabilities can be viewed as a more basic objective of development. It seems, the psychological conceptualization of poverty and disadvantage is congruent with the emerging paradigms in welfare economics. Therefore, instead of looking at the psychological concomitants of poverty as merely its consequences, psychologists can relate the cognitive-motivational aspects of poverty to the notion of capability deprivation. In his analysis of issues relating to use of minority mother tongues in India, Mohanty (Chapter 6, this volume) shows how treatment of languages as unequal deprives some groups of individuals of their choices perpetuating inequality and putting such groups at a disadvantage. The chapters in Section II of this volume show the limitations of taking a simplistic cause and effect view of the relationship between poverty and disadvantage and their cognitive, motivational and other psychological correlates. Simple demonstration of statistically significant differences between the poor and the upper class, the low and the high SES or the disadvantaged and advantaged does not further our understanding of the nature of poverty and disadvantage. It is necessary to analyse how the total context of poverty including its psychological concommitants limits the freedom and choices of individuals and groups restricting their chances of having a desired life style. Authors in Section I of this volume show how a contextual and holistic view of poverty and disadvantage can promote such an understanding. Similarly, intervention strategies can also be viewed in terms of their effects on expansion of human capabilities. Intervention efforts in terms of economic inputs as relief measures may bring about temporary changes in the quality of lives in poverty, but they do not ensure enduring and sustainable development. Noncontingent economic aids which are doled out as support for the economically backward classes are unlikely to reinforce forces from within for expansion of capabilities. The review of various intervention efforts for alleviation of poverty and disadvantage by Misra and Dash shows the limitations of interventions through simplistic economic inputs. Chapters by Dalal and Suar show that it is necessary to promote self-reliant and community based interventions to generate forces to motivate development out of poverty. In their chapters, Mishra and Vajpayee and Rath demonstrate that psychological interventions can promote expansion of capabilities at the level of the individual. Such interventions may not directly promote economic development but enable the individuals or groups to bring about such development. Human capabilities are not just products of economic inputs, they are "among the chief means of economic success" (Dreze & Sen, 1996, p. 184). Dreze and Sen (1996) also recognise the "intrinsic importance of human capabilities and effective freedom as the ends of social and political organization" (p. 184), in pleading for such macro-level interventions as education and health care "in promoting participatory economic growth and, through it, further advancing the quality of life that people can enjoy" (p. 185). Thus the loci of poverty as well as the loci of intervention are economic, social and psychological. In this perspective, psychological processes, such as cognition, motivation, values and other characteristics of the poor and the disadvantaged are to be viewed both as consequences as well as antecedent conditions which are ultimately related to human capabilities.

Such a view of poverty seems to locate the phenomenon in the context of human functioning and freedom of choice rather than in the elusive nature of economically defined conception of poverty line. This approach has some advantage since poverty defined in terms of economic subsistence may not suffice in a changing consumeristic society. As new wants are created, perceived basic needs for subsistence assume greater importance than the objective economic indicators. In this context, the relative nature of poverty and affluence, disadvantage and advantage in a changing society needs to be appreciated and future research in this area must study poverty in *transition* rather than poverty in *isolation*. This requires going beyond a fixed set of variables such as caste, income, sex etc. and focusing more on the processes underlying poverty as a changing or evolving phenomenon. Methodologically this would also call for more longitudinal and qualitative observational analyses rather than the more popular cross-sectional and quantitative ones. Similarly, psychological interventions in conditions of poverty need to reassess the basic assumptions underlying the strategies, going beyond a simplistic comparative analysis of the efficacy of a preconceived, theory driven treatment. Both at the social and individual levels, it has become necessary for us to ask "What is the most critical (and cost effective) input to change the conditions of poverty or rather, to expand human capabilities?" While there seems to be a general consensus among economists, psychologists and other social scientists that education is perhaps the most crucial input (e.g. Atal, 1997a) at the societal level and motivation at the individual level, there is a need for greater attention to the role of these inputs and the manner in which these and other inputs can be made more cost-effective.

Poverty and Deprivation: Changing Views

The study of poverty and deprivation in the context of third world countries has drawn considerable attention of social scientists in the later half of this century. This was a reflection of realization that social sciences have to be problem oriented. The interest of Indian researches in deprivation', however, owes largely to the influences of sensory deprivation research and studies of cultural deprivation in the United States. The increased concern with the weaker sections of society such as scheduled caste (SC), scheduled tribe (ST), minority groups and the people below poverty line has worked as an additional impetus to this end. The focus of psychological research has been on mapping of the differentials in psychological functions in the deprived people. The issues related to deprivation have implications for planning of human resources in developing nations.

Disparities/inequalities in opportunities do exist in different societies to different extent leading to the formation of advantaged/ privileged and disadvantaged/ underprivileged categories of people. The formation of these groups, however, is linked with specific socio-cultural, historical and political contexts. This makes the nature, magnitude and extent of deprivation an essentially relative phenomenon conditioned by differences in the quality life and distribution of resources. The relative nature of deprivational experience is further illustrated in the feeling of deprivation as reflected in the notion of 'relative deprivation'. The absence of necessary social, economic and physical support results in different degrees of discomfort for different individuals or groups. It must occur above the adaptation level if it is to be considered deprivational. Such a threshold obviously depends upon the comparison level opted by the people. Thus one feels deprived in relation to other individuals or groups. This makes deprivation a subjectively contingent phenomenon and the analogy of Black-White contrast becomes irrelevant while comparing Harijan vs. Brahman, urban vs. rural and tribal vs. non-tribal. The Indian society still evinces wide gaps and disparities in socio-cultural experiences, economic sufficiency, residential conditions, facilities for health and educational experiences. This situation offers vast differences in the experiential background of people which makes deprivation an important problem for study in its own right. However, in modern analyses, the Euro-American models have dominated. This has led to proliferation of studies, multiplicity of concepts, equivocal findings and misconstrual of the Indian social reality. While some researchers did venture methodological refinements and conceptual innovations to make their work pertinent to Indian conditions, the nature and consequences of deprivation in India are yet to be understood in a comprehensive and systematic manner. As has been documented in the various chapters of this volume, researchers working in this area have used a variety of expressions for deprivation and poverty and have used them independently as well as interchangeably. Some of them are value loaded and go against the growing interest in alternative life styles and pluralist vision of societies. It is not adequate to label cultures/groups/individuals as deprived or poor simply because they do not conform to a chosen set of standards used to define a privileged culture. The use of phrases like 'culturally deprived' often reflects such biases and value preferences.

Literally the term 'deprivation' means the process of dispossession. In experimental paradigm, deprivation assumes the status of a treatment involving reduction of sensory inputs available to an individual. It can take different forms depending on the number of sense modalities involved. However, its extension to natural life conditions has led to confusion in our understanding. Generally, 'deprivation' represents the lack of experiential base considered necessary for the growth and development in a society. An analysis of the various uses of the term 'deprivation' suggests that it consists of deficient, substandard and inadequate environmental conditions which interfere with development and growth of individuals. In other words, an environmental condition is deprived to the extent it adversely influences individual's attainment across various domains or his/her freedom to choose a life style. Unfortunately the focus of attention has shifted from environmental deprivation to deprived persons attributing the features of environment to the individual. This point needs some elaboration as it has direct policy implications. If we focus on the deprived persons (who behave in a given manner), the strategy of intervention will be directed towards the individual rather than the environment. Perhaps we need a two-pronged strategy aimed at changing the individual and also bringing changes in the socio-economic environment.

The way cultures facilitate the growth and development of individuals is a long term and complex process. The necessary and sufficient conditions for a definite form or/ and level of development are yet to be precisely specified. While these gaps in our knowledge have to be taken as stimulants rather than constraints for future research, a meaningful analysis of deprivation can hardly ignore the issues of development and its context. The human context of development consists of several sub-systems of environment which interact and influence the course of psychological development of a self-regulating human being. Recent investigations of cognitive functions have illustrated that very young children are also characterized by an effective cognitive apparatus. Also, the shaping and growth of higher order complex mental operations require cognitive inputs from several inter-related environmental systems. However, owing to preference for individual-focused and micro approaches, psychologists have largely treated 'deprivation' as an organismic phenomenon. Attempts at understanding the consequences of deprivation have been limited to documenting the differences across groups formed along caste/ region/ socio-economic status (SES)/ sub-culture designated as deprived or privileged. In fact, those who have viewed deprivation as an environmental phenomenon have also reduced it to the level of the individual. Such reductionism shifts the locus of intervention. Instead of enriching the deprived environment, efforts are made to change the deprived people through training, motivation, and attitudinal changes. These efforts often create even greater frustration as the raised expectations add to the problems of coping with environmental constraints. The deprived environment is maintained and nurtured by certain aspects of the vertically arranged traditional Indian social structure and ineffective implementation and monitoring of poverty alleviation programmes. It has been documented that such programmes are largely exploited by the privileged people rather than the deserving ones. This makes deprivation a social and political problem.

Empirical studies of deprivation and poverty have employed three major strategies of operationalizing and measuring deprivation. They distinguish between different degrees of deprivation in terms of environmental categories (e.g., residential background, institutionalization), social categories (e.g., membership of special cultural, economic, ethnic or caste groups) and experiential units (e.g., home environment and other indices of deprivation in terms of environmental inputs and individual's experiences). While all the three approaches consider deprivation in term of deficient environmental condition, the first two approaches are confined to characterization of these deficiencies. The third makes it explicit and takes into consideration the extent of within-category differences in the deprivational experience making it easier to examine the processes underlying poverty and disadvantage.

Psychological Correlates of Poverty and Disadvantage: Trends and Prospects

In the last two decades considerable data have accumulated pertaining to the relationship between poverty/ disadvantage and psychological functions in Indian context. It is, however, difficult to draw firm conclusions as there are marked differences in the criteria of deprivation, type and quality of measures used and regional variations. As has been pointed out, efforts at understanding the consequences of deprivation have largely been confined to demonstration of differences across groups formed along variables such as caste, region, SES, and sub-cultures labelled as deprived and privileged. The differences noted in the areas of cognition, intelligence, affective and personality functions, mental health, attitude and academic attainment are not unequivocal and are also fraught with several methodological limitations. The lack of comparability in terms of sampling and appropriateness of dependent measures often complicate our understanding of deprivational effects. These limitations notwithstanding, some trends can be deciphered.

Indian studies have generally shown a negative effect of poverty and deprivation on perceptual, conceptual, Piagetian, problem-solving and representational tasks. Comparisons on long-term memory, recognition and learning tasks also evince similar trends. However, the measures of short term and incidental memory do not show such effects. Cognitive styles, linguistic achievement and syntactic ability show significant adverse effects of deprivation and so does the performance on scholastic and academic achievement measures. At the same time, some positive characteristics like boredom tolerance, adaptability, vigilance, and drawing ability are found in the disadvantaged children.

In general, the deprived people perform on majority of the cognitive and intellective tasks at a lower level than their privileged counterparts. However, on the measures of competence and ability to learn, the discrepancy between the two groups is minimal. The deprived and non-deprived groups do not evince substantial differences on cognitive and behavioural measures during early years. However, the gap between the deprived and non-deprived groups increases with age. This indicates the role of non-intellective factors (such as school climate, teacher expectations, parental support etc.) in accentuating the differentials between the two groups and often leading to cumulative deficit. The motivational and personality characteristics of the deprived groups include low achievement motivation, low aspiration level, low expectation, neuroticism, insecurity, rigidity, conformity, anxiety, extroversion, alienation, low self image, past orientation, lack of future orientation, external attribution for success and internal attributions for failure, and use of dysfunctional coping strategies like escape, helplessness, hopelessness and denial. Viewed against the main stream, the deprived groups lack the qualities, dispositions, skills, and values supposed to be necessary for success and upward mobility in the contemporary competitive world. They show low level persistence and frequently leave the field. They are not equipped with the necessary skills nor prepared to cope with the demands of society. The goals aspired by them are beyond their reach.

The picture which emerges from these differentials suggests that the deprived or disadvantaged people display less efficient functioning than their advantaged counterparts. Such differences increase with the complexity of task demands and advancing age. The explanations of deprivational effects put forward favour a *difference* or *deficit* position or a combination of the two. The difference hypothesis explains performance differences on the basis of inadequacy of measures and procedures and considers such differences as artifacts. The deficit hypothesis assumes that the deprived are deficient in their cognitive, motivational and personality characteristics. In its extreme form, it considers that the differences reflect underlying genetic differences. In its mild form it assumes that the differences reflect lack of cognitive structures or skills owing to lack of necessary environmental support. The third possibility subscribes to the view that the performance differences involve deficit as well as difference depending upon the nature of skill and domain assessed.

We would like to aver that poverty and disadvantage are basically environmental phenomena. They stand for situations in which alternatives for human growth and development are drastically curtailed and people are subjected to limited choice conditions. The poor and the disadvantaged experience an environment which generates, sustains and promotes helplessness by making their actions unrelated to outcomes. They gradually come to subscribe to the view that their behaviour is inefficient and irrelevant. The resultant feelings of helplessness and apathy restrict them from undertaking steps to become self efficacious. The studies on achievement attributions by the deprived and disadvantaged students tend to suggest that the students from disadvantaged and deprived backgrounds show internal attributions for failure and external attributions for success while their advantaged counterparts evince an opposite trend. This implies that deprivation transforms their perspective in such a way that one can neither enjoy success in terms of self-enhancing experience nor reduce the sufferings of failure by attributing to the external factors. The low level of self-esteem and somewhat negative self- image of the deprived people further restrict their achievement efforts.

Psychologically the experience of helplessness entails the belief that poor people's actions are unimportant or redundant and the environment is non-supportive. These beliefs contribute to the development of an expectancy frame which is substantiated by their experiences in different walks of life. The outcome may take any one of the following forms: withdrawal, resignation, confrontation, hostile reaction, and alienation. The actual outcome depends on particular situational characteristics as well as individual's dispositions. In this context, it may be pointed out that the welfare provisions of the state in terms of loan, subsidy and other provisions are expected to play important role. But, it is generally observed that such measures have not been able to uplift the conditions of the poor since they tend to strengthen the feelings of dependence and inadequacy. The chain reaction continues to perpetuate the cycle of poverty. Involving these people in developmental efforts in order to create experiences of positive outcomes seems to be a way out of this vicious cycle. Mere provision of assets does not guarantee social uplift, unless they are contingent upon personal efforts and initiative leading to positive outcomes in respect of self-perception and independence.

It is expected that the future work in this area would be conscious of the tendency of blaming the victims and seek to identify the structure and components of environment at individual as well as collective levels which make the people deprived and to evolve effective strategies to help the deprived people realize their potentials. However, isolated changes in the person or in the environment would not be enough, since both jointly work and constitute a system in which changes in one need to be supported by changes in the other. Failure in coordinating the two will add to the existing problems. Enrichment programmes, attitude change and motivational training with a focus on the individual, in the absence of necessary environmental support, would not yield long-term success.

Unfortunately, psychologists have largely been focusing on decontextualized individual, proposing changes mainly in the individual and not in the socio-economic situation. The unfavourable experiences in one's life are attributed largely to shortcomings within the person. Psychology has a dual responsibility. It has to develop awareness of the prevailing circumstances and ideologies and must provide a vision of human welfare. These processes are known as conscientization and annunciation. Conscientization refers to the process whereby people attain an illuminating awareness of not only the critical environmental conditions that are shaping life but also of their capacity to transform that reality. Annunciation, on the other hand, is viewed as the act of convincing a just social arrangement in which the well being of the population is fostered. It is hoped that these challenges will be perceived as opportunities and psychologists will respond to them in a creative fashion.

While generalization from the studies showing a modal pattern of negative relationship between conditions of poverty/ deprivation/ disadvantage and development of competence has helped development of our understanding of the psychological nature of poverty and interventions necessary, this has also led to ignoring the few individuals who do not conform to the modal pattern despite the condition of disadvantage. While a majority of the poor and the disadvantaged shows low performance on psychological measures related to competence as well as inadequate motivational patterns, there are some individuals who show much better performance on these measures. Unfortunately, our usual statistical techniques of data analysis do not allow us to focus on those who show remarkable resilience to the adverse effects of poverty and disadvantage. Instead of showing the expected poor cognitive performance, poor motivation and learned helplessness, these individuals perform quite well on cognitive tasks, show healthy patterns of motivation and learned resourcefulness under the same conditions of poverty and disadvantage to which the poor performance of the others are attributed. What makes these individuals resistant to the adverse effects of growing up under poverty and disadvantage? Our understanding of the psychology of poverty and disadvantage would remain incomplete unless due attention is paid to this phenomenon.

The Invulnerable Deprived People: The Lotus of Mud

Studies investigating the role of environmental variables in the development of cognitive competence generally report a negative linear relationship between deprivation and cognitive growth. Based on this, attempts have been made to isolate environmental factors that have deleterious effects on cognitive development. The generalizations made by various investigators in this connection appear to be somewhat narrow if we remember that deprivation is an essential condition for acquisition of skills. An inverted U-shaped relationship between deprivation and performance is postulated by many researchers. It is, therefore, surprising that the facilitative effects of deprivation have gone unnoticed and uninvestigated. This point was driven home in the study by Misra and Tripathi (1980). In this study, the role of prolonged experiential deprivation in cognitive functioning was investigated. It was found that individuals who lived in physically and psychologically impoverished environments were generally inferior in their cognitive functioning, such as, intellective performance, conceptual categorization, perceptual identification of embedded figures, etc., as compared to individuals living in enriched environments. However, about ten per cent of such individuals in the highly deprived environments showed far superior functioning than their counterparts in the low deprived environments. Those who believe in a linear relationship between deprivation and cognitive functioning are not likely to take cognizance of this fact and treat such cases as part of the error variance. But, how does one explain the phenomenon of Abraham Lincoln who rose to the highest office of his country after being born to a set of extremely poor parents, or Napoleon Bonaparte in France and Ishwar Chandra Vidyasagar in India? All of them lotuses with their roots in the mud! It is not rarely that one comes across individuals who have risen to the top, although, they were born and brought up in highly deprived environments. How do such children, growing up in the most impoverished settings, attain an extraordinary degree of cognitive and behavioural competence and come out successful in life? A systematic scientific answer to this question is not yet available. Nevertheless, there are some pointers. It has been noted that environmental support significantly influenced the motivational levels of students coming from depressed backgrounds (Pandey & Tripathi, 1987). We, therefore, believe that a study of such individuals (the so called 'Lotuses of mud') in their context is likely to provide us an answer to the above question. By analyzing their environments and by understanding the ways in which such individuals cope up with their environmental impediments, it should be possible to arrive at a better understanding of the role environmental factors and, more significally, person-environment interactions play in development of cognitive competence. It is also hoped that the findings will be able to throw light on the controversy currently raging the field about the role of environmental factors vis-à-vis genetic factors.

The relative significance of genetic and experiential factors in determining competence is an issue which has been much debated. Without getting involved in this controversy, it can be said that the characteristics of environment play a crucial role in cognitive growth because human behaviour takes place within a context which not only elicits it but also places certain limits on it. Various psychological theories view environment as a major causal factor in cognitive growth and psychological functioning, in general. Indian studies on prolonged experiential deprivation and impoverished social settings have demonstrated restrictive or inhibitive effects of environment on acquisition of cognitive competence and motivational dispositions. However, no attempt has been made to measure and dimensionalize the environmental variables. Therefore, it has not been possible to find out the differentially facilitative or restrictive effects of specific environmental variables on developmental processes and outcomes.

Although, the term 'lotus of mud' is used here in an allegorical sense, it may be considered a new concept. Other concepts such as, 'gifted child', 'talented', 'genius', 'high or over achiever' are only its rough approximations. By 'lotus of mud' our reference is to individuals who are born in deprivational and deprived environments and who turn out to be cognitively competent, high achievers in school and successful in life. Thus, the lotus of mud refers to a special type of individuals who forge ahead in life by turning adversity to their advantage. Earlier, the names of Abraham Lincoln, Napoleon Bonaparte and Ishwar Chandra Vidyasagar were mentioned. There are countless other cases to illustrate this concept. There are professors, engineers, doctors, managers, and civil servants and others who rose to the highest wrung of the ladder in their professions, although they came from grossly deprived environments. The concept of competence appears relevant here. It is defined as an "organism's capacity to interact effectively with its environment". According to White (1971, 1976), competence involves skills and knowledge that are instrumental to successful coping with one's needs and environmental demands. It refers to personal characteristics (e.g. knowledge, skills, and attitudes) which lead to achievements having adaptive payoffs in significant environments. It is this broadened concept of competence which appears appropriate to study the lotus of mud phenomenon. The question which one would like to answer is what forces or combination of forces derived from environments produce lotuses of mud.

The lotus of mud phenomenon shows that it is possible for the least advantaged to overcome all odds against them and to develop effective coping strategies to maximally realise their potentials. Evidently the factors that make some among the poor and the disadvantaged invulnerable to the adverse effects of impoverished environmental conditions are individual as well as social in nature. Objectives of intervention programmes for the poor and the disadvantaged must, therefore, include individual as well as societal level changes to enable them to outgrow the limitations imposed on them by the characteristics of the groups to which they belong. Thus, both micro-level interventions at the individual level and macro-level programmes (such as the state sponsored welfare measures) are needed. As we have pointed out earlier, micro-level interventions at the individual level are common as psychological interventions. But they are less effective without macro-level changes. At the same time, macro-level interventions also need to be viewed from the micro-level and psychological perspectives.

Macro Level Intervention: Need for a Fresh Look

Since the independence, poverty alleviation has been attended to in India in three broad phases. In the first phase (1950-1960s) the major emphasis was on redistribution of land, abolition of intermediaries and tenancy reforms. Land reforms failed due to strong opposition from interest groups as well as lack of a strong political will. The dominant development strategy adopted during this period was industrialisation oriented. This strategy could not improve the plight of the poor in India as they did not have the capacity to respond effectively to the growth stimuli and utilise the opportunities created. By the late 1960s, the second phase of PAPs started with measures that were aimed at the poor in rural areas. This target oriented approach had emphasis on creating employment opportunities and distributing renewable assets among the poor. The performance of these programmes was distinctly better in the infrastructurally developed regions where the awareness levels and bargaining power of the beneficiaries were higher. Weak integration of self-employment activities and wage-employment programmes with the overall development strategy has led to inefficient use of a large chunk of resources. These programmes did not provide sustained livelihood to the poor. In the third phase, starting from the beginning of the 1990s, emphasis shifted to measures aimed at accelerating economic growth through market oriented strategies and economic liberalisation. Economic reforms are likely to affect the poor adversely because the costs will be felt quickly whereas, the benefits may take time to materialise. Therefore, it is desirable that the government must take care of the poor by maintaining the social sector expenditure during the adjustment period. On the whole during the post independence period income/ consumption approach has played a dominant role in measuring and analysing poverty. The policies emphasised increase in the income or the income earning capacity of the poor, rather than sustainable livelihood. The linkage of income earning capacity to social infrastructure, human development and socio-political environment was of limited concern. In this process, the central government played the key role. Apart from setting targets and allocating resources it issued guidelines about how to implement the schemes as well as framed the monitoring and evaluation criteria. It has a top-down structure with little scope for incorporating the views of target groups and implementing agencies. This is one of the causes of partial success of the poverty alleviation programmes. Further, such poverty alleviation programmes often involve economic and material assistance doled out not on the basis of effort and initiative but on the basis of extent of poverty and need. As has been said earlier, from a psychological point of view, such noncontingent benefits or need satisfiers become incentives to foster dependence and contribute little towards generating motivation for sustainable development.

Considering various facets of macro-level planning for poverty alleviation, economists and other social scientists have been pleading with increasing vigour for treating education as the most critical input at the societal level for development. Amartya Sen speaks of availability of education, health care and other basic services as essential aspects of social opportunities which (along with economic entitlements, political rights, transparency guarantees, and protective security) constitute a part of the five "instrumental freedoms" as criteria for human development. In India, implementation of universal primary education has been severally emphasised as the most critical priority for development (e.g. Inamdar, 1997). It has been noted that tangible reductions in birth and death rates are not possible without a significant improvement in other areas like literacy rate; and initial push to literacy and demographic achievement is a necessary condition for social development as is evident in the case of Kerala. The poorest states like Bihar, Madhya Pradesh and Uttar Pradesh also have a very low rate of literacy, high birth rate and high infant mortality rate. Literacy, health and poverty are closely linked and any attempt to increase the income alone will not trigger forces for sustainable livelihood as illiterate and undernourished people cannot take advantage of the economic opportunities. Atal (1997b) has also argued that education has an important role in poverty-eradication strategy. In addition, he pleads for food security, employment, access to basic services and political, social and cultural participation as necessary supplements to education.

On the whole, given the research input and the state of our knowledge in psychology as well as other social sciences, there seems to be a need to reassess the nature, quality and consequences of the macro-level intervention programmes for poverty alleviation. The strategies underlying such programmes need to be reviewed from multidisciplinary perspectives. Unfortunately, recent contributions from various disciplines have generally gone unnoticed as a result of which long term benefits of these programmes are not assured. While it is true that some disciplines like psychology are yet to come up with convincing demonstrations of the applicability of their positions and principles in large scale poverty alleviation programmes, others like economics have suffered the vagary of unpredictable political processes in decision making and implementation. Thus, the real and effective input of social sciences remains lamentably low.

Before we conclude, a note must be taken of the dominant negative tenor in social sciences' focus on poverty and disadvantage which are, more often than not, viewed as a lack of something or as absence of such qualities as are more typical of the affluent. Studies on poverty, deprivation and disadvantage usually view them as a disease and with an attitude of blaming the victim. Starting with a negative concept biases the study, definition of problems and even the findings in respect of poverty. Unfortunately, with such biases in our approach the positive facets of the phenomena of poverty and social deprivation are often undermined. That states of poverty can go with asceticism, austerity and puritanic life style and, as such, can be considered a desired state, at least for some, is often not brought to focus in our zeal to uplift the poor out of their conditions. Indian social scientists, in particular, need to balance their views of poverty in recognition of the dominant value of renunciation in the Indian psyche. Development out of poverty, affluence, sense of well being and happiness are not necessarily compatible goals. While our major preoccupation with poverty is understandable, there is also a need to appreciate that economic growth is not linearly related to subjective well-being and happiness.

Human well-being, Poverty and Affluence: The Economistic Fallacy

We have said earlier that in the emerging views of poverty, economic indicators *per se* are being deemphasised as other socio-cultural and psychological parameters are brought in into a multidisciplinary view of the phenomenon. Even then, economic growth is still considered a very significant aspect of poverty. The limitations of the 'economic growth' approach are exposed when one considers the relationship between economic growth and human well-being. Not only does human well-being often remains elusive despite economic growth but also it can be argued that, at a certain level of affluence, economic growth perhaps leads to a decline in well-being. Goodwin (1997) speaks of three worldviews in respect of the relationship between economic growth and well-being.

One view looks at all economic growth as contributing to human well-being which may also depend on factors other than economic growth. A second view suggests that, while some aspects of economic growth may contribute to well-being, there are other aspects which do not affect or are neutral in respect of well-being. The third view conceives of aspects of economic growth which "not only do not contribute to, but actually detract from the more general human well-being (p. 4)". Many aspects of economic growth such as pollution, stress and other concomitants of affluence can be cited as supporting this third view that, beyond a certain level, economic growth may detract from human well-being. Quality of life or subjective well-being is not always indicated by consumeristic or purchasing behaviour. There is no denying the assumption that people in extreme poverty would be better off with economic development, but the extent and nature of economic development will have to be carefully monitored if human well-being is the goal. Beyond a certain point, economic growth may not contribute significantly to human well-being.

As pointed out earlier Amartya Sen's view of poverty as "capability deprivation" is based on the assumption that capability for a good life is more fundamental than consumeristic satisfaction of market preferences. Such a view directs our attention to social, cultural, political and contextual conditions as necessary parameters of human well-being the absence of which is generally characterised as poverty. The implication of such a view is that poverty need not be contrasted with affluence nor seen as a disease. In fact, a case can also be made to view both poverty and affluence as somewhat undesirable states or conditions of pathology in a society. Indian view of 'happiness' perhaps comes quite close to being equidistant or even tangential to both these conditions. Material well-being is but a limited aspect of human well-being and the former, far from ensuring the later, at least partially, may even detract from it. As Lane (1996, cited and summarised in Ackerman, Kiron, Goodwin, Harris & Gallagher, 1997) says, "The economistic fallacy is the belief that even when one is beyond the poverty line, higher levels of income still contribute to increasing well-being. In reality, most evidence from advance countries suggest that above the poverty line this relationship holds only weakly at best; the rich are no happier than the merely comfortable" (pp. 30-31). The so called *affluence effect* may be limited in the sense that on the average the richer societies are somewhat happier than those in poverty but the difference is not linear nor systematic. As one moves out of poverty, happiness may and does increase perhaps briefly but following a short plateu, the trend is downward as economic growth reaches a point of affluence. Unfortunately, those who view poverty as a disease, are often not sensitive to the possibility that, affluence, particularly, extreme affluence, can also be treated as somewhat nonfunctional under certain conditions. Poverty is not simply absence of affluence nor is affluence absence of poverty. Both these concepts are necessarily multidimensional with certain degree of mutual overlap. One need not glorify poverty but one can, at least, recognise the possibility of some strengths, such as effective coping strategies, hardiness, and resilience acruing to the individual growing up under conditions of poverty.

Thus, it is quite evident that one has to go beyond the economic faces of poverty and affluence and look at their human sides. Economic conditions apart, the poor as well as the affluent display human strengths and weaknesses. The biasing effects of economic criteria compel a negative view of poverty as a problem while affluence not seen as a problem is least studied. Strangely, this selective attention makes us ignore the possibility that, in a sense, both the ends of economic development may share some common characteristics. For example, while the poor are characterised by several forms of experiential deprivation, it is possible that the affluent, devoid of much exposure to grass roots level reality and engaged in an overprotected material environment, also suffer from experiential deprivation of different forms. Poor social and emotional development of children in poverty has been much talked about. But, it is also possible that children growing up in conditions of opulence show problems in their social and emotional development. Their environment dominated by material possessions is likely to foster individualistic orientation with inadequate social support which, in turn, may lead to anomie, alienation, poor emotional and social development and loss of sensitivity. Similarly, while poor cognitive and intellectual development of children in poverty and disadvantage have been severally highlighted, that the highly affluent children may evince poor social and emotional intelligence, and lack of adaptability in constrained environments is a possibility which needs to be examined. It is necessary to compare and contrast the patterns of development in extreme ends of distribution of economic wealth to appreciate that the poor and the disadvantaged need not be blamed for the characteristic psychosocial patterns that they evince. Rather, the dynamics and profile of environmental conditions may lead to certain negative outcomes among the poor as well as the affluent. Thus, it is not poverty *per se* but the linkages between poverty and inequality and inequity, the concentration of wealth in the hands of a few widening the disparities and the relative nature of disadvantage due to unequal treatment of human resources which need to be recognised for their social and psychological ramifications.

To conclude, these years of psychological research on poverty and disadvantage in India have definitely added to our knowledge and understanding of the phenomena. But psychologists must appreciate inherent biases and limitations in their approach. In any society, the relative nature of poverty as well as unequal distribution of wealth and opportunities puts some into a position of disadvantage. Sociocultural disadvantage accrues to individuals and groups not just due to poor economic conditions as such but due to a host of other factors including experiential deprivation and lack of opportunities to live a life of choice and freedom. Regardless the level of economic growth in a society like ours, the relatively poor, the women, the minor and minority cultural and linguistic groups and otherwise disabled are more likely to suffer a position of disadvantage. Poverty and disadvantage are not just economic conditions; they are psychological states perpetuated by complex social conditions. Understanding and amelioration of these states need a broader perspective than what psychology or, for that matter, any other social science discipline has to offer. Psychology of poverty and disadvantage in India has come close to appreciating such a perspective and contributing to the alternative views on development.

Bibliography

Achiever-Gent, J. (1992). Public participation and poverty alleviation: The experience of reform by communists in India's West Bengal. *World Development, 20*, 1401-1422.

Ackerman, P., Kiron, D., Goodwin, N.R., Harris, J.M., & Gallagher, K. (1997). *Human wellbeing and economic goals*. Washington: Island Press.

Agarwal, A., & Mishra, G. J. (1993). Communication and rural development in deprivational environment. *Indian Journal of Community Guidance Service, 10*, 1-9.

Agarwal, A., & Tripathi, K.K. (1980). Temporal orientation and deprivation. *Journal of Psychological Researches, 24*, 144-152.

Agarwal, A., & Tripathi, K.K. (1984). Influence of prolonged deprivation, age and culture on the development of future orientation. *European Journal of Social Psychology, 14*, 451-453.

Agarwal, K.N., Agarwal, D.K., & Upadhyaya, S.K. (1987). Malnutrition and mental functions in school children. In K.N. Agarwal & B. Bhatia (Eds.), *Update growth* (pp. 137-149). Varanasi: Department of Paediatrics, B.H.U.

Agran, M., Fodor, D.J., & Moore, S. (1986). The effects of self instructional training on job task sequencing : Suggesting a problem solving strategy. *Education and Training of the Mentally Retarded. 21*, 273-281.

Ahluwalia, M. (1986). Rural poverty, agricultural production and process: A re-examination. In J. Mellor, & G.M. Desai (Eds.), *Agricultural change and rural poverty: Variations on a theme (pp. 59-75)*. Delhi : Oxford University Press.

Ahmad, S. (1980). Effect of socio-cultural disadvantages on creative thinking. *Journal of Psychological Researches, 24*, 96-106.

Ahuja, R. (1988). Development and collective violence: A theoretical perspective. In K.S. Shukla (Eds.), *Collective violence: Genesis and response* (pp. 213-215). New Delhi: Indian Institute of Public Administration.

Allen, V.L. (1970). Theoretical issues in poverty research. *Journal of Soical Issues, 26*, 149-167.

Ameerjan, M.S., & Thimappa, M.S. (1988). Self attitude as related to caste affiliation and socio-economic level. *Indian Journal of Applied Psychology, 25*, 11-15.

Anandalakshmy, S. (1975). Socialization for competence. In J.W. Berry & W.J. Lonner (Eds.), *Applied cross-cultural psychology*. B.V., Amsterdam : Swets and Zeitlinger.

Anandalakshmy, S. (1982). There's a method to the measurement. In D. Sinha, R.C. Tripathi, & G. Misra (Eds.) *Deprivation: Its Social roots and psychological consequences* (pp. 37-48). New Delhi: Concept.

Anandalakshmy. S. (1985). Cognitive competence in infancy. *ICSSR Research Abstracts Quarterly, 14*, 1-14.

Anandalakshmy, S. (1990). Toward enhancing cognitive development: Stimulating play in infancy. In U.K. Bevli (Ed.), *Researches in child development: A book of readings* (pp. 100-113). New Delhi: NCERT.

Anandalakshmy, S. (1994). *The girl child and the family: An action study*. New Delhi: Department of Women and Child Develoment, Government of India.

Annamalai, E. (1982). The poverty of language: A linguistic appraisal. In D. Sinha, R.C. Tripathi, & G. Misra (Eds.) *Deprivation: Its social roots and psychological consequences* (pp. 123-138). New Delhi: Concept.

Arnold, S.C., & Forhand, R. (1978). A comparison of cognitive training and response cost procedure in modifying cognitive styles of impulsive children. *Cognitive Therapy and Research, 2*, 183-187.

Atal, Y. (Ed.) (1997a). *Perspectives on educating the poor*. New Delhi: Abinav Publications.

Atal, Y. (1997b). Education for the poor and against poverty. In Y. Atal (Ed.), *Perspectives on educating the poor*. New Delhi: Abinav Publications.

Awasthi, B., & Janbandhu, D.S. (1988). Effects of socio-economic status and intellectual ability on self identity disparity in adolescents. *Psycholingua, 13*, 1-6.

Backman, J.G., & O'Melley, P.M. (1977). Self-esteem in young men : A longitudinal analysis of the impact of educational and occupational attainment. *Journal of Personality and Social Psychology, 35*, 365-380.

Baker, R.L. Shutz, R.E., & Hinze, R.H. (1961). The influence of mental ability on achievement when socio-economic status is controlled. *Journal of Experimental Education, 30*, 155-158.

Baksi, A. (1993). *Developing and implementing an infant stimulation programme to mothers through Anganwadi workers*. Unpublished manuscript, University of Baroda.

Bandura, A. (1977). *Social learning theory*. Englewood Cliffs, N.J.: Prentice-Hall.

Bardhna, P. (1970). On the minimum level of living and the rural poor. *Indian Economic Review, 5*, 129-136.

Barker, R.G., & Wright, H.F. (1954). *Midwest and its children*. New York : Row Paterson.

Basvana. M. & Rani, M.U, (1984). Differential impact of social and economic factors on intellectual and scholastic abilities. *Journal of Psychological Researches, 28*, 121-128.

Baxi, U. (Ed.) (1988). *Law and poverty*. Bombay: N.M. Tripathi Pvt. Ltd.

Beck, A.T. (1976). *Cognitive therapy and the emotional disorders*. New York: International Universities Press.

Beck, T.C. (1994). *The experience of poverty : Fighting for respect and resources in village India*. London : Intermediate Technology Publications.

Berland, J. (1988). *No five fingers are alike : Cognitive amplifiers in social context*. Cambridge, M.A. : Harvard University Press.

Bernstein, B. (1962). Social class, linguistic codes and grammatical elements. *Language and Speech, 5*, 31-46.

Berry, J.W. (1976). *Human ecology and cognitive style : Comparative studies in cultural and psychological adaptation*. New York : John Wiley.

Berry, J.W. (1990). Psychology of acculturation: Understanding individuals moving between cultures. In R.W. Brislin (Ed.), *Applied cross-cultural psychology*. London : Sage.

Berry, J.W., van de Koppel, J.M.H., Sehechal, C., Annis, R.C., Bahuchet, S., Cavalli Sforza, L.L., & Witkin, H.A. (1986). *On the edge of the forest : Cultural adaptation and cognitive development in Africa*. Lisse : Swets & Zeitlinger.

Bevli, U.K. (Ed.) (1990). *Researches in child development: A book of readings*. New Delhi: NCERT.

Bevli, U.K., Kapoor, R., Bharti, K., & Tiwari, L. (1990). *The growth of logical thinking in children*. New Delhi: NCERT.

Bharatraj, J., Bhawani, B.D., & Vidyasagar (1983). Can intelligence be improved among socially disadvantaged children? In S. Dube & P.S. Sachdev (Eds.), *Mental health problem of the socially disadvantaged children*. New Delhi : Tata McGraw Hill.

Bhargava, A. (1974). *Maternal and child Language in two socioeconomic groups*. Unpublished master's dissertation, University of Delhi, Delhi.

Bhargava, M., & Mittal, M. (1991). Second order personality factors of four castes in traditional Indian *Varna* system. *Indian Journal of Community Guidance Service, 8*, 79-87.

Bhatia, M.S., Singhal, P.K., Nigam, V.R., & Malik, S.C. (1989). Nail biting: An analysis of 160 children. *Indian Medical Gazette, 73*, 188-191.

Bhogle, S. (1991). Child rearing practices and behaviour development of girl child. *Indian Journal of Social Work. 52*, 62-69.

Biswal, P.N. (1992). A comparative study of intelligence, self concept, academic achievement and SES of the students joining vocational and academic streams at +2 stage in Himachal Pradesh. *Journal of Educational Research and Extension, 28*, 104-110.

Block, L. & Dwarking N. (1976). *The IQ controversy*. London : Quaver Press.

Bogin, B., & MacVean, R.B. (1983). The relationships of socioeconomic status and sex to body size, skeletal maturation, and cognitive status of Guatemala city school children. *Child Development, 54*, 115-128.

Brofenbrenner, U. (1974). Development research, public policy and the ecology of childhood. *Child Development, 45*, 1-5.

Bronfenbrenner, U. (1975). Nature with nurture : A reinterpretation of the evidence. In A. Montagu (Ed.), *Race and IQ* (pp. 114-144). New York : Oxford University Press.

Bronfenbrenner, U. (1977). Towards an ecology of human development. *American Psychologist, 32*, 513-531.

Bronfenbrenner, U. (1979). *The ecology of human development*. London : Harvard University Press.

Broota, K.D., & Pahwa, A. (1984). Socio-cultural factors in the development of colour, form, and size perception. *Indian Journal of Psychology, 3*, 8-17

Brown, M. (1983). *The structure of disadvantage*. London: Aldershot Avebury.

Brunswick, E. (1952). *The conceptual framework of psychology*. Chicago : University of Chicago Press.

Burte, J.M., & Burte, C.L. (1994). Ericksonian hypnosis, farmacotherapy and cognitive-behavioural therapy in the treatment of ADHD. *Australian Journal of Clinical Hypnotherapy and Hypnosis, 15*, 1-13.

Caplin, N., & Nelson, S.D. (1973). On being useful : The nature and consequences of psychological research on social problems. *American Psychologist, 28*, 199-211.

Chadha, J., & Sen, Anima. (1993). Mental ability and social maturity of the children of ICDS and the children of non-ICDS. *Indian Journal of Community Guidance Service, 10*, 47-58.

Chalip, L., & Stigler, J.W. (1986). The development of achievement and ability among Chinese children : A new contribution to an old controversy. *Journal of Educational Research, 79*, 302-307.

Chambers, R. (1991). Poverty in India: Concepts, research and reality. In B. Harriss, S. Guhan, & R.H. Cassen (Eds.), *Poverty in India: Research and policy.* (pp. 301-332). Bombay: Oxford University Press.

Chambers, R. (1995). Poverty and livelihood : Whose reality counts? *Discussion Paper*, 347, University of Sussex : Institute of Development Studies.

Chambers, R., Saxena, N.C., & Shah, T. (1989). *To the hands of the poor: Water and trees.* New Delhi: Oxford & IBH.

Chan, L.K. (1991). Promoting strategy generalization through self instructional training in students with reading disabilities. *Journal of Learning Disabilities, 24,* 427-433.

Chand, A. (1987). *Poverty and underdevelopment.* New Delhi: Gian Publishing House.

Chatterjee, B.B. (1982). Methodological implications of using the socio-economic status scale as a control variable in disadvantage-deprivation studies. In D. Sinha, R.C. Tripathi, & G. Misra (Eds.), *Deprivation: Its social roots and psychological consequences* (pp. 73-100). New Delhi: Concept.

Chaturvedi, M.G., & Singh, S. (1981). *Third all-India educational survey - languages and media of instruction in Indian schools.* New Delhi: NCERT.

Chaudhary, P., & Minhas, B.K. (1993). Psychological problems of adolescents in relation to intelligence and socio-economic status. In A.K. Srivastava (Ed.), *Researches in child and adolescent Psychology* (pp. 140-146). New Delhi: NCERT.

Chaudhary, U.S., & Bindal, V.R. (1986). Caste differences in creativity, experimental attitude and parents' attitude towards creativity. *Asian Journal of Psychology and Education, 17,* 22-26.

Chauhan, S.S., & Singh, H, (1985). The study of habits of children in relation to sex and economic status. *Journal of Educational Research and Extension, 22,* 9-16.

Codd, J.A. (1985). The TOSCA controversy : Political and ethical issues. *Delta, 36,* 39-52.

Cole, M. (1990). Cognitive development and formal schooling : The evidence from cross-cultural research. In L.C. Moll (Ed.), *Vygotsky and education : Instructional implications and application of sociohistorical psychology.* Cambridge : Cambridge University Press.

Cole, M. (1992). Context, modularity and the cultural constitution of development. In L.T. Wenger & J. Valsiner (Eds.), *Children's development within social context,* Vol 1. Hillsdale, N.J. : Lawrence Eribaum.

Cole, M., & Bruner, J.S. (1971). Cultural differences and inferences about psychological processes. *American Psychologist, 26*, 867-876.

Copestake, J. G. (1992). The integrated rural development programme: Performance during sixth plan, policy responses and proposals for reform. In B. Harris, S. Guhan, & R.H. Cassen (Eds.), *Poverty in India: Research and policy* (pp.301-332). Bombay: Oxford University Press.

Corno, L. (1987). Teaching and self regulated learning. In D.C. Berliner & B.V. Rosenshine (Eds.) *Talks to teachers*. New York: Random House.

Coward, B.E., Feagin, J.R., & Williams Jr., J.A. (1974). The culture of poverty debate: Some additional data. *Social Problems, 21*, 621-634.

Craighead, W.E., Meyers, A.W., & Craighead, I.W. (1985). A conceptual model for cognitive-behavior therapy with children. *Journal of Abnormal Child Psychology, 13*, 331-342.

Cummins, J. (1979). Linguistic interdependence and the educational development of bilingual children. *Review of Educational Research, 49*, 222-251.

Cummins, J. (1984). *Bilingualism and special education: Issues in assessment and pedagogy*. Clevedon, England: Multilingual Matters.

Dalal, A. K. (1991). School performance of disadvantaged children: The educational resourcefulness model. *Indian Journal of Social Work, 52*, 313-323.

Dalal, A.K., & Pande, N. (1995). A community intervention programme for changing attitude toward disability. *The Social Engineer, 4*, 16-25.

Dandekar, V.M. (1981). On measurement of poverty. *Economic and Political Weekly, 16*, 1241-1250.

Dandekar, V.M., & Rath, N. (1971). Poverty in India- I and II. *Economic and Political Weekly, 6*, 25-49.

Danzinger, K. (1990). *Constructing the subject : Historical origins of psychological research*. New York : Cambridge University Press.

Das, I., & Mona, P.K. (1990). The effect of poverty upon intelligence. *Indian Journal of Community Guidance Service, 7*, 34-48.

Das, J.P. (1973). Cultural deprivation and cognitive competence. In N.R. Ellis (Ed.), *International Review of Research in Mental Retardation*, Vol. 6 (pp. 1-53). New York: Academic Press.

Das, J.P., & Khurana, A.K.S. (1988). Caste and cognitive process. In S.H. Irvine & J.W. Berry, (eds.), *Human abilities in cultural context*. New York : Cambridge University Press.

Das, J.P., & Singha, P.S. (1975). Caste, class and cognitive competence. *Indian Educational Review, 10,* 1-18.

Das, R. (1993). *Testing for the effect of practice on attention and planning performance of high and low achievers.* Master Thesis, Utkal University, Bhubaneshwar.

Dash, A. S., & Rath, S. (1985). Effect of cognitive stimulation on disadvantaged and non-disadvantaged preschool children: An experimental study. *Journal of Psychological Researches, 29,* 121-129.

Dash, A.S., & Rath, S. (1986). An experimental study of effects of cognitive stimulation on disadvantaged preschool children, *Psucho-Lingua, 16,* 17-26.

Dash, R., & Dash, A.S. (1982). A study of perceptual-motor and intellectual abilities of tribal and non-tribal children. In R. Rath, H.S. Asthana, D. Sinha, & J.B.P. Sinha (Eds.), *Diversity and unity in cross-cultural psychology* (pp. 57-59). Lisse: Swets and Zeitlinger.

Das, U.N., & Das, J.P. (1984). Development of concrete operational thought and information coding in schooled and unschooled children. *British Journal of Developmental Psychology, 2,* 63-72.

Davis, A. (1960). *Socioeconomic influences upon children's learning.* Speech delivered at the mid-century White House conference on Children and Young.

Davis, D.L., & Boster, L.H. (1993). Cognitive-behavioral expressive interventions with aggressive and resistant youth. *Residential Treatment for Children and Youth, 10,* 55-68.

Dayal, E. (1989). Rural poverty in India: A regional analysis. *Journal of Rural Studies, 5,* 87-98.

Desai, A. S. (1989). Education of the child in urban slums: An overview of factors affecting learning and responsive action through social work. *Indian Journal of Social Work, 50,* 506-524.

Deshpande, S.S. (1985). *A critical study of the effect of deprivation on language ability of children studying in a municipal corporation school in standard I: A comparison with children in a private school and a village school.* Unpublished doctoral dissertation, Poona University, Pune.

Dey, R.R. (1992). *Developmental and socio-cultural differences in the effect of verbal labelling on memory for pictures.* Unpublished doctoral dissertation, Banaras Hindu University, Varanasi.

Dhillon, P.K., & Mehra, D. (1990). The influence of social class and sex on primary school children's creative thinking. *Indian Journal of Psychology, 63,* 9-19.

Doise, W. (1978). *Groups and individuals : Explanations in social psychology*. Cambridge : Cambridge University Press.

Douglas, J.W.B. Ross, J.M., & Simpson. H.R. (1968). *All our future : A longitudinal study of secondary education*. London: Peter Davis.

Dreze, Jean, & Sen, Amartya. (1985). *Indian economic development and social opportunity*. Delhi: Oxford University Press.

Dube, V.K., Mishra, R.C., & Pandey, K.N. (1987). Radio in support of women's empowerment for child survival, protection and development in India. *Interaction*, *5*, 1-14.

Dubey, S.N. (1984). Characteristic need patterns of scheduled caste Indians. *Psychologia, 27*, 122-124.

Dulcan, M.K. (1986). Comprehensive treatment of children and adolescents with attention deficit disorders: The state of the art. *Clinical Psychology Review*. *6*, 539-569.

Dusek, J.B., & Joseph, G. (1983). The base of teacher expectations : A meta analysis. *Journal of Educational Psychology, 75*, 327-346.

Dush, D.M., Hirt, M.L., & Schroeder, H.F. (1989). Self statement modification in the treatment of child behavior disorders: A meta analysis. *Psychological Bulletin, 106*, 97-106.

Dutt, S. (1988). Relationship of creativity with achievement in science and SES of Xth grade students. *Journal of Educational Research and Extension, 25*, 106-111.

Dutta-Banik, N.D. (1982). Semi longitudinal growth evaluation of childen from birth to 14 years in different socio-economic groups. *Indian Paediatrics, 19*, 353-359.

Edwards, J.R. (1979). *Language and disadvantage*. London: Edward Arnold.

Eldering, L. (1991). Intervention programmes for preschoolers from immigrant families : The Dutch case. In N. Bleichrodt & P.J.D. Drenth (Eds.), *Contemporary issues in cross-cultural psychology*. Amsterdam : Swet & Zeitlinger.

Eldering, L., & Liseman, P. (Eds.) (1993). *Early intervention and culture*. The Netherlands : UNESCO.

Eldering, L., & Vedder, P. (1993). Culture sensitive home intervention : The Dutch HIPPY experiment. In L. Eldering & P. Liseman (Eds.), *Early intervention and culture*. The Netherlands : UNESCO.

Ellis, A., & Grieger, R. (1977). *Handbook of rational emotive therapy*. New York: Springer-Verlag.

Entwistle, H. (1958). *Class, culture and education*. London : Methuen.

Eotovs, L.U. (1983). Szocialis Helzet, Intelligencia es Kreativitas Ovodal Korban, *Magyar-Pszichological Szemle, 40*, 323-339.

Evans, B., & Waites, B. (1981). *IQ and mental testing : An unnatural science and its social history*, London : Macmillan.

Everett, J., & Savara, M. (1984). Bank loans to the poor in Bombay: Do Women benefit? *Signs, 10,* 272-290.

Farren, D.C. (1990). Effects of intervention with disadvantaged and disabled children : A decade's review. In S.T. Meisels & J.P. Shonkoff (Eds.), *Handbook of early childhood intervention,* Cambridge : Cambridge University Press.

Feagin, J. (1972). Poverty: We still believe that God helps them who help themselves. *Psychology Today, 6,* 109-129.

Feagin, J. (1975). *Subordinating the poor.* Englewood cliffs, NJ: Prentice Hall.

Feather, N. (1974). Explanations of poverty in Australian and American samples: The person, society, or fate? *Australian Journal of Psychology, 26,* 199-216.

Feuerstein, R. (1980). *Instructional enrichment.* Baltimore, MD: University Park Press.

Firkowska Mankiewicz, A., & Czarkowski, M.P. (1981). Polozne Spoleczne a Poziom Timyslowy Dzieci Warszawlkich (Social position versus mental performance of Warswa children), *Studia-Sociologiczne, 3,* 177-194.

Fisher, R.A. (1951). Limits to intensive production in animals. *British Agriculture Bulletin, 4,* 317-318.

Furnham, A. (1982a). Perception of poverty among adolescents. *Journal of Adolescence, 5,* 135-147.

Furnham, A. (1982b). Why are the poor always with us? explanations for poverty in Britain. *British Journal of Social Psychology, 12,* 335-342.

Ganguli, M. (1989). Socio-economic status and scholastic achievement. *Indian Educational Review, 24,* 84-95.

Gangwar, H.N.S. (1992). Study habit as a function of SES and cultural setting in first division high school students. *Indian Psychological Review, 23,* 33-37.

Gans, H. (1972). The positive functions of poverty. *American Journal of Sociology, 78,* 275-289.

Gaur, R. (1992). *Machiavelleanism among adolescent boys and girls of different SES as a function of their parental Machiavellianism.* Unpublished doctoral dissertation, Meerut University, Meerut.

Gergen. K. J. (1973). Social psychology as history. *Journal of Personality and Social Psychology, 26,* 309-320.

Gergen, K.J. (1985). The social constructionist movement in modern psychology. *American Psychologist, 40,* 266-275.

Gewirtz, J.L. (1972). Deficiency conditions of stimulation and the reversal of their effects via environment. In F.J. Monks, W.W.

Hartar, & J. de Wit (Eds.) *Determinants of behavioral development* (pp 349-375). New York : Academic Press.

Ghosh, S. (1991). Girl child: A life time of deprivation and discrimination. *Indian Journal of Social Work, 52*, 221-227.

Ghurye, G.S. (1961). *Caste, class and occupation*. Bombay : Popular Book Depot.

Ginsberg, H. (1972). *The myths of deprived child : Poor children's intellect and education*. New Jersey : Prentice Hall.

Giriappa, S. (1992). IRDP and poverty alleviation. *Journal of Rural Development, 1*, 481-490.

Goedhart, T., Halberstadt, V., Kapteyn. A., & Praag. B.V. (1977). The poverty line: Concept and measurement. *Journal of Human Resources, 12*, 503-520.

Goodwin, N.R. (1997). Interdisciplinary perspectives on well-being: overview essay. In F. Ackerman, D. Kiron, N.R. Goodwin, J.M. Harris, & K. Gallagher (Eds.), *Human well-being and economic goals* (pp. 1-14). Washington: Island Press.

Gottesman, I.I. (1966). Genetic variance and adaptive personality traits. *Journal of Child Psychology and Psychiatry, 7*, 199-208.

Government of India (1986). *National policy on education*. New Delhi: Ministry of Human Resource Development.

Gunthey, R.K., & Sinha, P. (1983). SES as a determinant of anxiety and affiliation in teenagers. *Indian Psychological Review, 24*, 1-5.

Gupta, P.P., Malhotra, S.S., Bhalla, J.N., & Tripathi, V.N. (1985). Growth and development in urban slums. *Indian Paediatrics, 22*, 829-833.

Gupta, R., Mukherjee, M., & Chattarjee, S. (1993). A comparative study of the factors affecting academic achievement among four groups of adolescents. *Indian Journal of Applied Psychology, 30*, 30-38.

Gupta, S.P. (1987). *Structural dimension of poverty in India*. New Delhi: Mittal Publication.

Hanumanth Rao, C.H. (1992). Integrating poverty alleviation programmes with development strategies: Indian experience. *Economic and Political Weekly*, 27, 2603-2607.

Heider, F. (1958). *Psychology of interpersonal relations*. New York : Wiley.

Helode, R.D., & Kapai, N. (1986). A study of psychopathic tendency and locus of control as a function of SES among adolescents. *Indian Journal of Applied Psychology, 23*, 91-97.

Hess, R.D., & Shipman, V.C. (1965). Early experience and socialization of cognitive modes in child. *Child Development, 36*, 869-886.